The Teacher's Grammar Book

Second Edition

The Teacher's Grammar Book

Second Edition

James D. Williams
Soka University

LEA LAWRENCE ERLBAUM ASSOCIATES, PUBLISHERS

2005   Mahwah, New Jersey   London

Lawrence Erlbaum Associates, Inc., Publishers
10 Industrial Avenue
Mahwah, New Jersey 07430
www.erlbaum.com

Cover design by Kathryn Houghtaling Lacey

Library of Congress Cataloging-in-Publication Data

Williams, James D. (James Dale), 1949–
    The teacher's grammar book / James D. Williams.—2nd ed.
        p. cm.
    Includes bibliographical references and index.
ISBN 0-8058-5221-2 (pbk. : alk. paper)
    1. English language—Grammar. 2. English language—Grammar—
    Study and teaching.   I. Title.

PE1112.W46 2005
428.2—dc22   2004056421
                                                            CIP

Books published by Lawrence Erlbaum Associates are printed on acid-free
paper, and their bindings are chosen for strength and durability.

Printed in the United States of America
10   9   8   7   6   5   4   3   2   1

Contents

Preface

The Teacher's Grammar Book is designed for students who are preparing to become English or language arts teachers, as well as for credentialed teachers who want to know more about grammar. Most grammar books focus on terminology. Some add a discussion of the connection between grammar and writing. *The Teacher's Grammar Book,* however, is different. Certainly, it treats terminology thoroughly, but it is far more than just a list of grammar terms. It is not a handbook and was never intended to be one. *The Teacher's Grammar Book* was designed to offer an easy-to-use guide to teaching methods and grammar and usage questions, a combination that has not been readily available before. In addition, it provides an overview of English grammar that is informed not only by historical developments in the field but also by a variety of pedagogical, research, and philosophical issues that underlie grammar and our efforts to understand grammar, language, writing, and teaching. Out of this wide-ranging exploration emerges the view that a teacher's choice of grammar reflects philosophical and pedagogical orientations that influence both the content and the methods of language arts instruction.

The Teacher's Grammar Book grew out of my experience teaching grammar and composition methods courses to education students since 1981. What I discovered early in my career is that large numbers of prospective teachers do not feel confident about their knowledge of English grammar. They experience a certain degree of anxiety as a result. Most have recognized that they will be required to teach grammar—and they aren't happy about it. Many have had bad experiences with grammar in the past. They "didn't get it," or, sadder still, they "just didn't like it." Nearly all are surprised when, a few weeks into my grammar courses, they discover not only that they are "getting it" but that grammar is actually fun. *The Teacher's Grammar Book* aims to take readers on a similar voyage of discovery.

What's New in the Second Edition

The many teachers and students who used the first edition of *The Teacher's Grammar Book* provided various suggestions over the years intended to make the text better. I've tried to incorporate their suggestions into the second edition as much as possible, and I hope they are happy with the result of this indirect collaboration. In many respects, the finished product is significantly different from the original. The more important changes are:

- A new chapter providing a short history of grammar and its role in education.
- A new chapter on teaching grammar that examines not only the challenges teachers face but also what research, theory, and classroom experience tell us constitutes "best practices."
- A significant reduction in the formalism associated with phrase structure grammar so as to focus more on the descriptive goals of this approach to language analysis.
- A complete revision of the chapter on transformational–generative grammar that significantly reduces the discussion of transformation rules and tree diagrams so as to focus more on other features of this approach, such as its influence on teaching and psychology; also new is a summary of the model—the minimalist program—that Noam Chomsky developed to replace transformational–generative grammar.
- A complete revision of the chapter on cognitive grammar that not only makes the discussion more current but also more detailed, addressing how cognitive grammar provides insight into common problems associated with teaching writing, such as creating meaning and errors in language.
- A thorough revision of the chapter on dialects to make it both more current and more detailed; the discussion of Chicano English is significantly expanded, and new in this edition is a brief analysis of Spanglish and an exploration of code switching.
- Also new is the focus on teaching grammar and language as a thread that winds through each chapter, making the text more thoroughly a tool to help teachers meet the challenge of grammar instruction.

Chapter One.   The first chapter offers a brief history of grammar in the Western tradition. Although there are some interesting stories to tell about the study of grammar in places like India, China, and the Middle East, they are not very relevant to American public education, based as it is on Greek and Roman models. The goal of this chapter, therefore, is to give readers a sense of the place grammar has held in Western education since the days of Plato and Aristotle so that they can better understand and appreciate why we expect students to learn something about the English language.

Chapter Two. Chapter 2 explores various approaches to teaching grammar, and in many respects it is central to developing an effective classroom methodology. There are many different ways to teach grammar, and this chapter examines the most common, assessing their strengths and weaknesses with the aim of identifying best practices.

Central to this chapter is the section on grammar and writing. Most teachers and many textbooks, such as Weaver's (1996) *Teaching Grammar in Context* and Noden's (1999) *Image Grammar: Using Grammatical Structures to Teach Writing,* advocate teaching grammar in the context of writing. However, few recognize the difficulties and faulty assumptions inherent in this approach as it usually is applied. Emphasizing the linguistic perspective that informs the entire book, this section makes an important distinction between *grammar* and *usage*, explaining why most of the sentence errors we see in student writing are not problems of grammar but rather problems of usage. An important feature of *The Teacher's Grammar Book* are the **Usage Notes** that appear at key points to explain a wide range of common usage problems. Finally, the chapter examines existing research and explores the most pedagogically sound ways to link grammar and writing.

Chapter Three. Although chapter 2 is important for every English/language arts teacher, chapter 3, "Traditional Grammar," may be even more important because it provides the foundation for actually teaching grammar. The subsequent chapters are built on this foundation, and together they will eliminate any lack of confidence readers may have about their knowledge of grammar. The chapter begins by introducing basic grammatical terms and explaining their role in language study. It does not assume that readers have any significant knowledge of grammar at all so as to create a comfortable space for learning. Taking a standard approach, grammar is divided into two categories of analysis, *form* and *function.*

Chapter 3 also builds on the grammar/usage distinction by introducing a fundamental feature of modern language study—*appropriateness conditions.* Based in part on Hymes' (1971) principles of communicative competence, appropriateness conditions contextualize language use and allow students to understand more thoroughly the factors that make writing different from speech and that enable us to recognize that the language we use when talking with friends over pizza and beer will be different from the language we use during a job interview. In addition, chapter 3 examines traditional grammar's prescriptive approach to language study and explores the implications for teaching.

Chapter Four.   Chapter 4 introduces phrase–structure grammar and explains how it emerged during the early part of the 20th century as an alternative to traditional grammar. Because phrase–structure grammar provides the analytical basis for all modern grammars, the chapter devotes considerable attention to helping students understand phrase–structure notation. The primary focus, however, is on understanding the *descriptive,* as opposed to the *prescriptive,* nature of phrase structure and how this orientation is central to differentiating modern grammars from traditional grammar.

Chapter Five.   Chapter 5 introduces transformational–generative (T–G) grammar as an historical evolution of the work in phrase structure. Many students find T–G challenging, and others resist its complexities by arguing that it is irrelevant to teaching high school language arts. They often are put off by the fact that T–G grammar has undergone numerous changes over the years. Nevertheless, in the United States, T–G grammar remains an influential tool for analyzing language and therefore should be part of any language arts teacher's training. The first part of the chapter examines the fundamental features of T–G grammar and explains in simple terms how transformations work. The second part of the chapter examines the principles that underlie the latest evolution of the generative approach: *the minimalist program* (MP). This new approach has dropped many of the features that characterized T–G grammar, simplifying the rules associated with language production while simultaneously increasing the level of abstraction regarding the relation between grammar and language.

Chapter Six.   T–G grammar and the MP can be characterized as "formalist" approaches to language because of their emphasis on rules and the application of those rules. Advocates of formalist grammars—most importantly, Noam Chomsky—have claimed consistently that they reflect the underlying psychological mechanisms of language. That is, they have viewed the study of grammar as a means of developing a theory of mind. This claim is powerful, but to date scholars have had little success in supporting it. Numerous studies have failed to reveal any connections between formalist grammars and underlying cognitive mechanisms, leaving them with the unhappy status of unsubstantiated theories. As a result, various scholars began developing an alternative approach. What emerged was *cognitive grammar,* the subject of chapter 6. This grammar draws heavily on work in cognitive science to develop a model of language processing that is more congruent with mental operations and that can provide important insights into teaching grammar and writing.

Chapter Seven.   Many of our public schools, especially in the nation's cities, have a majority student population of nonnative English speakers and speakers of a nonstandard dialect. As a result, the need for teachers to have some knowledge of dialects and English as a second language is greater than ever before. Chapter 7 is designed to provide an introduction to the critical issues related to teaching these students. As such, it offers a solid foundation for additional studies in dialects and English as a second language.

ACKNOWLEDGMENTS

Books like this are never the product of a single person's efforts, and many people have figured significantly in the writing of *The Teacher's Grammar Book*. My linguistics professors at the University of Southern California—Jack Hawkins, Steve Krashen, and Sue Foster Cohen—were inspiring teachers who encouraged me to look deeper into language than I thought I could. I am grateful to the many fine students I've worked with over the years who have shared my enthusiasm for grammar and who have stimulated me to find better ways of teaching an often complex subject. I greatly appreciate the comments and suggestions of the following reviewers: Stuart C. Brown, New Mexico State University; Gerald Delahuntt, Colorado State University; Susana M. Sotillo, Montclair State University; and Rosalind Horowitz, University of Texas, San Antonio. They offered valuable advice for this second edition. I could not have completed this work without the help of my assistants, Lynn Hamilton-Gamman and Ceclia Ocampos. And I am ever grateful for the support of my wife, Ako, and my son, Austin.

—*James D. Williams*
Chino Hills, California

1

A Short History of Grammar

AGREEING ON A DEFINITION

Grammar is a term used to mean many different things. When teachers and administrators grow frustrated over errors in student writing, they often call for a return to "the basics," which they define as *grammar*. And English teachers know very well what the response will be when they tell anyone what they do for a living: "Oh, I better watch what I say!" In this situation, grammar is being defined as how one speaks.

Many years ago, Hartwell (1985, pp. 352–353) organized some of these different meanings in an attempt to clarify our understanding of grammar by offering five different definitions, summarized here:

1. A set of formal patterns in which the words of a language are arranged to convey a larger meaning.
2. The branch of linguistics concerned with the description, analysis, and formulation of formal language patterns.
3. Linguistic etiquette.
4. School grammar, or the names of the parts of speech.
5. Grammatical terms used in the interest of teaching writing.

Hartwell's (1985) taxonomy is certainly useful, and there is no question that teachers need to be aware of the many ways the term *grammar* is used throughout education and society. Nevertheless, it can be confusing. The taxonomy seems to separate "school grammar" from writing instruction when the two usually are connected. Also, it does not tell us much about the differences between spoken and written language, nor does it tell us anything about dialects.

For this reason, I have chosen a definition of *grammar* that is concise but that is sufficiently broad to include a wide range of language features and forms:

Grammar is the formal study of the structure of a language and describes how words fit together in meaningful constructions.

This definition is not complete, and perhaps no single definition can be. Being generic, it does not, for example, take into account the fact that there are multiple ways—and therefore multiple grammars—to study the structure of a language. Nevertheless, this definition is essentially congruent with how specialists in language study—*linguists*—use the term. Indeed, grammar is an important area in *linguistics,* which includes not only grammar (often referred to as *syntax*) but also several other features of language, such as meaning (semantics), sound (phonology), dialects, pragmatics, and language acquisition. Furthermore, this definition has the advantage of linking grammar to education, which is important because this book is designed for teachers and because grammar has been such an important part of education throughout Western history. In fact, until modern times, grammar was the most important part of a young person's education. Even now, we often refer to elementary school as *grammar* school.

GREEK BEGINNINGS

Like so many other elements of Western culture, the formal study of grammar began in ancient Greece, probably in the late 6th century BC, when a number of factors combined to motivate the Greeks to examine the structure of their language. However, the emergence of grammar study may not have occurred if the ancient Greeks had not already placed a high value on language. Homer's *Iliad* and *Odyssey,* put into written form between 900 and 800 BC, provide some insight into the nature of Greek education before the 6th century. In the *Iliad,* we find that the hero Achilles was tutored as a youth to be "a speaker of words and a doer of deeds" (9.454–455), and the work includes numerous speeches that illustrate the importance of speaking well. As Wheelock (1974) noted, "All this foreshadows the conspicuous place of … elocution and rhetoric in later Greek education" (p. 4).

In earlier times, education was in the hands of parents, with mothers educating their daughters and fathers educating their sons. But we see in *The Iliad* that by Homer's time (and possibly much earlier), wealthy families commonly employed professional tutors. By the end of the 6th century, education had become systematized and more or less universal for boys, who began attending private schools at the age of 6 and continued at least until the age of 14. The government did not require attendance, but education was highly valued among all classes, and it seems that even poor parents somehow found the means to provide tuition.

Young students were taught by a *grammatistes,* who provided instruction in the alphabet *(grammata),* reading, writing, and grammar. A *grammatistes* also gave instruction in other subjects, such as music and mathematics. When students were proficient readers and writers, they were deemed *grammatikos,* or literate. At this point, they began studying literature in earnest. Plato wrote in *Protagoras* that "when the boy has learned his letters and is beginning to understand what is written, as before he understood only what was spoken, they [the teachers] put into his hands the works of the great poets, which he reads sitting on a bench at school" (ll. 325–326).

The study of Homer was a central part of elementary education in Greece because his poems contain moral messages that were deemed vital for children. In addition, the poems represented the ideal form of language that students were expected to mimic so as to preserve the "purity" of Homeric Greek. Thus, Greek education developed a prescriptive stance with respect to language and grammar, defining notions of "correct" and "incorrect" language use in terms of adherence to literary norms that characterized Greek hundreds of years in the past.[1] To better understand the educational difficulties associated with this approach, we might consider what our language arts classes would be like today if we used the language of Shakespeare as a model for correct English.

Greeks of 6th century Athens obviously knew that their language was different from what Homer used. The language had changed, as all living languages do. This troubled the Greeks greatly, because they viewed the Homeric period as a golden age. Change necessarily meant decline. And although it may seem ironic to us because we honor the great contributions to civilization that Greece made from about 600 to 300 BC, the Greeks of the period often saw themselves as living in the dark ages after a fall from the golden age of their legendary heroes. They appear to have responded, in part, by initiating the study of language in an effort to understand its structure and stem the tide of change.

The 6th century also marked the beginning of what might be called an "intellectual explosion," typified by the emergence over the next 350 years of heretofore unparalleled art, drama, mathematical discoveries, political theory, and philosophy. As intellectuals began pondering the nature of the world around

---

[1]Glenn (1995) and Kolln (1996) argued a different view. Glenn, for example, proposed that the ancient Greeks viewed grammar as being related to style rather than correctness. This view, however, does not seem entirely congruent with the realities of Greek education; grammar was taught to children as part of their elementary education and style was taught to older students as part of rhetoric.

them, it was natural that they turned their attention to language and began asking questions about its structure. In addition, the rise of democracy and public debate of civic issues exerted a significant influence on all facets of Greek life, especially in Athens.[2] Citizens needed to speak persuasively and correctly if they were to guide the ship of state. Power was linked to speaking ability, which was the result of study and practice. Thus, the careful study of language, both grammatical and rhetorical, grew to paramount importance and formed the basis of Greek education.

During their first 3 years of classes, from about age 6 to 9, students studied the alphabet, reading, spelling, and the beginnings of writing. At around age 9, they began studying grammatical terminology and relations: nouns, verbs, conjunctions, prepositions, and so on. By age 12, students were focusing on literature, memorizing long passages that celebrated moral virtues, courage, duty, and friendship, and they were introduced to the fundamentals of rhetoric. A majority of young boys finished their formal education at age 14 and began working, either with their fathers or as apprentices. Those from families with the means went on to secondary education, concentrating on rhetoric, music, and mathematics. All males were required to complete 2 years of military duty at age 18, and afterwards it was possible to participate in advanced studies—what we might think of today as college—with a private tutor. The most well-known private tutors, called *Sophists,* focused their teaching on rhetoric, although their courses of study included other topics.

Even though this book is about grammar, a brief discussion of rhetoric is necessary here. Rhetoric, like grammar, has many different definitions today, but in the ancient world it was understood primarily to be the art of persuasive public speaking. The nature of Greek democracies was such that important decisions, made by a large group of citizens sitting in assembly, often hinged on a leader's speaking ability. The court system also demanded speaking skill, for all persons appearing in court were required to represent themselves. There were no attorneys. The most famous example of this system at work is the trial of Socrates, reported by his student Plato, in which we see the philosopher answering the charges against him and arguing his case.

Rhetoric was a highly organized field of study in the ancient world. It focused on what are called "the five offices": *invention, arrangement, style, memory,* and *delivery. Invention* may be best understood as a process of developing

---

[2]The two major powers during the classic period of Greek history were Athens and Sparta. Athens and its allies were democracies, whereas Sparta and its allies were aristocracies. Spartan society was dedicated wholly to military prowess, and Spartans never developed the love of language that characterized Athens. In fact, Athenians commonly mocked the Spartans for being inarticulate. Although we have no way of accurately assessing their relative speaking abilities, the Athenian view prevails even today. The term *laconic,* which describes brief, pithy speech, comes from *Lacedaemonians,* another name for the Spartans.

topics and arguments. When students in a literature class interpret a novel, for example, they must practice invention not only to develop an interpretation (deciding what to write) but also to find ways to support it. *Arrangement* involved how best to organize a speech, whereas *style* was related to the tone or voice of the speech, whether it would be formal or informal, sophisticated or plain. *Memory* was very important because speakers did not use notes or talking points but had to give the appearance of speaking extempore; also, their speeches were usually quite long—1 or 2 hours—so developing the ability to memorize was crucial to success. *Delivery* was related to style but focused more on gestures and postures. Many handbooks on rhetoric during the Renaissance, for example, provided numerous illustrations of hand gestures and postures intended to evoke specific responses from audiences.

A counterpart of rhetoric was *dialectic,* or what is sometimes referred to as "philosophical rhetoric." Rhetoric was almost completely pragmatic; that is, its aim was to get things done through persuasive discourse either in the governing assemblies or in the law courts. Dialectic, however, was not pragmatic but rather sought to discover truth. Plato claimed that philosophical rhetoric would convince the gods themselves *(Phaedrus,* 273e*),* and his Socratic dialogues are examples of dialectic. Over the centuries, the understanding of both rhetoric and, especially, dialectic changed, gradually moving closer together. By the time of the late Roman period, St. Augustine could declare in *On Dialect (De dialectica)* that "Dialectic is the science of arguing well" (I.1). By the Middle Ages, dialectic had changed again and was understood primarily as *logic,* which was considered a part of grammar.

Both Plato and his student Aristotle wrote about grammar, but the first complete grammar book we know about was written around 100 BC by Dionysius Thrax, a native of Alexandria who taught in both Athens and Rome. His *Art of Grammar (Techne grammatike)* set the standard for all grammar books until the 20th century. The following excerpt illustrates how his influence exists even today and should seem very familiar: "A sentence is a combination of words, either in prose or verse, making a complete sense.... Of discourse there are eight parts: noun, verb, participle, article, pronoun, preposition, adverb, and conjunction" (Dionysius, 1874, pp. 326–339).

GRAMMAR IN ROME

Greece had several prosperous colonies in Sicily and southern Italy, and the sheer vitality of Greek culture meant that it exerted an important influence on Rome from the earliest days. As Rome grew in power and size, it assimilated numerous Greek customs and practices, including the educational system.

Therefore, grammar also held a central place in Roman schools. Dykema (1961) noted that Romans, like the Greeks, believed that knowledge of grammatical terms was fundamental to correct language use.

Indeed, the influence of Greece ran throughout Roman education. Students studied both Greek and Latin poets, following the Greek tradition of basing grammar study on literary texts. The most influential grammars of the Roman period were written by Donatus *(Ars grammatica)* in the 4th century AD and Priscian *(Institutiones grammaticae)* in the 6th century AD. These writers were so popular that their texts became the basis for grammar study throughout the Middle Ages.

One of the foremost teachers during the Roman period was Quintilian (circa 35–95 AD), who wrote *The Education of the Orator (Institutio de oratoria),* a collection of 12 books on education from childhood through adulthood. Quintilian described an educational program that was clearly Greek in almost every respect, with grammar instruction in the early years, followed by logic and rhetoric. This three-part taxonomy came to be called the *trivium.* Education was not compulsory, but, as in Greece, nearly every child, regardless of status, attended school. In an age without electricity, all work, including school work, began at dawn and ended around 2 p.m. We know from Quintilian that students were expected to devote considerable time to homework, or "private study" (1974, I.ii.12). The length of the school year is uncertain, but we do know that classes began toward the end of March and may have ended around the time of the Saturnalia religious festival on December 17.

From ages 6 to 12, students studied the alphabet, reading, writing, and arithmetic.[3] Secondary education was from ages 12 to 16 and was not nearly as universal as primary education owing to the higher cost and the need for children without means to go to work. At the elementary level, students began studying Greek, and this study intensified at the secondary level. Educated people in Rome were expected to be bilingual. The emphasis on grammar—both Latin and Greek—increased as a result, and Quintilian reported that the secondary teacher should be prepared to address the parts of speech, declensions, conjugations, inflections, pronunciation, and syllables (I.iv). Quintilian was a strong advocate for correctness in language, and he argued that the study of grammar would enable students to produce error-free speech and writing. He described the ideal student as one "who is spurred on by praise, delighted by success, and ready to weep over failure" (1974. I.ii.7)—an indication that teachers' views have changed little in the last 2,000 years.

---

[3]Rome, unlike Greece, allowed girls to attend grammar school, but they generally did not continue formal education beyond age 12 or 13. Some women from wealthy families apparently did study with private tutors, however, and became quite well educated.

GRAMMAR IN THE MIDDLE AGES

Roman education concentrated on what is known as *the seven arts* of the trivium (grammar, logic, and rhetoric) and the *quadrivium* (music, arithmetic, geometry, and astronomy). When the Roman Empire collapsed around 475 AD, the educational system that had been in place throughout the Mediterranean for a thousand years disappeared. Within two generations, near universal illiteracy replaced near universal literacy.

The significance of the Greco-Roman education system with respect to grammar was at least twofold. As the Empire expanded, it provided schools or modified curricula in existing schools to meet Roman standards. Grammar instruction throughout Europe therefore had a coherent orientation that emphasized adherence to a literary norm. However, after the Empire collapsed, the fragmented European societies had a new Golden Age—the time of the Empire—and Latin was their bridge to a more civilized and sophisticated past.

The Church emerged from the collapse of civilization not only as the most powerful social force in Europe but also as the sole repository of classical knowledge. Soon it found itself in a difficult position. For at least 200 years before the fall of the Empire, the Church had been a fierce opponent of education. "The wisdom of man is foolish before God" was a favorite expression among the clergy. But rampant illiteracy was an obstacle to priesthood; a priest who could not read could not instruct parishioners in the lessons of the Bible. In this context, knowledge of Latin also became a source of power. Although the Venerable Bede translated portions of the Bible into English as early as the end of the 7th century, vernacular translations were rare and essentially uncirculated. Nearly all copies of the Bible existed only in Latin. Thus, even as the Latin language was changing rapidly into Spanish, Italian, French, and Portuguese, the Church schools continued to use Latin as the basis of instruction and continued to teach Latin grammar. When Latin ceased being a living language—that is, when it no longer had any native speakers—the only way to learn it was through mastering its complex grammar.

In the Middle Ages, then, we see a fundamental shift in the nature of education from the secular to the religious. The focus was not on providing universal education but rather on providing a religious education to a select few. Moreover, the goal was not to develop more enlightened and productive citizens but rather to maintain a steady flow of literate priests. Even many kings were illiterate. Latin became the prestige language, much as Greek had been during the Empire, and educated people—that is, members of the priesthood—were expected to be bilingual, with Latin as their second language.

Nevertheless, Church leaders saw no need to reinvent the wheel. The system of religious education that developed drew heavily on the Roman model. The course of study continued to be divided into the elementary trivium and the more advanced quadrivium; the trivium, however, was altered to include a heavier emphasis on the study of literature. Rhetoric no longer dealt exclusively with the means of persuasion but now included the study of law. More striking is that the trivium no longer was limited to elementary education; instead, it was expanded greatly, encompassing elementary, secondary, and college education. Completion of the trivium entitled students to a bachelor of arts degree. The quadrivium still included arithmetic, geometry, and astronomy, but geography and natural history, as well as astrology, were added to the curriculum. Music study, on the other hand, was reduced almost completely to signing and composing hymns. When students finished the quadrivium, they were awarded a master of arts degree. The seven arts of the Roman period became the "seven liberal arts," a phrase that eventually was reduced simply to the "liberal arts," which form the basis of our undergraduate education today.

Throughout the Middle Ages, the study of grammar maintained its important place in education. R. W. Hunt (1980) stated that, during the 11th and 12th centuries, "everyone had to study grammar, and it was regarded as the 'foundation and root' of all teaching" (p. 1).

It is easy to understand why. When a language has no native speakers, nuances of expression and structure are easily lost and difficult (if not impossible) to retrieve. Consequently, students and teachers during the Middle Ages had to rely on the Latin grammars produced by Donatus and Priscian to understand the form and function of the language. Written in the 4th and 6th centuries, respectively, these grammars were comprehensive and authoritative but difficult to understand because they were written for native speakers of Latin and were not intended to teach Latin as a *second language*. Consequently, teachers and students alike faced a dual challenge: mastering Latin grammar and also trying to understand exactly what Donatus and Priscian meant. Scholars during this period did not write new grammar books—rather they wrote glosses, or explanatory commentaries, on Donatus and Priscian in an effort to understand the nuances of the language (R. W. Hunt, 1980).

These commentaries usually referred to classical literary texts to illustrate difficult points. The approach to instruction was similar in many respects to the grammar-translation method still used today in some schools to teach foreign languages. Students would study Latin grammar and vocabulary and then apply their knowledge to translating (and in some cases explaining) the text of an ancient author, such as Cicero.

By the end of the 13th century, the curriculum began to change. Throughout the Greek and Roman periods and during the early Middle Ages, grammar and logic were distinct areas of study. This distinction started to disappear toward the end of the 13th century, perhaps as a result of new developments in mathematics. Logic and grammar often were studied and taught together as language scholars connected the two areas in an attempt to approach language with the orderliness found in logic. For many years, Latin was viewed as the logically normal form of speech, but the growing influence of mathematics led to more formal logical structures that increasingly became the norm by which to measure language. Scholars began comparing the natural language of speech to the artificial languages of math and logic and asserted that natural language should conform accordingly. We see the outcome of this effort in the argument that double negatives, such as *I ain't got no money,* are incorrect because two negatives make a positive, which is certainly true in math. These scholars (as well as many of today's teachers) failed to recognize that language and math operate on different principles and that no one would ever understand a sentence like *I ain't go no money* to mean that the speaker actually *has* money.

The appeal of order may have been the result of fundamental changes in the way Europeans viewed the world. Before 1250 AD, people viewed reality in qualitative terms. For example, the cardinal directions were not viewed merely as points on a map—they had a more profound signification. As Crosby (1997) noted:

> South signified warmth and was associated with charity and the Passion of Jesus. East, toward the location of the terrestrial paradise, Eden, was especially potent, and that is why churches were oriented east-west with the business end, the altar, at the east. World maps were drawn with east at the top. "True north" was due east, a principle to which we pay respect every time we "orient" ourselves. (p. 38)

The shift to a quantitative world view may well have altered reactions to language that deviated from both the literary norm and assumed connections between speech and logic. We know that during this same period scholars produced a variety of general grammars that were different from their predecessors in that they attempted to show how linguistic structure was based on logical principles. What emerged was the view that people who spoke "incorrectly" were not only violating the rules of the grammar but also were being *illogical*. In a world increasingly dominated by logic rather than faith, the label of "illogical" was damning—and still is. Grammar study, therefore, was believed to improve the quality of mind.

THE AGE OF ENLIGHTENMENT

Between the 13th and 17th centuries, grammar instruction changed very little. Schools remained extensions of the Church, and the focus was on training students in Latin so they could enter the priesthood. The Renaissance, however, with its celebration of the human as well as the divine, gave rise to a sense of individualism that had been absent in Medieval society. Perhaps more important for societies and civilization was the significant increase in commerce, which grew almost without interruption after the early 1400s. By creating a middle class, which had not existed since the fall of the Roman Empire, commerce altered the very structure of Medieval society. For example, the law of primogeniture required transfer of property from parents to their firstborn sons. As a result, large numbers of young men who were not firstborn had for centuries turned to the Church and priestly orders for their livelihood. Commerce offered opportunities where none had previously existed: These second sons could look forward to a future in business. Thus, the middle class recognized that literacy had value that extended beyond commerce, and private secular schools, often sponsored by wealthy burghers, were opened throughout Europe and North America to meet the needs of family and enterprise.

Another important factor in educational change was the Protestant Reformation, led by Martin Luther and John Calvin. For 1,500 years, the Church had insisted that priests were spiritual mediators who alone could explain the Bible. Most people were illiterate and knew no Latin, so this role went unchallenged. Martin Luther (1483–1546) and John Calvin (1509–1564) preached that spiritual mediation was unnecessary and that faith and biblical knowledge should be in the hands of the individual believer, not the priesthood or the religious hierarchy. Such a personal relationship with God was not possible, however, as long as the Bible existed only in Latin, so Luther translated the Bible into German to give the common people access to all priestly authority: the Word of God. The invention of the printing press in 1440 ensured this access. Prior to Gutenberg's invention, books were so extremely rare and expensive that only the Church and members of the nobility could afford them. The printing press altered this situation completely. Eisenstein (1980) reported that by 1500 there were 1,000 printing shops in Europe, an estimated 35,000 titles, and 20 million books in print. The first English grammar book, explaining Latin grammar, was published in 1586.[4]

In this context, the 18th century—the Age of Enlightenment—saw a surge in the number of schools throughout Europe, both private and public. Germany took the lead, establishing compulsory education in 1717. John Locke

---

[4]Illiteracy was still a problem, however. St. Ansgar had produced the *Biblia Pauperum,* or *Poor Man's Bible,* in the 9th century, a picture book of biblical scenes for the illiterate that was widely used for hundreds of years. When Niccolò Malermi published the first Italian translation of the Bible in 1490, *Biblia vulgare istoriata,* he was careful to include numerous illustrations to aid the illiterate and semiliterate. The *Biblia vulgare* proved so popular that it went into six editions in 15 years, no doubt in part because the pictures helped people learn how to read through matching words and pictures.

had published *Some Thoughts Concerning Education* in 1693, in which he argued that the goal of education was to prepare the child to achieve future independence in the world. This preparation required the development of a logical mind, but it also entailed controlling the child's true, unruly nature through moral instruction. Grammar study was believed helpful in both regards, an idea with roots in ancient Greece, as already noted. Grammar study was seen as the foundation for literacy, and literacy allowed students to read literature rich in moral lessons.

During the 18th century, the spread of education and industrialization created greater socioeconomic mobility, which in turn led to a mingling of people from different backgrounds that had not been possible for more than 1,000 years. Increasing numbers of people from the growing middle class started having regular contact with the upper class. Although in England both upper-class and middle-class people spoke the same language, there were noticeable differences in pronunciation, structure, and vocabulary—what we term *dialect*—much like the differences we notice in the United States between speakers from different parts of the country. Because the upper-class dialects identified one with prestige and success, mastering the upper-class speech patterns became very desirable, and notions of grammar became more normative than ever.

The vision of grammar as a normative power was perhaps most strongly expressed in Bishop Robert Lowth's *A Short Introduction to English Grammar,* a book (first published in 1762) that many scholars believe influenced the teaching of English grammar more than any other. Not surprisingly, Lowth based his discussion of English grammar on Latin. What distinguished his book, however, was that he moved beyond the view that grammar study disciplined the mind; he sought to provide a guide to those who wanted to use correct English. The problem, as Kapel (1996) noted, is that "rather than basing his grammatical rules on the usage of the best educated speakers and writers of English, he erringly and foolishly based them on the Latin grammatical system, a system wholly inappropriate and incapable of dictating usage in a language as different from Latin as German-based English" (p. 1).

It was Lowth who first claimed that infinitives in English cannot be split and that sentences cannot end with a preposition. According to Lowth, the following sentence is ungrammatical:

- Our 5-year mission was *to boldly go* where no man had gone before.

The italics identify the part of the sentence that is supposedly problematic. The phrase *to go* is an infinitive verb phrase and is separated by the word *boldly*. An infinitive verb phrase in English always is formed by putting the word *to* in front of the verb. In Latin, however, infinitive verb phrases are single words, not two words. We can use Spanish to illustrate this principle because Spanish is a Latin-based language. In Spanish, the infinitive verb phrase *to speak* is *hablar,* one word. It is not possible to split the infinitive, and any attempt to do so would be both impossible and ridiculous. But because English forms the infinitive verb phrase using two words, it is possible to split the infinitive, and, indeed, speakers and writers do so all the time. In claiming that the infinitive in English should not be split, Lowth and his often witless adherents were trying to force English to fit the structure and grammar of Latin.

Language scholars during this time suffered from a fundamental confusion that had its roots in the notion of linguistic decay first formulated by the Greeks. They noted that well-educated people wrote and spoke good Latin; those who were not so well educated, on the other hand, made mistakes. These scholars did not recognize that reproducing a dead language is an academic exercise, and they applied their observation to modern languages. In this view, those without education and culture corrupt the language with their deviations from the prescribed norm. Accordingly, the discourse forms of books and upper-class conversation represented an older and purer level of language from which the speech of the common people had degenerated.

THE AGE OF REASON

The 19th century—The Age of Reason—witnessed fundamental shifts in society that inevitably affected grammar study. Although industrialization is often cited as the most significant social change during this century, equally important was the population explosion in Europe and the United States that industrialization set off.

As Greenword, Seshadri, and Vandenbroucke (2002) indicated, industrialization had the greatest influence on poor farmers. In 1800, 80% of Americans lived on farms. During the 1850s alone, approximately 23% of American males between the ages of 20 and 30 migrated to cities to work in factories (Ferrie, 1999). The material improvement was modest, but it was enough to trigger a population explosion. Greenword et al., for example, noted that "the baby boom [of the 19th century] is explained by an atypical burst of technological progress in the household sector that ... lowered the cost of having children" (p. 1). Census data reflect the extent of the baby boom. The National Center for Education Statistics (1993) reported that the U.S. population in 1800 was 5.3 million; by 1850 it was 23 million, of which only about 4 million was the result of immigration. England experienced similar growth. Aldrich (1999) reported that the population of England and Wales doubled between 1800 and 1850.

Both the middle class and the wealthy saw the huge increase in the poor population as a threat. The French Revolution (1789–1799) was fresh in everyone's memories, and many recognized it as a struggle between the haves and the have-nots in which the peasants of France had overwhelmed the ruling class and turned society upside down. Understandably, concern in England and America over the proper education of the multiplying poor escalated in the first half of the century. Civic and corporate leaders saw the need to instill moral and social values in the young to maintain stability and a reliable workforce. But the baby boom children were from families who could not pay private school tuition, and even if they had been able, there simply were not enough schools for everyone. In an effort to meet the sudden need for mass schooling, communities everywhere transformed their Sunday schools to include the basics of reading, writing, and arithmetic. According to Aldrich (1999), "by 1851, three-quarters of … working-class children aged five to 15 were enrolled in Sunday schools" (p. 1). These schools comfortingly ensured that rowdy poor children received lessons steeped in morality and civic virtue. They provided the added benefit of keeping these youngsters busy all day every Sunday—the only day that most were not at work.

This approach could not serve over the long term, however, and politicians began exploring options. Although Massachusetts had decreed in 1647 that any settlement of 50 families must have a grammar school and all states had encouraged universal education, Massachusetts did not implement compulsory education laws until 1852. Most of the other states soon followed suit, and by the end of the 19th century, America essentially had nationwide compulsory education.

Mass education led to a reconceptualization of how grammar was taught. Elementary schools retained the first function, linking grammar and reading to provide students access to important moral lessons. Published in 1835, *Cobb's Juvenile Reader* was a very popular text with a preface that included the following statement: "Containing interesting, moral, and instructive reading lessons, composed of words of one and two syllables: designed for the use of small children in families and schools" (1835, n.p.). Even more popular were the McGuffey readers, first published in 1836. These books were used throughout the United States until World War I and were noted for their moral lessons.

In addition, the normative, prescriptive function of grammar became more pronounced, with teachers drawing on the dictates of Lowth and inventing some of their own, such as the injunction against the word *ain't*. As Cmiel (1991) noted, the ability to speak correctly became a matter of class distinction, in part as a result of the Civil War and the demonization of Southern dialects. Soon, failure to follow the prescriptions for correct speaking was deemed not only an error in logic but also a sign of moral inferiority.

Not long after the war, the prescriptive function found its way into writing as, in 1874, Adams Sherman Hill offered the nation's first composition courses at Harvard. The 18th century had seen grammar instruction alter its focus from the study of Latin to include prescriptive notions of what constituted correct English. Another change was related to the connection between grammar and rhetoric. Throughout much of Western history, grammar and rhetoric were distinct areas of instruction. Grammar was concentrated at the elementary level and was used to develop basic literacy, whereas rhetoric was for advanced students and provided facility in speaking. The study of logic usually was part of the study of rhetoric, following Aristotle, who provided a lengthy discussion of logic as a method of argumentative proof in his *Art of Rhetoric.* Starting in the Middle Ages, grammar was studied at the advanced level, but primarily to further the understanding of Latin. However, rhetoric had been undergoing a transition since the 4th century, when St. Augustine's work on biblical exegesis and a variety of social forces reduced the status of speaking (primary rhetoric) and elevated the status of writing (secondary rhetoric).

This shift accelerated during the Middle Ages. Advances in science increased the importance of logic and diminished the importance of rhetoric's five offices—invention, arrangement, style, memory, and delivery—which historically had been vital components of rhetorical studies. Then, in the 16th century, Peter Ramus launched an attack on rhetoric with his master's thesis, entitled "All of Aristotle's Doctrines Are False," and went on to make some striking claims. He argued that rhetoric should be subsumed under logic, rather than the reverse, and that rhetoric itself involved nothing more than style and delivery.

Ramus' martyrdom in the Massacre of St. Bartholomew (1572) ensured that his ideas were disseminated throughout Europe. The consequences of their influence become clear when we consider that invention in rhetoric had always provided the *content* of discourse. If rhetoric has no content and no means of developing content, all that remains is style. In addition, the close connection between logic and grammar inevitably led to a perception that style—that is, rhetoric—was largely about the study of grammar. This was the message of Alexander Bain's (1866) *English Composition and Rhetoric,* in which he argued that *rhetoric was composition,* thereby completing the subordination of primary rhetoric that had begun with St. Augustine. Teaching rhetoric ceased being about public speaking and became all about teaching writing.

Furthermore, as Crowley (1990) noted, the focus on style ended the centuries-long emphasis in rhetoric on *generating* knowledge—its epistemic function—and rhetoric became a vehicle for merely *transmitting* knowledge, what was already known. Crowley stated that "the best to be hoped for from writing was that it would copy down whatever writers already knew. What writers knew, of course, was the really important stuff—but this was not the province of writing instruction" (p. 160).

Adams Sherman Hill developed the composition courses at Harvard in this context, after two thirds of the 1872 freshman class failed the writing exam that the school required for the first time as a way of separating the wheat from the chaff. Although today we think of Harvard as being an elite institution with a history of educating the children of wealthy and influential parents, it was a different place in the 19th century. Many of its students certainly came from affluent families, but it also had a fair number of students of middling means. Moreover, as Geiger (1999, p. 48) noted, the goal of higher education in America during this period was to discipline the minds of unruly students, not to provide them with knowledge. Indeed, most professors saw their students as intellectual midgets with little knowledge of and even less appreciation for the liberal arts, so there was no expectation that they could actually produce anything worth reading.

On this account, Bain's (1866) reduction of rhetoric to composition and composition to style was astutely in tune with the educational spirit of the times and provided the perfect theoretical and pedagogical framework for composition instruction. Teachers did not have to concern themselves with how to teach content or with how to help students generate content on their own. Instead, the question that teachers had to answer was this: How do we teach style? The answer lay in pedagogical structures that already were in place—the study of literature and grammar. If literature represented an older and purer level of language, and if grammar provided a set of prescriptive rules for producing such language, writing instruction necessarily must focus on reading literature and studying grammar. Reading literature would edify the spirit, making students better persons, and studying grammar would improve student writing, making it clear, concise, and error free. It is this legacy that teachers bring into today's classrooms whenever they teach writing.

MODERN GRAMMARS

Much of what follows in this book is about modern grammars, so a lengthy discussion is inappropriate here. I will note, however, that the 19th century witnessed two important events related to the study of grammar: (a) the fossilization of the idea that grammar is a prescriptive set of rules for producing correct English, and (b) the establishment of the foundation for modern grammars, which are *descriptive* rather than prescriptive. Chapter 4 relates this story in detail, but suffice it to say that scholars investigating the languages of American Indians discovered that Latin-based rules could not be made to fit what was being observed and recorded on reservations. What followed was a major reassessment of grammar and the development of new grammars that provide insight not only into the structure of language but also into how people use language.

But the new grammars also created a paradox. Today, language scholars use the new grammars and fully embrace their descriptive orientation. Language teachers, on the other hand, continue to use the prescriptive, Latin-based grammar of the 19th century, as though the world has stood still for more than a hundred years.

2

Teaching Grammar[1]

RECOGNIZING THE CHALLENGES

Grammar instruction is a significant part of the language arts curriculum at all levels of public education. Because performance expectations are high, prospective teachers face several challenges before they enter the classroom. They must know English grammar exceptionally well. Meeting this basic requirement is hindered by the fact that nearly all language arts teachers receive a degree in English, which inevitably focuses on literature, not grammar. Most future teachers take one college-level grammar course before obtaining their credentials, but these courses have been criticized as being mere introductions to a complex subject that do not adequately prepare teachers for the task ahead. In some instances, the content may not be current. In others, the course may focus on what is called *traditional grammar* (the subject of chapter 3) rather than modern grammars, in which case the syllabus will slight or even ignore developments that have occurred since the early 1900s.[2]

On this account, many new teachers feel underprepared to teach grammar and resort to following the instructor's manual for whatever textbook their schools have adopted. Although following the textbook may seem like a reasonable pedagogical approach, it usually isn't. Such textbooks tend to give

---

[1]This chapter deals with teaching grammar to native speakers of English. Some observations and principles do not apply to those for whom English is not the home language.

[2]No criticism of these courses or their professors is intended here. From a practical perspective, the decision to base a college-level grammar course on traditional grammar is understandable, for this is the pedagogical orientation of most schools. My view, however, is that all language arts teachers need to know as much about grammar as possible. For this reason alone, limiting instruction to traditional grammar is problematic.

modern grammars short shrift and focus just on terminology. In addition, prospective teachers must know how to teach grammar effectively, and this information is not going to be found in a textbook for high school students or in the associated teacher's manual, particularly if the textbook is based on the drill and exercise method, as most are.

Another approach is to follow the model of one's own grammar instruction, but this also can be problematic. As I've noted elsewhere (Williams, 2003a), "A commonplace in education is that most teachers teach the way they themselves were taught" (p. 42). Because the college model may be too intense and too fast for middle or high schoolers, there's a strong urge to draw on one's memories of, say, his or her 10th-grade English class and its lessons on sentence structure. For most people, these memories will be dim—and essentially useless.

When we consider grammar pedagogy in our schools, one fact should strike us as both bizarre and unacceptable: Grammar instruction begins in third grade and continues unabated through high school, and yet our students graduate knowing very little about grammar. Think about this for a moment. Is there any other single subject in the curriculum that students study as long? After nine years of instruction, shouldn't our students be *experts* in grammar?

There are several reasons for such woeful results. The idea that grammar is just too complicated is not one of them. We explore some of these reasons shortly, but at this point one should begin to suspect that perhaps the grammar instruction we provide year after year is not very effective and that a new approach is warranted (see Williams, 2003b).

The content of instruction also presents a challenge. What exactly do we teach under the heading of "grammar"? Everyone may agree that grammar includes the parts of speech, but what about punctuation and spelling? We have different conventions that govern both. Moreover, punctuation is often viewed as a matter of writing style, and spelling is not related to sentence structure at all. Are they really part of grammar? Deciding the content of grammar instruction is not a simple matter, and the new teacher's task is further complicated by the observation that, as Patterson (2001) indicated, all facets of grammar instruction are usually dictated by the district, by the school principal, or by senior teachers without any consideration of research, theory, or outcomes. Of course, the number of experienced teachers who faithfully adhere to district guidelines is notoriously small, but for beginners the thought of modifying established practice can be daunting.

The students themselves present another challenge. Even the best teacher using a sound approach must face the resistance students have to grammar. Because many teachers make studying grammar an extremely painful experience—and because it only takes one such experience to get students to shut down whenever they hear the word "grammar"—successes are always hard-won. And although a lengthy critique of popular culture isn't appropriate here, it is clear that our society has lost the interest in language that led to the exploration of grammar in the first place. The focus today is on entertainment to such a degree that society expects even learning to be "fun," an attitude that trivializes the hard work necessary to master any subject (see Williams, 2002). Large numbers of students automatically label grammar study as "stupid" or a "waste of time"—expressions that are commonly applied today to anything that is difficult. Society does not make our job easier when, in the name of anti-elitism, we see Standard English ridiculed in the media and nonstandard English, with its vulgarisms and slang, celebrated.

LEARNING OUTCOMES

Any meaningful discussion of teaching grammar must begin by considering learning outcomes. Learning outcomes specify what students will know or be able to do after instruction, and they require that we *match instruction to expected outcomes*. Learning outcomes always are linked to *outcomes assessment*.

Let's consider a simple example. When teaching children addition, teachers commonly use objects such as blocks to introduce the idea of putting items into groups. The goal is to help students understand how addition is a grouping procedure, and the learning outcome is that they will be able to add 2 + 2 and get 4. Instruction might involve asking students to take two red blocks, put them with two yellow blocks, and then count the total number of blocks. If the instruction is well grounded and successful, students will, indeed, learn addition, which we would assess by asking them to add some numbers.

But there are many ways to teach addition, and we can easily imagine some that are ineffective because they are based on flawed theory or faulty assumptions about what contributes to learning how to add. For example, a teacher might propose that understanding the shapes of numbers is related to addition. In such a case, we probably would find this hypothetical teacher asking students to engage in activities related to number shapes, tracing 2s and 4s or looking at them from different angles. Because outcomes always must be tied to instruction, we would have to ask in this scenario whether studying the shapes of numbers leads to student mastery of addition. It should be obvious that the answer is *no* for the simple reason that the shapes of numbers are unrelated to the nature of addition.

We must apply this kind of critical analysis when teaching grammar. We must decide in advance what we want students to know and be able to do after studying grammar, and we must plan lessons that enable them to achieve objectives.

Faulty Assumptions

Successful grammar instruction involves matching instruction to expected outcomes and then assessing whether the instruction was effective. As I've already suggested, there is ample anecdotal evidence that these crucial considerations are absent in typical language arts classes. More evidence follows, but at this point we need to consider why years of instruction might not produce students who have much knowledge or understanding of grammar.

One factor is that the long history of grammar instruction has instilled in us certain pedagogical assumptions that are difficult for most teachers to challenge and that make developing viable learning outcomes extremely difficult without a radical change in perspective. The most influential assumptions are the following:

- Grammar instruction leads to correct speaking.
- Grammar instruction develops logical thinking.
- Grammar instruction improves writing and reduces or even eliminates errors.

Grammar and Speech. Let's take the first assumption and use it to formulate "correct speaking" as a learning outcome. The most common approach to teaching grammar is drill and exercise. Students drill on grammar terminology—*noun, verb, preposition,* and so on—and then complete exercises in which they are required to identify the various parts of individual sentences. Given enough encouragement and practice, students can become very good at these activities. But it should be obvious that there is no match between such activities and speaking and that the fundamental requirement of learning outcomes is not met. These activities can be completed successfully without speaking at all, which no doubt accounts for the fact that we just don't find any language arts classes in which there is an attempt to link grammar lessons explicitly with speaking.

Still, the hope exists that something from these drills and exercises will have an influence on students' speech. Somehow, the ability to identify nouns in workbook sentences is supposed to transfer to speech. This hope is ill-founded. Consider the following: Nearly all young people today use the word *like* repeatedly when speaking, and the expression *goes like* has in most instances replaced the word *said.* As a result, sentence 1 below typically appears in current speech as sentence 2:

1. And then Macarena said, "I'm not going to dinner with you."
2. And then Macarena goes like, "I'm not going to dinner with you."

For anyone who uses sentence 2, no amount of drilling and exercising will result in a change in speech patterns to sentence 1, which outcomes assessment and even casual observation reveal (see Wolfram, Adger, & Christian, 1999). To influence speech, instruction would have to focus on speech. Grammar instruction doesn't.

Grammar and Logical Thinking. A similar situation exists with regard to the second assumption. Some people believe that certain logical mental operations are innate. For example, if someone tells us that a friend fell into a pool of water, we seem to understand intuitively that the friend will be wet. We do not have to see the person to reach this logical conclusion. But scholars who study logical mental operations, such as Johnson-Laird (1983, 2001), have suggested that logic is based on experience. In other words, we can logically conclude that the person who fell into the water got wet because we have experience with water and its properties.

Johnson-Laird's (1983) investigations into our ability to process and comprehend logical statements led to a widely accepted model for logical reasoning. This model posits that our logical performance depends on a grasp of how the words in statements relate to the world. Stated another way, our ability to reason logically depends on our ability to develop a mental model of the relations expressed in logical statements.

On this basis, we can see why it is rather easy to process syllogisms of the following type:

All men are mortal. (statement 1)

Socrates is a man. (statement 2)

Therefore, Socrates is mortal. (logical conclusion)

We have experience with men and mortality, so we can relate these statements to the world.

However, if we change the wording of a syllogism slightly, such that it is difficult to develop a mental model of the real-world relations, logical operations become nearly impossible. Johnson-Laird (1983) found that none of the subjects in his research could arrive at a valid logical conclusion for the following two statements:

All of the students are athletes.

None of the writers is a student.

Many subjects proposed "None of the athletes is a writer," but that is incorrect because some of the writers could be athletes without being students. Equally incorrect is the conclusion that "None of the writers is an athlete." The only valid conclusions are "Some of the writers are not athletes" and "Some of the athletes are not writers." Only when subjects were allowed to draw diagrams to represent the relations expressed in the given statements could they arrive at the correct logical conclusions.

The question of transfer is central to the assumption. What the research suggests is that logical reasoning is situation specific, in which case it is not readily transferable. But the ease with which we process simple syllogisms makes it appear as though exercises in syllogistic reasoning will increase our logical abilities overall. Furthermore, the history of grammar instruction, as well as the folk psychology that informs much of what we do in education, inclines us to believe not only that grammar is an exercise in logic but also that logical reasoning is as innate as breathing. If we can do it at all, we can do it anywhere.

This is probably an illusion. As Johnson-Laird (1983) reported, no amount of practice with syllogisms of the "all of the students are athletes" type makes formulating a valid logical conclusion easier. It's the equivalent of trying to prepare for a marathon by running 50-yard dashes. Running is involved in both cases, but 50-yard dashes will do little to prepare one for a marathon. On this account, even if we accept the premise that grammar instruction exercises logical reasoning, we can predict that no amount of grammar study will have a significant influence on students' logical thinking in general. It will affect only their logical thinking with regard to grammar. The situation-specific characteristic of logical reasoning suggests that students may fully master grammar and still reason illogically on a regular basis.[3]

Furthermore, a wide range of research suggests that general logical reasoning is related to intelligence, which increasingly has been viewed not only as the ability to develop multiple mental models to process experiences and solve problems but also as the ability to select the best one consistently from among the competing alternatives (Alcock, 2001; DeLoache, Miller, & Pierroutsakos, 1998; Herrnstein & Murray, 1994; Pinker, 2002; Rumelhart & McClelland, 1986; Steinberg, 1993).[4] Formal instruction, of course, does not have a significant effect on intelligence (Pinker, 2002).

At this point, our analysis of the first two assumptions indicates that a significant disconnect exists between grammar instruction and learning outcomes. The final assumption, that grammar instruction improves writing and reduces

---

[3]Following a suggestion by Bloom (1994), Pinker (2002) stated that "The logic of grammar can be used to grasp large numbers: the expression *four thousand three hundred and fifty-seven* has the grammatical structure of an English noun phrase like *hat, coat, and mittens*. When a student parses the number phrase she can call to mind the mental operation of aggregation, which is related to the mathematical operation of addition" (p. 223). To the best of my knowledge there is no supporting evidence for this claim. Also, what Pinker described here is merely a mnemonic, not a logical operation.

[4]Although educators have thoroughly accepted Gardner's (1983, 1993, 2000) theory of multiple intelligences, the majority of scholars in psychology and cognitive science seem to have dismissed it, largely on the grounds that the theory lacks empirical support (Klein, 1998; Morgan, 1996).

or even eliminates errors, is the most powerful and misunderstood. Consequently, it warrants special consideration.

GRAMMAR AND WRITING

Any principled discussion of grammar and writing necessarily must consider a number of factors associated with writing instruction, a topic that could easily fill an entire book. What follows cannot possibly be comprehensive but covers some of the central issues.

First, it is important to recognize that our approach to teaching writing has changed very little since the first composition classes were offered at Harvard in 1874. The Harvard model was adopted quickly at colleges across the country, and high schools with any ambition of getting their graduates admitted to institutions of higher learning had to follow suit. As noted in the previous chapter, this model is predicated on the idea that students are empty headed, so the focus of instruction is on the structure, or form, of writing.

Today, labeling students empty headed is not acceptable or tolerated. Nevertheless, the writing curriculum in most schools treats them as though they are. The modern application of the Harvard model is congruent with two powerful beliefs in English education. The first is that the study of literature does not involve content beyond plot summaries and character descriptions. Instead, it emphasizes *reactions* to literature. The second is that self-esteem should be bestowed rather than earned and that negative evaluations are at odds with the goal of enhancing students' sense of worth. As a result, our language arts classes typically focus on personal experience or reaction papers.

This approach does not require any attention to or assessment of content because one student's reaction to a reading assignment cannot be judged as being any better than another's. The same principle applies to personal experiences. Everything is relative. There is no "right" or "wrong" in self-expressive writing—there is only the expression of true feeling. It also has the perceived benefit of helping to equalize evaluations by removing a significant criterion from assessment.[5] As Haussamen, Benjamin, Kolln, and Wheeler (2003) noted, "We're not comfortable encouraging students to be original and authentic one minute and then assigning them exercises in sentence structure the next" (p. xi). This sentiment is so strong that even after identifying the problem, Haussamen et al. could not address the probability that the emphasis on originality and authenticity in our public schools is profoundly misplaced. Instead, we have to turn to a keener observer, David

---

[5]See Williams (2003a) for fuller discussion of the Harvard model and its influence on contemporary writing instruction.

Fleming (2002), to find the hard but accurate word on the state of the profession. He surveyed the field and concluded that the typical composition curriculum is lacking "substance" and is "intellectually meager" (p. 115).

If instruction and evaluation do not address content, then the only legitimate factor in assessment is form, or style. This is where grammar instruction comes in. However, the stress on style forces us to adopt a peculiar view of what constitutes good writing—form without substance, the mechanically correct essay that contains absolutely nothing worth reading. In an attempt to skirt the inherent problems in this definition, several scholars and many teachers, as already intimated, have sought to define good writing as "authentic writing," which expresses an "authentic voice" (see Davis, 2004; Elbow, 1973, 1981; Macrorie, 1970; Coles & Vopat, 1985). "Authentic writing" consists exclusively of personal experience writing. Lindemann (1985) noted, for example, that "Good writing is most effective when we tell the truth about who we are" (p. 110). But as I've noted elsewhere (Williams, 2003a), the "authentic writing" that receives the highest praise seems inevitably to be that in which students reveal their most painful personal experiences (p. 64). Writing becomes a form of confession and the teacher a voyeur. Private writing is made public by the misguided authority of the classroom. A moment's reflection should prompt us to question not only how this approach prepares young people for real-world writing tasks in business, education, and government, but also whether the role of voyeur is professionally appropriate.

College teachers of 1st-year composition see the consequences of such writing instruction every year: Students who received good grades in high school English, where personal experience writing served them well, are stunned when they get their first papers back with low grades largely because the writing is vacuous. One unfortunate result is that college teachers in all disciplines complain bitterly that high school writing instruction fails to teach students how to produce academic discourse. They blame high school teachers.

It therefore seems that current practices in the public school language arts curriculum may minister to certain intangible goals, such as convincing large numbers of students that they are reasonably good writers and thereby artificially enhancing their self-esteem, but they do not appear to have any beneficial effect on actual writing performance. Of course, anecdotes from college professors may not be compelling, but National Assessment of Educational Progress (NAEP) data should be. They show that writing skills among our students at all levels have been in steady decline for more than 20 years. A 1999 assessment of writing in grades 4, 8, and 12 found that the percentages of students performing at the basic (below average) level were 84, 84, and 78, respectively.

Only 1% of students at each grade level performed at the advanced (above average) level (U.S. Department of Education, 1999).[6]

On this account, we should begin to understand that we cannot continue to define good writing merely in terms of form, of structure. Good writing—and thus good teaching—should focus on content, on having something worthwhile to share with readers. The focus on form, on grammar, therefore seems fundamentally flawed. Equally important, we should begin to recognize that the unrestrained emphasis on private writing, on personal experiences, fails mightily to help students master the kind of writing that will be demanded of them in college and the workplace.

A Comment on Errors

That people sometimes make mistakes whenever they use language is a given. We are all familiar with slips of the tongue and malapropisms. Because speech is transient, we tend to let these mistakes pass by and to focus on the substance of what is being said.[7] Writing is different because it is more or less permanent and exists on the page for us to study and analyze. Any mistakes in writing, therefore, are much more apparent and annoying, so the world expects writers to demonstrate control over their work by making it largely error free. Errors that appear (such as the ones that inevitably will be found in this book) are deemed to be the result of copyediting or printing problems that somehow were overlooked, not the result of the writer's lack of knowledge or control of writing conventions. When writers cannot produce essentially error-free writing, they are viewed either as incompetent or as having no regard for readers. Neither judgment is desirable, so we rightly devote a vast amount of effort in our schools to produce competent, if not good, writers.

An Empirical Question. Without a doubt, underlying this effort is the most pervasive assumption in language arts—that grammar instruction improves writing and reduces or even eliminates errors. Chapter 1 traced the roots of this assumption, and now we need to examine it closely. An important first step is to understand that this is an empirical question: It can be tested. Moreover, *informal* testing has been going on for countless years and takes place daily in our schools.

Operating under the grammar-improves-writing assumption, teachers instruct students in grammar terminology and rules, and they do an admirable

---

[6]At the time of this writing, the 1999 NAEP report is the most current available.

[7]There are obvious exceptions. President George W. Bush inspired several websites and books devoted to "Bushisms."

job. The governing expectation is that when teachers ask students to write an essay in a week or two, they will see fewer errors and greater clarity. Yet when they collect those essays for grading, they find that the papers are riddled with errors of all kinds: subject–verb agreement problems, faulty and even haphazard punctuation, incorrect word use, and the like. In other words, assessment of student performance indicates that the outcomes have not been achieved.

We can understand the problem easily if we consider that grammar instruction, especially the drill and exercise kind, does not involve writing essays. Any valid assessment of what we are teaching via grammar drills and exercises must assess students' performance on grammar drills and exercises. The educational principle here is fundamental: We assess what we teach. We obviously are not teaching writing when we teach grammar: Our grammar instruction is about identifying form and function—parts of speech, sentence types, and so forth. Writing instruction is about audience, intention, revision, argument, support, documentation, and so on. The substance of grammar instruction is so different from the substance of writing instruction that only centuries of confusion, as summarized in the previous chapter, could blind us to the point that we mistake one for the other. Many of us also blithely ignore the violation of a fundamental educational principle when we assess grammar instruction on the basis of student essays. We are engaged in invalid assessment each time we use students' writing to measure how well they have mastered grammar. We just aren't assessing what we teach.

Our public school culture leads teachers to react to students' writing errors in predictable ways. Rather than question the underlying assumption, they generally conclude that they did not present the grammar lessons effectively and will repeat them. They may conclude that their students were careless or perhaps resistant and will lecture their students on the need for error-free writing and greater attention to mechanics. Or they may conclude that their students are dull and did not understand the lessons, although they seemed to be able to complete the assigned exercises without too much difficulty, and will repeat them. In other words, more grammar instruction inevitably follows, as well as another essay in a couple of weeks. And when teachers grade these new papers, they find the same errors, again.

What should be most surprising is that this cycle will continue without anyone ever reaching the conclusion that the governing assumption is false and that the entire enterprise is misguided. The outcomes are explained and rationalized so that the failure to improve student writing performance is blamed on the students or the teacher, where it does not belong. Only the most reflective teachers begin to suspect that their instruction does not match learning outcomes.

The Research on Grammar Instruction: A Brief Summary

Formal testing of the assumption began in the 1950s. In the early 1960s, the National Council of Teachers of English (NCTE) asked Braddock, Lloyd-Jones, and Schoer to examine the existing research and assess the status of the field. Published in 1963, their report offered what has become the most widely known statement on grammar and writing:

> In view of the widespread agreement of research studies based upon many types of students and teachers, the conclusion can be stated in strong and unqualified terms that teaching formal [traditional] grammar has a negligible or, because it usually displaces some instruction and practice in actual composition, even a harmful effect on the improvement of writing. (pp. 37–38)

This assessment was strong, but it did not stop various researchers from further investigating grammar instruction and writing performance. Whitehead (1966), for example, compared a group of high school students who received no grammar instruction in writing classes with one who received instruction in traditional grammar, with an emphasis on sentence diagramming. The results showed no significant difference in writing performance between the two groups. White (1965) studied three classes of seventh graders. Two of the classes studied grammar, whereas the third used this time reading popular novels. At the end of the study, White found no significant difference in terms of writing performance. The students who had been reading novels wrote just as well as those who had studied grammar.

Gale (1968) studied fifth graders, dividing them into four groups. One group received no grammar instruction, whereas the other three studied one of three different types of grammar. Students in two of the grammar groups, but not the students who studied traditional grammar, ended up being able to write slightly more complex sentences than students in the other two groups, but there were no measurable differences in overall writing ability.

In another investigation, Bateman and Zidonis (1966) conducted a 2-year study that started when the students were in ninth grade. Some of the students received instruction in grammar during this period, the rest received no grammar instruction. Again, there was no significant difference in overall writing performance.

Elley, Barham, Lamb, and Wyllie (1976) began with a relatively large pool of subjects (248), which they studied for 3 years. Some critics of the earlier studies had suggested that the lack of any measurable differences might be the result of different teaching styles, so the researchers were particularly careful to control this variable. The students were divided into three groups. The first studied grammar, various organizational modes (narration, argumentation, analysis, etc.), and literature. The second group studied the same organizational modes and literature as the first group but not grammar; instead, they practiced creative writing and were given the chance to do additional reading. The third group studied traditional grammar and engaged in reading popular fiction.

At the end of each year of the investigation, students were evaluated on a range of measures to determine comparative growth. These measures included vocabulary, reading comprehension, sentence complexity, usage, spelling, and punctuation. Students also wrote essays at the end of each year that were scored for content, style, organization, and mechanics. No significant differences on any measures were found among the three groups at the end of the 1st year. At the end of the 2nd year, the students who had studied traditional grammar produced essays that were judged to have better content than those of the students who had not studied any grammar, but the raters found no significant difference on other factors, such as mechanics and sentence complexity, which were judged similar for all groups.

At the end of the 3rd year, the various factors related to writing were evaluated a final time. A series of standardized measures showed that the students who had studied grammar performed better on the usage test than those who had not, but no significant differences on the other measures were found. After 3 years of work and effort, the writing of the students who had studied grammar showed no significant differences in overall quality from that of students who had studied no grammar. Frequency of error in spelling, punctuation, sentence structure, and other mechanical measures did not vary from group to group. As far as their writing was concerned, studying grammar or not studying grammar simply made no difference.

Summarizing the research that was published after the Braddock et al. (1963) report, Hillocks (1986) noted that:

> None of the studies reviewed for the present report provides any support for teaching grammar as a means of improving composition skills. If schools insist upon teaching the identification of parts of speech, the parsing or diagramming of sentences, or other concepts of traditional grammar (as many still do), they cannot defend it as a means of improving the quality of writing. (p. 138)

Recently, the Institute of Education at the University of London published a review of more than 4,500 studies on grammar and writing (English Review

Group, 2004). Echoing previous investigations of this type, the report concluded that: "there is no high quality evidence ... that the teaching of the principles underlying and informing ... 'syntax' has ... [any] influence on the writing quality or accuracy of 5 to 16 year-olds"; and that "there is no high quality evidence that the teaching of grammar ... [of any kind] is worth the time if the aim is the improvement of the quality and/or accuracy of written composition" (p. 4).

The consensus of language scholars, however, has not had much effect on the curriculum. Weaver (1996) proposed several reasons for this puzzling situation. She suggested, for example, that teachers and administrators may simply be "unaware of the research" (p. 23) or, even worse, "do not believe the research" (p. 24), perhaps owing to the observable tendency among some teachers to discount empiricism as being contrary to humanistic values. In this view, the goal of writing and writing instruction is not to prepare students to succeed on college writing tasks or in the workplace but to aid their personal development as human beings. Fueling this tendency are books on grammar that ignore scholarship so as to consider the act of writing through an artistic lens. Noden (1999), for example, wrote:

The writer is an artist, painting images of life with specific and identifiable brush strokes, images as realistic as Wyeth and as abstract as Picasso.... Hidden beneath ... [a writer's work] often unnoticed and unappreciated, lies a grammar of style, a combination of artistic techniques as worthy of respect and awe as any museum canvas. (pp. 1–2)

The artistic sentiment is rooted, as we've seen, in the classical notion that literature represents a purer and better expression of language than everyday speech. Many of us may agree with this sentiment whenever we imagine an ideal world. But we must understand that the idea of "the writer as artist" belongs to a bygone era, at best, when education catered to the privileged leisure class. Equally problematic is the fact that the "image grammar" Noden advocated is merely a repackaging of Christensen's (1967) work on sentence combining. Based almost exclusively on literary writing, it ignores research indicating that gains in writing performance through sentence combining are temporary, as well as research and theory suggesting that the primary focus of instruction should be on the whole essay (Callaghan, 1978; Crowhurst & Piche, 1979; Green, 1973; Kerek et al., 1980; Kinneavy, 1979; Perron, 1977; Sullivan, 1978; Witte, 1980).

Today's classrooms call for a more realistic view, given the large number of nonnative English speakers and native English speakers with limited language skills. In terms of sheer quantity, most writing is performed in the service of government and business, where there is no place for artistic writing. Teachers have a professional obligation to consider what will happen to students who are taught to "paint images of life" but who must inevitably meet the demands for analytical and interpretive writing in college and the workplace.

The Nature of the Problem

There are several reasons why grammar instruction does not lead to improved writing. One that can be hard to accept but that nonetheless is crucial to effective teaching is that *most of the errors we find in the writing of native English speakers are not related to grammar.* When Connors and Lunsford (1988) surveyed college composition teachers, for example, they found that punctuation was cited as the most frequent error. Although some knowledge of grammatical structures certainly makes correct punctuation easier, it isn't necessary. At the public school level, the most common errors also include spelling and capitalization—but not grammar.

Let's consider an excerpt from a student essay that is illustrative. The student was 11 years old and produced the following on an impromptu writing test that asked for a narrative about something interesting that happened to a friend:

> on wednesday Sam was on his way to school it was like a ordemerly day. on Friday though he got detenshon whitch was proberly a good thing because he found a book on the front cover it said "Lets go" so he took it home and opened it and then he was rushed forwards in. (Henry, 2003, p. 1)

Such writing is typical for students this age, and our initial response is likely to involve some shaking of the head and an inward moan over the abuses to the language. Close examination, however, indicates that the errors here are related almost exclusively to spelling, capitalization, and punctuation—which are conventions of writing that do not exist in speech. The student produced only one grammar error. In other words, what we see in this passage is the student's lack of knowledge and/or lack of control of writing conventions, not a problem with grammar. If we fix the convention problems, we have something that is quite readable:

> On Wednesday, Sam was on his way to school. It was like an ordinary day. On Friday, though, he got detention, which probably was a good thing because he found a book. On the front cover it said, "Let's go," so he took it home and opened it, and then he was rushed forwards in.

Notice that I left the single grammar error intact: "he was rushed forwards in." Although ungrammatical, we can understand what the student wanted to communicate—something along the lines of "the book pulled him in," or "he fell into the book," or "he couldn't put it down." The concept of being drawn into a book is novel for most 11-year-olds today, which means that the student not only was attempting to express an idea that doesn't come easily to him but also that he was trying to express something that he probably had never heard anyone ever articulate before. In this context, the error seems, if not predictable, less than fatal.

The Issue Is Usage, Not Grammar. What this example illustrates is that the most serious errors students make in their writing involve conventions of *usage,* not grammar. For this reason alone, it seems that we need to shift the focus of our instruction.

As the term suggests, *usage* is related to how we use language. If grammar is about how words fit together in meaningful ways, usage is about the *words we choose* to communicate meaning. On one level, these choices differentiate formal from informal language. On another—and this is important—they differentiate Standard from nonstandard English. Too often, our language arts classes confuse usage and grammar, even though they are distinct.

Standard English, Nonstandard English, and Formal Standard English. Every person speaks a dialect, a variation of the core language that usually is associated with geographic location and/or socioeconomic status. In the United States, we have West Coast dialects, Southern dialects, Midwestern dialects, East Coast dialects, and numerous variations within each region. *Standard English* may be thought of as a dialect that includes certain features of all dialects but that is nevertheless distinct from each. More important, it is identified as the spoken language of educated persons and the written language of journalism.

Nonstandard English, like its counterpart, also includes certain features of all dialects. It exists primarily as speech, although it frequently appears in student compositions when writers import conversational features into their work. They may do so for several reasons, but chief among them is failure to recognize or accept the need to use Standard English in certain situations and an inability to control the conventions of speaking and the conventions of writing. *Formal Standard English*, on the other hand, describes spoken language in certain professional settings and nonjournalistic writing, particularly the writing of government, business, law, and education.

With regard to writing, both Standard and formal Standard English have developed a set of conventions associated with spelling, punctuation, and capitalization that operate in conjunction with the words we choose in the application of appropriate usage: Sentences begin with capital letters, words have an established spelling, and so on. Historically, an important goal of language arts instruction has been to teach students the conventions of Standard and formal Standard English.

Students who use nonstandard English have a hard time mastering Standard English, and they have an even harder time with formal Standard English. Their home dialect has served them well for years, and they may question the need to change. For many, the message they may receive in their language arts classes—that Standard and formal Standard English are important tools for success in the adult world—is distorted or even blocked by youth, inexperience, and popular culture.

Standard and formal Standard English have identical grammatical structures, but they are governed by different usage conventions. Consider the example sentences below:

3a. Gabriel Garcia Marquez has written a lot of books. (Standard English)
3b. Gabriel Garcia Marquez has written many books. (formal Standard English)
4a. Macarena was the woman that stole his heart. (Standard English)
4b. Macarena was the woman who stole his heart. (formal Standard English)

Notice how the different usage conventions result in different word choices. We use "a lot of" in speech, but not in writing. Likewise, when speaking we commonly use the word "that" in sentences like 4a, but when writing or being more formal, we use "who."

The situation is not quite the same with regard to nonstandard English. The most widely studied variety of nonstandard English, Black English Vernacular (BEV), does differ grammatically from Standard English in a number of ways (see chapter 7). But at the sentence level, the grammar of BEV and Standard English is very similar, differing slightly with respect to certain word forms, as the following sentences illustrate:

5a. Ralph is working today. (Standard English)
5b. Ralph be workin' today. (BEV)

Sensitivity to Home Dialects.   Not everyone believes that our schools should be teaching students Standard and formal Standard English. The question has been debated among educators for many years and became heated in the early 1970s, in part owing to the growing sentiment that society in general and education in particular should be more tolerant and accepting of nonstandard English.

The issue is sensitive because language is inextricably linked to who we are. We define ourselves—and others define and assess us—on the basis of the language we use, which nearly always is a reflection of our upbringing, our community, and our social class. As a result, efforts to get students who speak nonstandard English to master the conventions of Standard English are frequently seen today as an attack on a child's heritage. Many educators also believe that teaching Standard English robs children of their ethnic or cultural identity because utilizing the Standard dialect can lead children to *redefine* themselves in ways that are incongruent with their home culture. Such views are reflected in the 1974 NCTE position statement—"Students' Right to Their Own Language"—that some have interpreted as a rejection of usage conventions in general and Standard English in particular on the grounds that Standard English is elitist and discriminatory.

Tracing the various sociopolitical factors that underlie these views is beyond the scope of this book. Some comment, however, seems necessary, given the tensions that teachers must face regarding the issue. Considering the matter of redefinition in historical terms can provide some insight. Until recently, giving students the tools to redefine themselves was a legitimate goal of education. Immediately after World War II, for example, working-class parents sent their children to school in the belief that education would afford them a better life, one that took them out of poor neighborhoods and reduced the prospect of dead end or dangerous jobs. As Weir (2002) noted, America invested heavily in schools following the war because "education offered occupational mobility to millions of Americans" (p. 178). For this reason, support for education as an opportunity for redefinition was strong and widespread.

A significant side effect was economic leveling as children of working-class parents entered the middle class and the lines separating the working class from the middle class became blurred. This obvious benefit was soon offset, however, by an inevitable consequence of increased attention to education. Weir (2002) described it thus: "Expanded education, even as it opens new avenues for upward mobility, sorts the population into educated and less-educated categories" (p. 179).

The sorting process accelerated as the 1970s wound down, when the nation shifted toward a service economy. This put pressure on the middle class and, in fact, caused it to start shrinking. Simultaneously, globalization and uncontrolled immigration provided a huge labor force willing to work for substandard wages. Beginning in the 1990s and continuing today at an increasing rate, millions of highly paid U.S. workers found themselves unemployed when their jobs were exported to China, Indonesia, India, and Mexico. As a 2003 article in the *Wall Street Journal* reported, "the U.S. could lose the bulk of its information technology jobs to overseas competitors in the next decade, largely to India and China" (p. 1), and as many as 700,000 jobs in information technology and manufacturing "have moved overseas [just] in the past three years" (Schroeder & Aeppel, 2003, p. 2). Displaced workers have had little choice but to seek employment in the service sector, the only area of job growth, even though success means a significantly reduced income. But their efforts have been greatly handicapped by competition from immigrants who, lacking education and skills, have flooded the job market. According to the Public Policy Institute, in 2003 more than 40% of all service sector jobs in California were filled by Hispanics, most of them illegal, nearly all from Mexico (Baldassare & Katz, 2003). Other states are currently undergoing a similar experience.

A shrinking middle class meant that upward mobility quickly required more and better education. Competition increased. Between 1960 and 1990, America's population doubled, without a corresponding increase in the number of colleges and universities. As Herrnstein and Murray (1994) noted, our schools became very efficient at identifying the "cognitive elite," children with the potential to excel academically. The problem is that a disproportionate number of successful students come from white and Asian families. In spite of our best efforts and vast expenditures, black and Hispanic children historically have lagged behind their white and Asian counterparts, as reflected not only in SAT scores and high school grades but also in dropout rates. Census Bureau data indicate that in 2000, the black dropout rate nationwide was 13.1%—double the rate for whites—whereas the Hispanic rate was 27.8%. In states like California, Arizona, New Mexico, and Texas, with large Hispanic populations, the dropout rate is higher, in some districts a staggering 50% (U.S. Census Bureau, 2000).

The future for those who cannot compete academically is grim. By the 1980s, rather than viewing education as the key to upward mobility, many in the black and Hispanic communities came to see the sorting inherent in education as a process of labeling that ensured *downward mobility*. The hope of desegregation—that attending predominantly white schools would lead to improved performance—faded in the face of persistent low grades, poor reading and writing skills, and low SAT scores. The many individual successes among black and Hispanic students were overshadowed by the pervasive lack of group success.[8]

The reaction in many quarters was to withdraw, to return to the community in both spirit and body through a process of indigenization in which group identity becomes more important than national identity and certainly more important than mainstream education and adherence to a linguistic standard. By the early 1990s, tens of thousands of black parents were choosing to resegregate their children, some enrolling them in the multitude of Afrocentric private schools that were opening their doors nationwide, others demanding that their local (and predominantly black) public schools shift to an Afrocentric curriculum—and getting it. In this context, any language arts curriculum that

---

[8]The No Child Left Behind Act of 2002 was developed specifically to improve academic performance among blacks and Hispanics and provided $53.1 billion in federal funding for FY 2003.

included lessons in Standard English, even implicitly, was viewed as discriminatory and oppressive.

One cannot overestimate the importance of being sensitive to these perceptions and to the admittedly complex issues surrounding Standard English and its usage conventions. But it also is important to recognize that there always is a cost involved when one fails to follow convention.[9] The National Commission on Excellence in Education sounded the alarm in 1983, when it issued its report on the state of American education in *A Nation at Risk*: "Each generation of Americans has outstripped its parents in education, in literacy, and in economic attainment. For the first time in the history of our country, the educational skills of one generation will not surpass, will not equal, will not even approach, those of their parents" (1983, p. 1).

In the two plus decades since *A Nation at Risk* was published, the federal government has provided approximately $1.4 trillion in funding to improve public education (funding for FY 2000 alone was approximately $123 billion), but not much has changed (U.S. Office of Management and Budget, 2004). Fewer classrooms have teachers who specialized in their subject areas than in 1983; the school year is more than a week shorter than it was in the 1970s; and students do less homework than their counterparts did in 1982. Although SAT math scores have improved, verbal scores have not and overall scores remain about 100 points below their 1970 levels, even though in 1992 the College Board "renormed" the SAT, which had the effect of raising all subsequent scores by 150 points. NAEP scores have remained either unchanged or, in the case of writing, have dropped along significant dimensions, such as sentence fragments, coherence, and substance (a word that already has appeared several times in this chapter) (U.S. Department of Education, 1999).

Asking nonstandard speakers to master the conventions of Standard and formal Standard English does not—and certainly should not—entail any explicit rejection or criticism of the home dialect. To counter the claim that it involves an implicit criticism, we need to adopt an additive stance with respect to language. That is, mastering Standard English conventions is not intended to subtract from students but instead is intended to add to their linguistic skills.

We should not be so naive, however, as to begin thinking that nonstandard English will ever shed its stigma. Many who argue against teaching Standard conventions seem to believe it will. The reality is that failure to teach the conventions of Standard and formal Standard English in our classes is unlikely to

---

[9]Consider this extreme example: *Judges* recounts how the Gileadites killed 42,000 Ephraimites simply because the latter pronounced the word *shibboleth* as *sibboleth* (12, 4–6). As Quintilian stated, "Usage … is the surest pilot in speaking, and we should treat language as currency minted with the public stamp" (1974, I.vi.1–3).

have any effect on society's attitudes toward speakers of nonstandard English, but it will most certainly have an effect on our students' lives. Their horizons will be limited, and many at the bottom of the socioeconomic scale will remain ghettoized. On this basis alone, I would argue that we must push students to reach their full potential, especially with regard to language. Our society is growing ever more competitive, not less, and Standard English, because it is inclusive rather than limiting, is a basic requirement for social and economic opportunities.

First Language Acquisition.   Language acquisition is such an important topic in discussions of grammar that we examine it here more than once. The goal is to consider acquisition from different perspectives to gain a full understanding of what it entails. In this context, the previous sections examined the assumption that grammar instruction leads to better writing, and they explored the confusion in education about the nature of grammar, what it entails, and how it differs from usage. Understanding why the errors in student writing are largely matters of usage rather than grammar requires us to look closely at the process of becoming a native speaker of a language.

Language acquisition begins at birth and is made possible by the existence of special features in the body and brain that became dedicated to language production and comprehension through evolution. An upright posture allowed our respiratory and articulation systems to shift to the vertical, which enabled easier control of breathing, necessary for nuanced articulation, a wider range of sounds, and effective management of intonation and rhythms (de Boysson-Bardies, 2001). We have a genetic predisposition to develop and use language, what Pinker (1994) described as "the language instinct." As Jackendoff (2002) stated, "It is part of being human that a child … learns to speak" (p. 70). This genetic predisposition underlies Halliday's (1979) observation that a 1-day-old child will stop crying to attend to its mother's voice and that a mother "will stop doing almost anything, including sleeping, to attend to the voice of her child" (p. 179).[10]

But language is not innate in the strict sense of, say, the ability to see or walk. The neurophysiological apparatus must be stimulated before it will become operational, as illustrated by several tragic cases of abused and abandoned children. One of the more famous involved a girl called "Genie," whose mother kept her tied up in a room for years and never spoke to her. "Genie" had no interactions with other people until authorities discovered her at age 13. She had not

---

[10]We should note that fathers display similar behavior but that it is more observable in women because they generally are primarily responsible for feeding and caring for infants.

developed any language. Subsequent efforts to teach her English were fraught with difficulty.[11]

Such cases confirm that language is inextricably linked to social interaction and will not develop without it. As Pinker (1995) noted, in all recorded cases in which children grew up lacking a social environment, "The outcome is always the same: the children, when found, are mute. Whatever innate grammatical abilities there are, they are too schematic to generate concrete speech, words, and grammatical constructions on their own" (p. 152).

Fortunately, the number of children who are abused in this way is small. The majority of parents delight in the presence of their children and seem compelled, perhaps owing to evolution, to talk to them at every opportunity. Other adults display similar behavior. As a result, infants are immersed in a language-rich environment during nearly all of their waking hours.

During the 1st year, infants produce a range of babbling sounds that are understood to be the precursors of language. Some scholars (de Boysson-Bardies, 2001; Pinker, 1994) have proposed that these sounds represent the full range of possible human utterances and that they are part of a procedure in which children strive to match the sounds of their home language. In addition to babbling, infants engage in preverbal communicative behavior involving gestures and expressions. An upward reaching gesture to a parent, for example, signals "pick me up!" Infants also learn a great deal about the world around them by observing the behavior of others; they seem to be highly motivated to structure their environment. By 8 months, they typically know that cups are used for drinking, spoons are for eating, beds are for sleeping, and so on. Stimulation in a meaningful context triggers language.[12]

Infants understand many simple words before they can produce them, such as "baby," "no," "night-night," and "bottle." Actual language appears in most children at around age 1, regardless of culture (Clark, 1993). Their first utterances are about their world, and Nelson (1973) reported that these fall into three main categories—animals, food, and toys—but they also include body parts and household items. The people they name most often are "dadda," "momma," and "baby," respectively. By age 18 months, children have a vocabulary of about 50 words, but they are able to use, first, single-word utterances and then

---

[11]In addition, "Genie" did not develop normal social skills after her rescue, and she never learned to care for herself. She has spent her adult life in a private facility with a staff that can accommodate her special needs.

[12]Note that the context must be meaningful, communicative, and involve direct human interaction. We easily understand that a dog's bark will be nothing but noise to an infant. By the same token, discourse that comes out of a TV or radio will not trigger language acquisition; to the infant, it will be as meaningless and noncommunicative as the dog's bark. Sitting infants in front of a TV and turning on a program, therefore, cannot lead to language development. This finding naturally has important implications for children's television programming, such as *Sesame Street*.

two-word utterances to accomplish a great deal of communication. This pattern of development is universal across all known languages. Some typical two-word utterances are:

- Go bye-bye.
- All gone.
- Baby fall.
- Me sleep.
- Doggie run.

These two-word utterances have a basic grammatical structure. In the case of "go bye-bye," they contain an action with an understood agent, whereas in utterances like "me sleep," the agent and the action are present. These agent-action utterances are very similar to the simplest grammatical sentences, such as "dogs bark." Between 18 months and age 2, children's language develops at a rapid pace; they acquire two or more new words per day, and within 6 months to a year they are producing complete sentences that are grammatically correct. That is, a 3-year-old child will produce sentences like 6a, but they will never produce sentences like 6b:

6a. I got a boo-boo.
6b. Got boo-boo a I.

What should strike us immediately is that this behavior allows us to understand why most of the errors students make in their writing are not related to grammar. *As native speakers of English, their language is necessarily grammatical.* There is no other option. Language is partially, but significantly, defined by grammar; that is, grammar is inherent in language and language cannot be acquired or produced without grammar. Newport, Gleitman, and Gleitman (1977) estimated that 99.93% of the speech produced by anyone older than age 6 is grammatically correct. If people produced ungrammatical sentences like 6b, they would not be using English.[13] This does not mean, of course, that native speakers of a language never produce ungrammatical sentences—they do—but such sentences represent a tiny fraction of all the sentences they generate. The majority of ungrammatical sentences we find in

---

[13]Linguists have developed a theory of universal grammar that proposes that languages do not vary arbitrarily or without limitations. This means that all languages share numerous properties, probably as a result of the way the mind is structured and operates. Example 6b violates the word order properties of universal grammar; no languages exist or can exist with this particular structure. Therefore, we would have to conclude that anyone who spontaneously produced 6b (as opposed to its deliberate construction as an example in this text) probably is not human. See Chomsky (1981, 1995, 2000), Culicover (1999), Jackendoff (2002), Newmeyer (1998), and Prince and Smolensky (1993) for more on universal grammar.

speech and writing typically are so established in everyday speech that they go unnoticed by all except the most astute observers. Generally, however, native speakers find it so difficult after about age 6 to produce an ungrammatical sentence that they cannot do so without a conscious effort, and even then they usually get it wrong and generate a sentence that is grammatical but that displays incorrect usage. Research on this phenomenon has led to two major models of language acquisition—the induction model and the association model.

Acquisition and Learning. The two models of language acquisition differ in many respects, and each has its supporters. But they also have many features in common. Both models recognize that language has a genetic foundation, that the brain is structured for language, and that children are able to produce grammatical utterances without any instruction in grammar. In addition, both propose that grammar operates in the background of language processing. A 6-year-old can produce grammatical utterances yet have no conscious knowledge of grammar. Furthermore, grammar is so deep in the background that it is extremely difficult for people to attend to grammar when they listen to a conversation; it is only slightly less difficult when they are reading. We are predisposed to focus on meaning, not structure—a fact that has significant implications for instruction. Finally, both models recognize that children acquire the language of their communities, what we call their *home language* or *home dialect.* The home dialect is so thoroughly ingrained that only significant motivation and conscious effort enable a person to adopt another dialect.

The problem teachers face is transparent. Although Standard English is the norm in many households, huge numbers of children are reared in families where the home dialect is nonstandard English, where books are rarely found and reading is seldom encouraged and practiced even less. It seems reasonable to assume that few if any children are reared in families where the home dialect is formal Standard English. Standard and formal Standard English are the targets of instruction, yet our students bring to school and to classroom writing assignments home dialects that are measurably different from these targets. *What we are striving to do when we teach the conventions of Standard and formal Standard English is help our students master a new dialect.*

The study of grammar is supposed to give students the tools they need to move their language closer to Standard and formal Standard English. It is viewed as the bridge between home language and Standard English. The assumption is that once this bridge is in place (once students learn the grammar), they will speak and write Standard English. This approach is misguided.

We must consider the following: Linguists describe the process of grammar study as *language learning* to distinguish it from language acquisition. Whereas acquisition involves the unconscious, easy mastery of grammar, learning is both conscious and difficult. The reason is that the mind processes acquired knowledge of language in a way that is different from learned knowledge of language. Whenever most people try to apply such learned knowledge, their language processing ability is impaired. Part of the problem is related to differences in form and meaning. As suggested previously, people focus on the meaning of an utterance or of writing, unless the form is so flawed as to be distracting. They find that when they also try to focus on form, it is harder to attend to meaning. It's a bit like trying to think about the mechanics of breathing. For most people, what we do unconsciously and without effort suddenly becomes labored.

We see extreme examples of this phenomenon among people with writer's block. Rose (1984) reported that students in his study were so concerned with getting the form correct that they could not focus on meaning; moreover, they never felt that the form they used was correct, so they became caught in a cycle of writing a couple of sentences, crossing them out, rewriting them, crossing them out, rewriting them, and so on. Most found it hard to complete even one paragraph.

On a less serious level, we see students who study and understand the difference between *who* and *whom,* for example, who can differentiate between these two words correctly and consistently in exercises, but who nevertheless either fail to make the distinction when speaking or writing or must think hard for several moments about which form is appropriate. And anyone who has ever written a paper of any length understands how difficult it is to spot errors when proofreading. The reason is that even when we try to focus on the structure of our writing, we tend to lose that focus and attend to the meaning, instead. Even professional writers and academics experience this problem, which is why publishers employ copyeditors to correct errors that the authors miss. The implication for instruction is clear: Training students to be editors is likely to have a greater effect on reducing errors in writing than grammar instruction.

Also worth considering is the fact that writing teachers at the college level regularly see how knowledge of grammar has little bearing on the quality of speaking and writing. Many foreign students, especially those from Asia, commonly have learned as much or more about English grammar than their teachers, but they nevertheless speak and write English quite poorly, on the whole. Their learned—rather than acquired—knowledge of English grammar does not help them much when it comes to actually using the language.

WHY TEACH GRAMMAR?

Given all the foregoing, any reasonable person might conclude that we are wasting our time, as well as that of our students, by teaching grammar. Such a conclusion would be incorrect, however. There are many legitimate reasons for teaching grammar. One of the more important is related to the fact that we use language to define ourselves and the world around us. Anything so important deserves study. In addition, knowledge of grammar *does* play a role in writing. It provides information about form and function that enables students to study language and how we communicate. When teachers and students share a common vocabulary, discussions of writing can be more efficient and clear. *Thus, grammar itself does not lead to better writing, but grammar study gives us tools that allow for more effective teaching of writing.*

Another answer—less palatable, perhaps—is that grammar is inherently interesting and intellectually challenging, at least when it is taught as an interesting subject. Many things are worth doing simply because they are hard. Finally, a knowledge of grammar has been deemed a characteristic of well-educated people throughout Western history. As Hirsch (1988) convincingly argued, there are certain things worth knowing.

BEST PRACTICES

The real question is not why we teach grammar, but how. We saw in the previous sections that native speakers have internalized the grammar of English. They may not know grammar terminology, but they are able to produce grammatical utterances and recognize ungrammatical ones with great consistency. Indeed, they rarely produce ungrammatical sentences. What they lack is mastery of the usage conventions that govern Standard and formal Standard English, which accounts for most of the errors we find in student writing. The typical language arts curriculum, however, ignores the native understanding of grammatical patterns and aims to teach students as though they are learning a foreign language. Usage is seldom addressed. This approach is at odds with the basic educational principle of building on what students already know, but it nevertheless remains the most widely used in our public schools. To make matters worse, this approach usually insists on grammar study without a context. There are few attempts to relate grammar to the lives of students outside the classroom, few attempts to encourage students to see grammar in the communication that they engage in on a daily basis.

How, then, are we to teach grammar effectively? What constitutes best practices? I would suggest that in an ideal world, we would teach grammar in our public schools for its own sake, as an independent and inherently interesting subject. One of the more effective ways to do so would be to focus on the sociological and psychological dimensions of grammar and language, using grammar as a tool to help students better understand themselves and others. But we don't live in such a world, so this untraditional approach is hard—although not impossible—to adopt. Change and innovation often are viewed very negatively in public education, and the resistance to any change in how we teach grammar is intense. As Lester (1990) noted:

> Traditional grammar has been used in English classrooms for generations.... It is what you do in an English class. Even the fact that students do so poorly with traditional grammar is not seen as a reason for questioning [its] ... importance because that failure is already built into the system as an expected norm. (p. 340)

Let's nevertheless consider other alternatives. When we examine grammar instruction in our schools, we observe three primary pedagogical orientations. The most pervasive is the traditional approach, based on the study of Latin centuries ago, which focuses on terminology and involves teaching grammar as though students are learning a foreign language. This entire chapter has explained why this approach does not work. Another—associated with the "ideal world" mentioned earlier and advocated most notably by Andrews (1995, 1998), Kolln (1996), and Wolfram (1998)—proposes that grammar be embedded in the broad context of *language study*. I call this the *linguistic approach*. The third orientation, often associated with Weaver (1996), argues for locating grammar instruction in the context of *literacy*. I call this the *literacy approach*. Both approaches provide the framework for best practices.

The Linguistic Approach

The linguistic approach, as the label suggests, is based on insights gained from linguistic research. A teacher using this approach focuses on introducing students to the various components of language, such as sound (phonology), meaning (semantics), and use (pragmatics). Grammar is taught as a tool for describing, rather than prescribing, language, a tool that can help students understand the nature of dialects and how they differ from one another while maintaining a core integrity.

In describing the essence of the linguistic approach, Wolfram (1998) argued that:

> the most effective way to develop an appreciation for the intricacies of language ... involves working through some actual linguistic patterns governing socially disfavored forms. Such an awareness affects not only the perspective of language arts instructors, but also how students feel about other students and themselves. (p. 91)

Likewise, Andrews (1998) noted that:

before students are likely to gain significant insight into how they and other speakers and writers might unconsciously or deliberately use language elements, patterns, and structures, or before they see a reason to pay attention to these issues, they need first of all to become more aware of language in general and how it varies, changes, and works in their world. (p. 6)

Andrews advocated what he called Language Exploration and Awareness, a program for teaching grammar based on assignments designed to help students consider how language works. One assignment, for example, asks students to question elderly people, such as grandparents, about whether during their lifetimes they have seen any changes in language.

The linguistic approach encourages students to observe how people use language and then to explain and interpret their observations. We can easily envision additional activities that engage students in this way, and several are listed at the end of this chapter. The pervasive use of the word *like,* for example, offers opportunities for students to observe their peers and to perform frequency counts to see how often the word is used in conversations and whether usage differs by age, occupation, gender, ethnicity, or socioeconomic class. Use of the expressions *I feel bad* and *I feel badly* tend to vary on the basis of education level. If students monitor conversations and news broadcasts, they can explore the nature of the variation. Teaching students the correct form and its grammatical basis takes only a few minutes, but the experience they have as researchers studying people to determine who uses which expression can make the lesson last a lifetime. It is hands-on and relevant, which textbook exercises are not.

A potential shortcoming of the linguistic approach is that it typically concentrates on speech and can be criticized for ignoring writing. As a result, this approach can be a hard sell in schools. It is important to recognize, however, that listening to oral discourse and attending to its structural patterns is a necessary first step in understanding and appreciating grammar. The linguistic approach can increase students' awareness that grammar permeates their world and, to a certain degree, defines it. An assignment on dialects, for example, can be very effective in motivating students to attend to matters of form not only in their speech but also in their writing.

A survey of popular language arts textbooks shows only a token recognition of the linguistic approach to grammar instruction. Houghton Mifflin's *English* (Rueda et al., 2001) offers a brief discussion of formal and informal language to show students that we change the way we use language on the basis of context, and it also has a brief discussion of cultural factors associated with language. On the whole, however, *English* is based on a traditional approach to grammar.

Holt's *Elements of Language* (Odell, Vacca, Hobbs, & Irvin, 2001) takes a similar approach, providing limited information about the history of language and dialects. Both texts emphasize dialects without offering much discussion of context. For example, *Elements* states that "everyone uses a dialect, and no dialect is better or worse than another" (p. 692), but it does not adequately address the question of appropriateness—important because in numerous situations one dialect *is* better or worse than another. The overall impression is that these texts include material related to the linguistic approach for political, not pedagogical, reasons.

Glencoe/McGraw-Hill's *Writer's Choice* (2001) takes a more principled approach. It includes an essay by Mark Lester on teaching grammar and usage that is both well informed and entirely congruent with the issues raised in this chapter—particularly the need to differentiate between grammar and usage. Moreover, he applied the linguistic approach to writing in effective ways, noting that "good grammar programs constantly connect grammar to usage problems in the students' own writing" (p. T28).

The Literacy Approach

The literacy approach, often associated with Constance Weaver (1996), is grounded not only in linguistics but also in contemporary writing pedagogy. Recall that language acquisition occurs when children are immersed in a language environment. If we view writing (or formal Standard English) as a dialect, then it is reasonable to conclude that students will acquire this dialect when they are immersed in the language environment, which exists primarily in texts (see Smith, 1983). What we know about language acquisition suggests that reading immerses students in written language in the way that a child's family immerses him or her in spoken language. Reading leads to acquisition of the features of language that characterize the formal standard of texts, which in turn facilitates composing. For these reasons, the literacy approach views reading as the most effective means of teaching grammar.

Reading activities lend themselves nicely to discussions of form and function as well as meaning. More important, they lend themselves to *indirect,* rather than *direct,* instruction. Indirect instruction is based on principles of language acquisition, whereas direct instruction is based on language learning. Specifically, indirect instruction involves embedding grammatical terms and concepts in daily lessons and avoiding stand-alone units. To understand how this works, we can envision a teacher who, while discussing a text, points out to students an interesting word or a provocative phrase, naming the word or phrase and explaining what makes it interesting. The cognitive process is similar to what we see when parents, playing with a child, hold up a ball and utter the word "ball." The connection between object and name develops in a meaningful context; the instruction is indirect because it is incidental to the play; and the child develops a lasting mental model of the term.

The influence of contemporary writing pedagogy is evident in the structure of the classroom: The literacy approach emphasizes a grammar curriculum that is based on writing as well as reading, and it is predicated on the notion that students must write and revise frequently, using feedback from peers and the teacher to move their revisions forward. Weaver (1996), for example, recommended that students read and write every day. Teachers facilitate the *writing process* by circulating as students produce drafts, reading work in progress, and providing helpful suggestions. In this context, grammar instruction is part of writing instruction. The pedagogy provides that when teachers see common problems in student work, they stop the writing activity and offer brief instruction on the spot (see Williams, 2003a).

A couple of examples will illustrate the approach. Student writers frequently have trouble with agreement owing to the influence of conversational patterns. They will produce sentences like "Everyone took their books to the library." *Everyone* is singular, but *their* is plural, which creates an error in agreement. Noticing this problem, teachers call a halt to writing activities and explain how to change the sentence in keeping with Standard conventions ("Everyone took his or her books to the library" or "All the students took their books to the library"). Likewise, they may observe several students who are using the word *impact* rather than *effect,* a very common usage error: "The new policy had a significant impact on school funding"/"The new policy had a significant effect on school funding." Teachers then intervene with a short lesson on the meaning of the words and their proper use in English.

Such minilessons never last more than 10 minutes, which means that they usually have to be repeated several times during the term before the instruction begins to influence student performance consistently. Nevertheless, this type of instruction is significantly more effective than the dedicated lecture or drills and exercises (Calkins, 1983). Students learn what they need to know to solve an immediate writing problem, and because they apply the knowledge directly to the problem, they retain it longer. In this respect, the approach is similar to what we see in sports and other hands-on tasks. The teacher assumes the role of a coach who intervenes and helps students correct faulty writing behavior the moment it appears.

The view that writing is a process that contains several phases, or stages, has become so widespread over the last three decades that it is hard to imagine a textbook that does not include it in part or whole. At least *mentioning* process has become de rigueur. But whether process is properly described and articulated as a pedagogy is an altogether different matter. Too often, it is presented as a fossilized system that, ironically, is antithetical to what process is actually about.

When we consider the three textbooks previously mentioned—Houghton Mifflin's *English* (Rueda et al., 2001), Holt's *Elements of Language* (Odell, et al., 2001), and Glencoe/McGraw-Hill's *Writer's Choice* (2001)—we find that they offer some process pedagogy, but little of it relates grammar instruction to writing as outlined in this section. *English* has an overview of process followed by a discussion of "grammar, usage, and mechanics," but this material obviously does not include any discussion of methodology, and it does not offer students many effective strategies for improving their understanding of grammar while improving their writing. The teacher's edition discusses process primarily as a concept and has few practical suggestions related to intervention techniques. Both *Writer's Choice* and *Elements* link grammar and writing by asking students to analyze sentences. Thus, they are very traditional and display little understanding of the principles that underlie the literacy approach.

Writer's Choice does link reading, writing, and grammar, but in a traditional way. For example, students are asked to read excerpts from novels with the aim of using them as models to make their writing interesting. This exercise would make sense only if students were writing novels. It makes no sense whatsoever for students who are writing essays. The opportunity to use these reading activities to learn grammar indirectly is never pursued. The result is a treatment of reading and writing that is thoroughly traditional.

The Blended Approach

The two approaches discussed are not in conflict; they merely apply different emphases to the task of teaching grammar. Both have much to offer as a means of developing best practices for teaching grammar in the context of language study and literacy. For this reason, my recommendation is for what I call the *blended approach,* which combines linguistics and literacy. The blended approach recognizes that grammar is a tool that allows teachers and students to talk more effectively about language in general and writing in particular. Although grammar has intrinsic value, the pedagogical focus of our schools is on improving writing; consequently, grammar study cannot be dropped from the curriculum, nor can it be separated from writing and considered a separate subject. At the same time, the blended approach is based on the understanding that students must be motivated to learn grammar before they can apply it to anything other than ultimately useless drills and exercises. It therefore emphasizes the social and psychological aspects of grammar by engaging students in observing and studying how people use language in a variety of settings. That is, it provides opportunities for young people to become students of language.

In this role, students quickly and easily come to understand the difference between usage and grammar, and they come to recognize the ways in which individual speakers and writers change their language depending on context and audience. These are important lessons that bear directly on writing performance. They help students understand the nature of their home dialects and how writing—formal Standard English—represents a new dialect that must be studied and learned in an additive, rather than subtractive, way.

Teacher intervention is a crucial part of the blended approach. Teachers must monitor students as they are writing in class, identify problems, and then offer a minilesson that students can apply immediately. More monitoring follows, with appropriate guidance to ensure that students apply the lesson correctly. Reading also is important in the blended approach because it provides many useful opportunities for grammar instruction and modeling of Standard and formal Standard English. But teachers also must serve as models. Linguistics has taught us two uncontrovertible facts over the last 30 years. First, language change occurs when someone is highly motivated to modify his or her language. Second, change must occur in an environment that immerses a person in, or at least exposes a person to, the target language. Addressing the issue of motivation is challenging and difficult. But teachers can do a great deal with respect to the learning environment by serving as models of spoken Standard English. Doing so, however, has one fundamental requirement that takes us back to the beginning of this chapter: Teachers must know English grammar exceptionally well. In addition, they must know the various usage conventions of formal Standard English. The chapters that follow are designed to provide knowledge of both.

SUGGESTED ACTIVITIES

The activities described here are illustrative rather than comprehensive and should be used as models for developing a wider range of assignments congruent with the blended approach. The activities appear in no particular order and do not represent a grammar curriculum. Note that some of the activities reference concepts and terminology that are discussed in later chapters.

1. Ask students to read a story or an essay, then ask them to write a couple of paragraphs on the effect the work has on readers. After discussing these paragraphs, ask students to explain how the work achieved the effect—not in terms of the elements of fiction or the ideas but in terms of the structure.

2. Instruct students on the nature of *style,* the choices writers make with regard to word choice and sentence structure. Ask students to read two stories, each by a different author. Then ask them to analyze the writing in terms of style by taking four paragraphs from each story and calculating the average sentence length, the different types of sentence openers (subject, introductory modifier, coordinating conjunction, verb phrase, etc.), the average number of adverbs and adjectives per sentence, and the average number of subordinate clauses. Have students use these data to write a couple of paragraphs comparing and contrasting the styles of the two writers. Follow-up activity: Have students read an essay and perform the same stylistic analysis on it. Then have them compare these data with the data they obtained from their analysis of one of the stories.

3. Ask students to perform a stylistic analysis on a paper they wrote for another class and then write a couple of paragraphs comparing their data with those from the professional essay examined previously.

4. Ask students to write an argumentative or analytical essay. Have them perform a stylistic analysis on it, then ask them to revise the paper so that it approximates the stylistic features of the professional essay. That is, if their average sentence length is 12 words and the professional average is 20 words, have them combine sentences to increase their average length; if the average number of adjectives in their writing is 4 per sentence and the professional average is .5, have them delete adjectives, and so on.

5. Assign research teams of 3 to 5 students. Provide a lesson on some features of dialect and usage, such as those listed here. Then ask the teams to listen unobtrusively to conversations in, say, the school cafeteria or a local shopping mall and record the observed frequency of the nonstandard usage, along with descriptions of the speakers (age, gender, etc.). They should then present an oral report on their findings.

- I feel bad/I feel badly
- Fred and I/Fred and me
- In regard to/In regards to
- She said/She goes like

6. Have the research teams in the foregoing activity perform the same observation with TV programs. They then should present an oral report comparing and contrasting these findings with those from their first observations.

7. Have students circle every prepositional phrase in a paper and then show them how to revise sentences to change prepositional phrases to adjectival phrases. Ask them to revise their papers so that no sentence has more than three prepositional phrases.

8. Provide students with a lesson on dialects. Assign research teams of 3 to 5 students. Ask them to watch three TV programs or movies and determine whether there are any dialectical differences among the characters. If so, what are they and

what conclusions can we draw about dialect and social status? Have them present an oral report on their findings.

9. Have students pair up. One person in the pair will assume the role of an employer, the other person the role of a job seeker. Each pair can decide the nature of the business, but it should be something in the professions. The employer has an opening and is looking for candidates. Have the employer write up a job description. Ask each job seeker to write an application letter to the employer outlining his or her qualifications and asking for an interview. Have each employer write a response letter that either rejects the application or accepts it. Then ask each pair to analyze the job description, the application letter, and the response letter for structures and word choices that do not conform to the usage conventions governing this context.

10. Give students a lesson on the semantic features of subordinating conjunctions that are commonly confused: *while/because, while/whereas, since/because,* and the like. In small work groups, have them examine a newspaper or magazine article to determine whether the writers used subordinating conjunctions in keeping with their semantic content. They should share their findings with the whole class. Next, have them pair up and exchange drafts of a paper in progress. Then ask them to examine each subordinate clause to determine whether it begins with the correct subordinating conjunction.

3

Traditional Grammar

PRESCRIPTIVE GRAMMAR IN OUR SCHOOLS

In nearly every instance, school grammar is traditional grammar. It is concerned primarily with correctness and with the categorical names for the words that make up sentences. Thus, students study grammatical terms and certain "rules" that are supposed to be associated with correctness. Grammar instruction is justified on the assumption that students who speak or write expressions such as *He don't do nothin'* will modify their language to produce *He doesn't do anything* if only they learn a bit more about grammar. Because society deems that affecting such change in language is a worthwhile goal, our grammar schools, like their ancient Greek counterparts, give much attention to grammar as a prescriptive body of knowledge.

We say that traditional grammar is prescriptive because it focuses on the distinction between what some people do with language and what they *ought* to do with it, according to a pre-established standard. For example, students who utter or write *He don't do nothin'* are told that they ought to use *He doesn't do anything*. The chief goal of traditional grammar, therefore, is perpetuating a historical model of what supposedly constitutes proper language. Those who teach traditional grammar have implicitly embraced this goal without recognizing that many of the assumptions that underlie school grammar are false. As the previous chapter explained, both experience and research show that learning grammatical terms and completing grammar exercises have little effect on the way students use language.

In addition to its foundation on flawed assumptions, there are two other problems in adopting a prescriptive grammar. First, prescription demands a high degree of knowledge to prevent inconsistency, and few people have the necessary degree of knowledge. That is, when teachers make prescriptive statements concerning language, they must be certain that their own speech and writing does not violate the prescription. This seldom is the case. Even a casual observation of how people use language illustrates that deviations from the prescribed standard are common. We can observe teachers correcting students who use a construction such as *Fred and me went fishing* (the problem involves case relations, discussed on pages 61–64). The formal standard is *Fred and I went fishing.* But if these same teachers knock on a friend's door and are asked *Who is it?* they probably will say *It's me*—even though this response violates the same convention. The formal standard is *It's I.*

This reality is related to the second problem, examined in chapter 2: Everyone acquires language as an infant, and the home dialect rarely matches the more formal standard used in prescriptive grammar, which generally is learned in school. The illustration in Fig. 3.1 suggests how one's home language and the formal standard overlap in some areas, but not all. In addition, the two forms coexist and compete with each other, as in the case of someone whose home dialect accepts *Fred and me went fishing* but who has learned that *Fred and I went fishing* is correct. Both sentences are grammatical, but the second is congruent with the conventions of Standard English, whereas the first is not.

The gap between acquired language and the formal standard can be narrowed through a variety of input: classroom instruction in usage, reading, writing, and association with people who speak Standard English. Unfortunately, such learning is slow and difficult. The home dialect acquired in infancy is so strong that it usually dominates, but not always. As a result, one may have learned that *Fred and I went fishing* is preferable in most situations, but when it

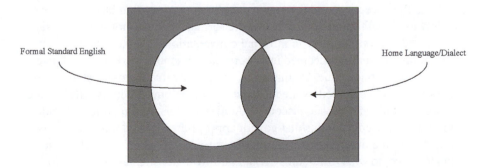

FIG. 3.1.   Formal Standard English and the home language/dialect coexist in the child's total language environment. Some features overlap, as indicated in the diagram, but many do not.

comes time to write or utter that statement, the home dialect wins the competition and one utters or writes *Fred and me went fishing*.

What is especially interesting is that, on a random basis, the competition between the coexisting constructions will cause the person to use the most familiar form—typically without even being aware of it. Such observations lead to important conclusions. One is that for most people the content, or meaning, of a message is more important than the form. We understand both *Fred and me went fishing* and *Fred and I went fishing* equally well. Another is that changing a person's language—or more precisely, dialect—is difficult and does not consist simply of giving students grammatical terminology and exercises. In some cases, students already will have the standard form coexisting with the nonstandard. These two conclusions lead to what is perhaps the most important and the most difficult to address: Students must be motivated to shift dialects before instruction will have any measurable effect.

Appropriateness Conditions

Although most teachers in our public schools are prescriptivists, linguists dropped prescription long ago, replacing it with the concept of *appropriateness conditions*. This expression signifies that language use is situation specific and that there is no absolute standard of correctness that applies in all situations. People modify their language on the basis of circumstances and conventions, which means that in some instances—as in the case of *It's me*—the preferred form of expression is technically nonstandard. Generally, what is appropriate (and acceptable) in one situation may not be appropriate (and acceptable) in another. However, this principle is not as clear-cut as we might wish because the issue of appropriateness is almost always unidirectional: *Standard usage is acceptable under most conditions, but nonstandard is not.*

With the exception of a few nonstandard expressions that have become so widely used that they are preferable to the formal standard, nonstandard usage is deemed appropriate only in informal conversations or notes among friends and family. It usually is deemed inappropriate for school work, the workplace, or any other public venue. On this basis, we can say that language study in our schools should be guided by the idea that we are helping students differentiate between public and private discourse. Achieving this goal requires an understanding of the conventions that govern appropriateness and public language. In addition, the unidirectional nature of appropriateness requires close attention to usage, to what differentiates Standard from nonstandard English. Much of what this text has to say about appropriateness and acceptability, therefore, is tied to mastering standard usage conventions.

Traditional grammar is not well suited to such mastery. It does not adequately meet the need of teachers or students for a means of analyzing and understanding language because it is based on the structure of Latin rather than English. The one important feature of traditional grammar is its terminology. Developed in ancient Greece and Rome, the names of the various components of language provide the vocabulary we must use to talk about language in general and writing in particular. Traditional grammar, on this account, always will play a role—albeit a limited one—in the study of language. Learning the names of the various constituents that make up sentences undeniably remains an important part of language study, and the rest of this chapter takes up this task, setting the groundwork for more interesting analyses to follow. This chapter, in other words, provides an introduction to and an explanation of grammar's basic terminology.

We must keep in mind at all times that people judge one another on the basis of language. As speakers of American English, we have a prestige dialect that to one degree or another accepts certain conventions and rejects others. These conventions usually don't involve grammar, but they do involve usage.[1] We may wish that language prejudice were not so intense, but simple denial does not provide a solution. For this reason, regular discussions of usage conventions appear throughout much of this text. They are designed to examine the nuances of usage rather than to be prescriptive, but it goes without saying that any notion of a standard presupposes some level of prescription. To reduce the inconsistency inherent in developing a text that focuses on description rather than prescription, discussions of standard usage conventions should be understood in terms of appropriateness.

FORM AND FUNCTION IN GRAMMAR

Grammar deals with the structure and analysis of sentences. Any discussion of grammar, therefore, must address language on two levels, which we may think of as *form* and *function*. Sentences are made up of individual words, and these words fall into certain grammatical categories. This is their form. A word like *Macarena,* for example, is a *noun*—this is its *form*. A word like *jump* is a *verb,* a word like *red* is an *adjective,* and so on.

The form of a word is generally independent of a sentence. Dictionaries are an exploration not only of meaning but also of form because they describe the grammatical category or categories of each entry. But language exists primarily as sentences, not individual words, and as soon as we put words into sentences they work together in various ways—this is *function.* For example, nouns can

---

[1]Of course, Black English and Chicano English do vary grammatically from Standard English. Both dialects are considered in chapter 7.

function as *subjects,* adjectives *modify* (supply information to) nouns, and verbs establish *predicates.*

Form and function are related in several ways. For example, on a simple level, the terms we use to describe grammatical form and function come from the Greco-Roman tradition. *Noun* comes from the Latin word, *nomen,* for *name; verb* comes from the Latin *verbum,* for *word; predicate* comes from the Latin word, *praedicare, to proclaim.* On a deeper level, the form of a given word often determines its function in a sentence—and vice versa.

Teaching Tip

It is important to be a bit cautious when discussing form because many words change their classification on the basis of their function in a sentence. For example, "running" is a verb in some sentences (Fred is running in the race), but it has all the characteristics of a noun in others (Running is good exercise). The ability of words to change classification in this way enhances the richness of language. It also causes great confusion among students. Therefore, form and function must be taught together, not separately.

The Eight Parts of Speech.   Traditional grammar usually describes form in terms of the *eight parts of speech: nouns, verbs, adjectives, adverbs, conjunctions, particles, prepositions,* and *articles.* This is a useful starting point. Likewise, traditional grammar identifies six functions that words may perform in sentences: *subject, predicate, object, complement, modifier,* and *function word.* The words that have the broadest range of function are nouns and verbs. Form and function usually are the same for adjectives, adverbs, conjunctions, particles, and prepositions.

In this chapter, we examine what these various terms mean so as to lay the groundwork for grammatical analysis. The goal is to introduce, or provide a review of, terminology and concepts. This review makes no attempt to be comprehensive; thus, those readers desiring a more in-depth presentation should turn to a grammar handbook.

SUBJECTS AND PREDICATES

Although sentences can be infinitely rich and complex, they are based on *nouns* and *verbs.* Nearly everything else provides information about the nouns and verbs in some way. We examine nouns and verbs in more detail later, but at this point we can say that nouns tend to be the names of things, whereas verbs tend to be words that describe actions and states of being. On this basis, we can see that sentences generally express two types of relations: (a) an agent performing an action; (b) existence. Sentences 1 and 2 illustrate the two types.

1. Dogs bark.

2. The tree was tall.

The word *dogs* is the agent of sentence 1. It performs the action conveyed in the word *bark*. We also can say that *dogs* is the *subject* of the sentence. Thus, *subject* is our first function category. The word *bark* supplies information about dogs, stating or describing what they do. Words that state an action of this sort and that supply information about the nature of subjects or what they are doing are referred to as *predicates*. Thus, *predicate* is our second function category. A predicate consists of the main verb of a sentence and all the words associated with it. Although in sentence 2 *the tree* is not an agent, the sentence expresses a fact about the tree's existence—it was tall. *The tree,* therefore, is the subject, and *was tall* is the predicate. Understanding *subject* and *predicate* is important because these are the two central functional parts of all sentences. If one is missing, we don't have a sentence. Functionally, everything else in a sentence is related to its subject and predicate in some way.

Teaching Tip

Many students find the concept of "agent" easier to understand than "subject." Using "agent" therefore seems to be a wise choice when introducing the two main functional relations in sentences. Begin with simple sentences with clear agents. Once students understand the concept, introduce "subject" and show how it is a more flexible term because it includes those sentences, such as "The tree was tall," that do not have an agent.

Clauses

All sentences in English can be divided into the two constituents of subject and predicate, even when, as sometimes occurs, the subject isn't an explicit part of a given sentence. Almost everything else that one may see in a sentence will be part of either the subject or the predicate. In addition, a subject/predicate combination constitutes what is referred to as a *clause*. This means that every sentence is a clause.

Teaching Tip

English allows us to truncate sentences—that is, to drop either the subject or the predicate—in certain situations. For example, if one is asked "Why are you going to the store?" an appropriate and grammatical response could be "Need milk." The subject has been dropped, producing a truncated sentence. Students need to understand that truncation is legitimate in speech but not in writing or formal speaking situations. Engaging students in role-playing activities in which they take on roles congruent with formal English is a good first step toward helping students recognize when truncation is appropriate and when it is not.

Independent and Dependent Clauses.   There are two major types of clauses: *independent* and *dependent*. One way to differentiate the two types is to understand that dependent clauses *always supply information to an independent clause*. That is, they function as *modifiers*. Another way is to understand that dependent clauses begin with a word (sometimes two words) that links them to an independent clause. A clause that begins with one of these words cannot function as a sentence. Only independent clauses can function as sentences. Listed in the following table are some of these words:

because	if	as
until	since	whereas
although	though	while
unless	so that	once
after	before	when
whenever	who	whom

Consider sentence 3:

3. Fred went to the market because he needed milk.

This sentence has two major parts. The first part, *Fred went to the market,* contains the subject *Fred* and the predicate *went to the market,* so it is a clause. The second part, *he needed milk,* also has a subject, *he,* and a predicate, *needed milk,* so it is another clause. Note, however, that the second clause: (a) begins with the word *because* and (b) also explains why Fred went to the market and provides information of reason to the first clause. Thus, we have two criteria with which to label *because he needed milk* as a dependent clause: It begins with the word *because,* and it modifies the first clause.

Phrases

Although nouns and verbs provide an adequate classification system for very simple grammatical analyses, they do not sufficiently account for the fact that sentences are made up of groups of words (and not just subjects and predicates) that function together. Subjects, for example, are not always composed of a single noun; more often than not they are made up of a noun and one or more other words working in conjunction with the noun. For this reason, the discussions that follow use the term *phrase* regularly. *A phrase can be defined as one or more words functioning together as a unit that does not constitute a clause.* On this account, the subject and predicate of *Dogs bark* are made up of a noun phrase (NP) and a verb phrase (VP), respectively, and in *The tree was tall,* the subject, *The tree,* also is a noun phrase.

We generally identify a phrase on the basis of a key word at its beginning, such as a noun or a verb. Consider these examples:

- *flowers* in her hair
- *running* with the bulls

In the first case, the phrase begins with *flowers,* which is a noun. In the second case, the phrase begins with *running,* which is a verb. We also refer to these words as *head words* because they are at the head of the phrase and the other words in the phrase are attached to them. (See pages 79–80 for a further discussion of head words.)

Objects

As it turns out, sentences like *Dogs bark* are not the most common type in English. Far more common are sentences that have an agent, an action, and what was acted upon, as in sentence 4:

4. Fritz hit the ball.

In this sentence, *the ball* was hit, so it is what Fritz acted upon. Such constructions are referred to as *objects.* Thus, *object* is our third function category. Objects always consist of a noun phrase. Nevertheless, because of the two-part division noted previously, *objects are part of the predicate.* In sentence 4, *Fritz* is the subject, and *hit the ball* is the predicate; the predicate then can be further analyzed as consisting of the verb *hit* and the noun phrase object *the ball.*

Complements

Sentence 2, *The tree was tall,* is different from sentences 1 and 4 in an interesting way: The word *tall,* though it follows the verb *was,* is not what is acted upon. It is not a noun and thus cannot be classified as an object. Also, *was* is not an action verb but an existential verb. Nevertheless, *tall* has something in common with *the ball,* even though it is not a noun: It serves to complete the predicate. Just as *Fritz hit* does not sound complete (and isn't), *the tree was* does not sound complete (and isn't). Because *tall* completes the predicate in sentence 2, it is referred to as a *complement.* Complement is our fourth major function category.

APPLYING KEY IDEAS

Part 1

Directions: Examine the following sentences and identify the constituents of *subject, verb phrase, object,* and/or *complement.*

Example: The police visited the casino.

- the police—subject
- visited—verb phrase
- the casino—object

Sentences:

1. Fred planned the party.
2. Fritz felt tired.
3. Macarena bought a dress.
4. Buggsy smoked cigars.
5. Fred borrowed $100.

Part 2

Directions: In the following sentences, put brackets around the independent clauses, underline the dependent clauses, and circle the word that marks the construction as dependent.

Example: Although Buggsy was overweight, he was strong.

Although Buggsy was overweight, [he was strong.]

Fritz called Rita when he finished dinner.

[Fritz called Rita] when he finished dinner.

Sentences:

1. Before they drove home, Fred and Buggsy ate lunch.
2. Macarena wore a gown, even though the party was casual.
3. Fritz loved the races, whereas Fred loved boxing.
4. Although he was retired, Buggsy kept his guns.
5. Fritz spent money as though he were a movie star.
6. Macarena and Rita danced while the boys played cards.
7. Fred felt bad because he had forgotten Rita's birthday.
8. Fritz loved Los Angeles because it was seedy.
9. Venice Beach was his home until he found a job.
10. His landlady was Ophelia DiMarco, who owned a pool hall, a pawn shop, and a taxi-dance club.

NOUNS

As noted earlier, subjects and predicates are related to nouns and verbs. Traditional grammar defines a noun as a person, place, or thing. However, this definition is not the best because it isn't sufficiently inclusive. The word *Monday,* for example, is a noun, but it is not a thing, nor is *freedom* or any number of other words. For this reason, it is tempting to define a noun in terms of function: *A noun is any word that can function as a subject.*

Although this definition is better than the traditional one, it is not completely accurate. A word like *running* can function as a subject, and when it does it has the characteristics of a noun, but some people argue that the underlying nature of the word—its form as a verb—doesn't change. To better describe the complexity and nuances of this situation, linguists call words like "running" *nominals.* This term can be applied to any word that has a classification other than noun that can be made to function as a noun.

If the situation seems complicated, it is. In fact, defining the term *noun* is such a problem that many grammar books do not even try to do it. Accepting the idea that the concept of *noun* is fairly abstract, however, can point us in the right direction, toward a reasonably acceptable definition. Also, we want a definition that students can easily grasp. From this perspective, *nouns are the labels we use to name the world and our experiences in it.*

As suggested earlier, nouns function as the head words for noun phrases. Thus, even complex noun phrases are dominated by the single noun that serves as head word.

Teaching Tip

Nouns can function as modifiers; that is, they can supply information to other words, typically other nouns. A good example is the word "evening," which is classified as a noun. But we can use it as a modifier in sentences like "Rita wore an evening gown." Words that modify nouns are called "adjectives," discussed in detail on pages 77 to 79. But when a noun like "evening" functions as a modifier, it retains its underlying form as a noun. For this reason, we call it an "adjectival." Students often are confused when they see nouns functioning as adjectives. Using the term "adjectival" can help them better understand the difference between form and function.

Common Nouns, Proper Nouns, and Mass Nouns

There are three major types of nouns. *Common nouns,* as the name suggests, are the largest variety. Common nouns signify a general class of words used in naming and include such words as those in the following list:

Typical Common Nouns		
car	shoe	computer
baby	disk	pad
elephant	book	star
speaker	politician	movie
picture	telephone	jacket
ring	banana	flower

Proper nouns, on the other hand, are specific names, such as Mr. Spock, the Empire State Building, Ford Escort, and the Chicago Bulls.

Mass nouns are a special category of common nouns. What makes them distinct is that, unlike simple common nouns, they cannot be counted. Below is a short list of mass nouns:

deer	air	mud
research	meat	knowledge
furniture	wisdom	butter

Teaching Tip

Nonnative English speakers, particularly those from Asia, have a very difficult time with mass nouns. Japanese and Chinese, for example, do not differentiate between count nouns and mass nouns, treating both as a single category. As a result, we often find these students treating a mass noun as a count noun. It is important to understand in such instances that the problem stems from a conflict between English and the students' home language. One way to help them better distinguish between count nouns and common nouns is to prepare a list of frequently used mass nouns for study.

PRONOUNS

English, like other languages, resists the duplication of nouns in sentences, so it replaces duplicated nouns with what are called *pronouns.* (No one is sure why languages resist such duplication.) The nouns that get replaced are called *antecedents.* Consider sentence 5:

5. *Fred liked Macarena, so Fred took Macarena to a movie.[2]

---

[2]The asterisk at the beginning of the sentence signifies that it is ungrammatical. This convention will be used throughout the text from this point on.

The duplication of the proper nouns *Fred* and *Macarena* just does not sound right to most people because English generally does not allow it. The duplicated nouns are replaced, as in sentence 5a:

5a. Fred liked Macarena, so he took her to a movie.

Notice that sentence 5b also is acceptable:

5b. He liked her, so Fred took Macarena to a movie.

In this instance, however, sentence 5b is not quite as *appropriate* as 5a because the sentence lacks a context. Real sentences, as opposed to those that appear in books like this one, are part of a context that includes the complexities of human relationships; prior knowledge related to past, present, and future events; and, of course, prior conversations. The pronouns in sentence 5b suggest that *Fred* and *Macarena* already have been identified or are known. This suggestion is contrary to fact. In sentence 5a, on the other hand, *Fred* and *Macarena* appear in the first part of the sentence, so the pronouns are linked to these antecedents without any doubt or confusion about which nouns the pronouns have replaced. At work is an important principle for pronouns: *They should appear as close to their antecedents as possible to avoid potential confusion.*

Personal Pronouns

Pronouns that replace a duplicated noun are referred to as *personal* or *common* pronouns. The common pronouns are:

Singular: I, me, you, he, him, she, her, it

Plural: we, us, you, they, them

In addition, there are several other types of pronouns: *demonstrative, reciprocal, possessive, indefinite, reflexive,* and *relative.* Possessive and relative pronouns are examined in detail later in the book, with special attention paid to relatives because they are part of an interesting construction called a *relative clause.* Therefore, discussion of these types here is brief.

Case. Before going forward with the discussion of pronouns, we need to pause and explore *case.* The functional relations in sentences are important in all languages, but not all languages signify those relations in the same way. English relies primarily on word order. On a basic level, we know that subjects normally come before the verb and that objects normally come after. Other languages, however, do not rely so much on word order but instead alter the forms of the words to signify their relations. Japanese, for example, uses word order *and* form, attaching particles to words to signify their function: *Wa* is used for subjects, and *o* is used for objects. Thus, "I read this book" is expressed as follows:

- *Watashi-wa kono hon-o yonda.*

We know that *watashi* is the subject because of the particle *wa* attached to it, and we know that *hon* is the object because of the particle *o*. Translated literally, this sentence reads, "I this book read." Notice, however, that we also could state:

- *Kono hon-o watashi-wa yonda.*

This shift in word order ("This book I read") would be appropriate if the speaker wanted to emphasize that it was a particular book that he or she had read. Even though the word order has changed, there is no confusion regarding subject and object because the particle markers always signal the proper function.

We use a special term to describe changes in the forms of nouns based on function—*inflections*. Some languages are more inflected than others, with modern English being largely uninflected. At one time, however, English was highly inflected, and it retains a vestige of this past in the various forms of its pronouns, some of which change on the basis of whether they are functioning as a subject or an object.

As indicated earlier, the relation of subjects and objects to a sentence is determined with respect to their relation to the action conveyed in the verb. More formally, these relations are expressed in terms of case. When a noun or pronoun is functioning as a subject, it is in the *subject,* or *nominative,* case; when functioning as an object, it is in the *objective* case. However, case does not affect nouns in English, only pronouns—they change their form depending on how they function.

Consider sentence 6:

6. *Fred* and *I* kissed Macarena.

Both *Fred* and the pronoun *I* are part of the subject, so they are in the nominative case. When these words function as objects, *Fred* does not change its form, but the pronoun *I* does, as in sentence 7:

7. Macarena kissed *Fred* and *me.*

Me is the objective case form of the personal pronoun *I.*

Analysis of case can become complicated. In fact, linguists have a hard time agreeing on just how many cases exist in English. Everyone recognizes nominative and objective case, but some linguists argue that others exist, such as *dative* (indirect objects) and *genitive* (possessive) cases. For our purposes, it is sufficient to recognize just three cases—nominative, objective, and possessive—illustrated in the following examples:

- *She* stopped the car. (nominative)
- Fred kissed *her.* (objective)
- The book is *his.* (possessive)

Teaching Tip

A few English nouns retain inflection for gender. Consider, for example, the two spellings available for people with yellow hair: "blond" and "blonde." Although pronounced the same, the former is used for males, the latter for females. "Actor" and "actress" are two other words that retain inflection. Over the last several years, there have been concerted efforts to eliminate all gender inflections, such that female performers increasingly are referred to as actors rather than actresses. An engaging activity for students is to have them form teams and observe how inflected forms are used for gender and by whom. They can report their findings and explore whether inflected forms are still useful and whether these forms should be retained.

Usage Note

Nonstandard usage commonly reverses nominative case and objective case pronouns, resulting in sentences like 8 and 9 below:

8. ?Fritz and me gave the flowers to Macarena.[3]
9. ?Buggsy asked Fred, Raul, and I to drive to Las Vegas.

Formal standard usage is illustrated in sentences 8a and 9a:

8a. Fritz and I gave the flowers to Macarena.
9a. Buggsy asked Fred, Raul, and me to drive to Las Vegas.

Note that sentences 8 and 9 are not ungrammatical, but they do violate standard usage conventions. Even though we may *hear* people violate these conventions on a regular basis, teachers are rightly concerned when the problem appears in students' speech and writing.

---

[3]The question mark at the beginning of the sentence signals that the sentence is nonstandard. This convention will be used throughout from this point on.

Nevertheless, it is important to consider that an equally troublesome problem with case gets little attention. When someone knocks on a door and is asked, "Who is it?" the response nearly always is *It's me*. In formal standard usage, the response would be *It's I* because the verb *is* establishes equality between the subject, *It*, and the noun complement that follows the verb. This equality includes case, which means that the noun complement in standard usage would be set in the nominative case, not the objective. Even so, few people ever use *It's I*, not even people who use Standard English consistently. The contrast between these forms can offer a meaningful language lesson for students.

In addition, the question of case in this situation is interesting because it illustrates the influence of Latin on notions of correctness. Latin and Latin-based languages are more inflected than is English, so problems of case rarely arise. For example, we just do not observe native Spanish speakers using an objective-case pronoun in a nominative position. If a Spanish speaker is asked, "Who is it?" the response always is *Soy yo*, never *Soy me*. All native Spanish speakers will reject *Soy me* as an appropriate response. This fact offers a useful foundation for a lesson on case in classes with a high percentage of native Spanish-speaking students.

In an uninflected language like English, on the other hand, speakers rely on word order not only to determine what is acceptable but also, on a deeper level, to determine what is grammatical. In a word-order-dependent language like English, case is largely irrelevant. As a result, *Fritz and me gave the flowers to Macarena* is acceptable to many people because it conforms to the standard word order of English. The pronoun *me* is in the subject position and is understood to be part of the subject regardless of its case. Likewise, *It's me* will be accepted because the pronoun is in what normally is the object-complement position. This analysis explains, in part, why most people think *It's I* sounds strange.

Demonstrative Pronouns

There are four demonstrative pronouns:

this, that, these, those

They serve to single out, highlight, or draw attention to a noun, as in sentences 10, 11, and 12:

10. *That* car is a wreck.
11. *Those* peaches don't look very ripe.
12. *This* book is really interesting.

Teaching Tip

The demonstrative pronoun "this" usually comes before a noun, but not always. In certain situations, it replaces an entire sentence, as in the following:

Fritz cleaned his apartment. This amazed Macarena.

Here, "this" refers to the fact that Fritz cleaned his apartment. In this kind of construction "this" is called an "indefinite demonstrative pronoun" because there is no definite antecedent. In the example given, with the two sentences side by side, the relation is clear; we understand what "this" refers to. However, inexperienced writers do not always use the indefinite demonstrative pronoun in ways that make the connection with the antecedent clear. As a result, they often will have several sentences separating the indefinite demonstrative "this" and the fact or action to it which it refers. Readers do not have an easy time figuring out the connection, as in this example:

> The romantic model that views writing as an independent and isolated process has dominated the classroom for years. The model may be poetic, it may feel good for teachers, but it is not practical. It does not take into account the pragmatic social factors that contribute to successful writing. Moreover, measures of student writing have shown a steady decline in proficiency over the last 15 years. This can present a major problem for teachers seeking to implement new models and strategies in the classroom.

The word "this" in the last sentence should refer to the idea in the previous sentence, but it doesn't; there is no real connection between them. The last sentence seems most closely linked to the first, but the relation is not clear, and it certainly is not strong, because of the intervening sentences. Using the indefinite demonstrative in this instance is not appropriate because it negatively affects clarity and understanding. The sentence would have to be moved upward to be successful.

The misplacement of sentences that begin with the indefinite demonstrative "this" occurs frequently in the work of inexperienced writers. In many instances, the situation is worse: There will not be any preceding sentence for the pronoun; the reference is to a sentence in the writer's mind that never was put on paper. A large number of experienced writers object to any usage of "this" in such a broad way, arguing that an alternative, more precise structure is better. They recommend replacing the indefinite demonstrative pronoun with an appropriate noun. In the previous example, replacing "this" with "the romantic model" would solve the problem.

Reciprocal Pronouns

English has two reciprocal pronouns—*each other* and *one another*—which are used to refer to the individual parts of a plural noun. Consider sentences 13 and 14:

13. The friends gave gifts to *each other*.
14. The dogs looked at *one another*.

Each other and *one another* do not mean the same thing; thus, they are not interchangeable. *Each other* signifies two people or things, whereas *one another* signifies more than two. Sentence 13 refers to two friends; sentence 14 refers to more than two dogs.

APPLYING KEY IDEAS

Although no strong connection between grammar and writing quality exists, it is easy to find one for usage. Most writing, for example, is improved when writers make certain that their indefinite demonstrative pronouns have clear antecedents. For this activity, examine some of your writing, especially papers you have submitted for classes, and identify any instances of indefinite demonstrative pronouns that lack clear antecedents. In each instance, revise your writing to provide an antecedent or to eliminate the pronoun. Doing so can help you avoid this problem in the future. You also may find it interesting to check your writing to see whether your use of reciprocal pronouns is congruent with the standard convention. If you can, you should share your revision efforts with classmates to compare results, which can give you better insight into revising.

Possessive Pronouns

Possessive pronouns indicate possession, as in sentences 15 and 16:

15. *My* son loves baseball.
16. The books are *mine.*

The possessive pronouns are:

Singular: my, mine, your, yours, her, hers, his, its

Plural: our, ours, your, yours, their, theirs

Teaching Tip

Many students confuse the possessive pronoun "its" with the contraction of "it is"—it's. Explaining the difference does not seem to have any effect on students' writing, nor do drills and exercises. An editing activity, however, appears to lead to some improvement. After students have worked on a paper and engaged in peer reviews of their drafts, shift the focus of students' attention to editing. Have students exchange papers and circle all instances of "its" and "it's." Then, with it's = it is and its = possessive written on the board, have them check each occurrence to ensure that the usage is correct. They should point out any errors to their partners, who should make corrections immediately. Circulate among students to offer assistance, as needed.

Indefinite Pronouns

Indefinite pronouns have general rather than specific antecedents, which means that they refer to general entities or concepts, as in sentence 17:

17. *Everyone* was late.

The indefinite pronoun *everyone* does not refer to any specific individual but rather to the entire group, which gives it its indefinite status.

Indefinite Pronouns in English		
all	any	anybody
anything	anyone	another
both	each	every
everybody	every	everything
either	few	fewer
many	neither	nobody
no one	none	one
several	some	somebody
something		

Usage Note

English requires agreement in number for nouns, verbs, and pronouns. For example, a plural noun subject must have a verb in the predicate that also designates plurality. Thus, we have *Dogs bark* but not *Dogs barks*. Likewise, if Fritz and Fred are getting cleaned up, we have *Fritz and Fred washed their faces* but not *Fritz and Fred washed his face*. We cannot understand *Fritz and Fred washed his face* as meaning that the two men washed their own faces, only that they washed someone other than themselves. To indicate the first meaning, the pronoun *their* must be plural to include *Fritz and Fred,* and the noun *faces* also must be plural.

With respect to the indefinite pronouns *everyone* and *everybody,* a problem arises. These pronouns are singular, not plural. Nevertheless, their semantic content is inclusive, indicating a group. Consequently, most people when speaking treat the pronouns as though they are plural, as in the following sentence:

- ?Everybody grabbed their hats and went outside.

Because *everybody* is singular rather than plural, correct usage requires a singular pronoun as well as a singular noun to provide the necessary agreement:

• Everybody grabbed his hat and went outside.

What we see in this sentence is the masculine pronoun *his* being used in a generic sense to include all people, regardless of gender. Beginning in the early 1970s, some educators and students expressed concern that the generic use of *his* was a manifestation of sexist language. Within a few years, NCTE published its guidelines on sexist language, and the major style guides and handbooks asserted that the generic use of *his* should be avoided at all costs.

Some educators advocated the arbitrary redesignation of *everyone* and *everybody* from singular to plural. Others proposed replacing the generic *his* with the generic *hers,* and still others suggested using *his/her* or *his or her.* Today, the first option is deemed unacceptable in most quarters; the second option is embraced only by those with an ideological agenda. The third option (note that *his or her* is always preferable to *his/her*) is most widely accepted and has been complemented with a fourth: Restructuring the sentence so as to eliminate the indefinite pronoun. Consider these examples:

• Everybody grabbed his or her hat and went outside.
• They grabbed their hats and went outside.
• All the people grabbed their hats and went outside.

Reflexive Pronouns

When subjects perform actions on themselves, we need a special way to signify the reflexive nature of the action. We do so through the use of *reflexive pronouns.* Consider the act of shaving, as in sentence 18, in which Macarena, the subject, performs a reflexive action:

18. *Macarena shaved Macarena.

This duplication is not allowed, but we cannot use a personal pronoun for the object, *Macarena.* Doing so results in a different meaning, as in sentence 18a:

18a. Macarena shaved her.

In sentence 18a, the pronoun *her* cannot refer to Macarena but instead must refer to someone else.

To avoid this problem, English provides a set of special pronouns that signify a reflexive action:

Singular: myself, yourself, himself, herself, itself

Plural: ourselves, yourselves, themselves

Thus, to express the idea that Macarena shaved Macarena, we would have 18b:

18b. Macarena shaved herself.

Usage Note

Sometimes reflexive pronouns work as *intensifiers,* as in sentences 19 and 20:

19. They *themselves* refused to sign the agreement.
20. We *ourselves* can't abide deceit.

On page 63, we saw how nonstandard usage confuses nominative case and objective case pronouns. People will use a nominative case pronoun in the subject position, and vice versa. Many people are aware of this problem in their language, probably as a result of instruction, but they do not know how to fix it. In an attempt to avoid the problem, at least with respect to the pronouns *I* and *me,* they will use a reflexive pronoun in either the subject or object position, as in sentences 21 and 22:

21. ?Macarena, Fritz, and myself went to Catalina.
22. ?Buggsy took Fred, Macarena, and myself to Acapulco.

Using a reflexive pronoun to replace a personal pronoun simply creates another problem because there is no reflexive action. Replacing a personal pronoun with a reflexive is a violation of standard usage.

Relative Pronouns

As we saw on page 56, dependent clauses begin with words that link them to independent clauses. An interesting and important type of dependent clause begins with a *relative pronoun* and therefore is called a *relative clause.* Consider these sentences:

23. Fritz knew a woman *who had red hair.*
24. The woman *whom Fritz liked* had red hair.

25. The book *that Fritz borrowed* was a first edition.

In these sentences, *who, whom,* and *that* are relative pronouns. These and others are shown in the following list:

Major Relative Pronouns in English		
who	whom	that
which	whose	where
when	why	

VERBS

Verbs are the words we use to signify an action or a state of being. They make up the head of the predicate (they are the head word of the predicate) and are interesting in large part because they convey so much information in sentences. For example, actions can occur in the past, present, or future, and verbs commonly change in relation to the time an action occurred. We call this feature *tense.*

Although three tenses are possible, *English has only two: past and present.* The future has to be conveyed in a way that does not involve changing the verb. Sometimes, we use the words *will* or *shall* to indicate the future, as in *We will eat soon,* but English is flexible and allows us to signify the future in other ways. We can, for example, use the present to indicate the future, as in *We eat soon.* In fact, English is so flexible that sometimes we also can signify the past by using the present, as in: *So last night he asks me for money. Can you believe it?*

Romance languages like Spanish have three tenses, whereas other languages, such as Hopi, have only one or no tense at all. Differences in verb tense across languages played an important role in the shift from traditional grammar to modern grammar in the early 1900s (a topic that we take up in the next chapter).

Comparing English and Spanish verbs illustrates the nature of tense and how English differs from a Latin-based language. Consider the verb *speak,* which in Spanish is *hablar:*

Past	Present	Future
spoke	speak	Ø
hablé	hablo	hablaría

Teaching Tip

Some languages, such as Chinese, do not mark verbs for tense. Instead, they indicate the time of an action through modifiers—words like "tomorrow," "yesterday," and "today." When students come to our classes with a home language that does not include tense, we must anticipate interference during speaking and writing activities. One effective way to help these students better grasp the concept of tense is to use contrastive pairs of sentences that illustrate tensed and untensed verbs. Contrastive pairs consist of examples of sentences written in nonstandard English beside sentences written in Standard English, as in:

- **The dog bark at Fritz.*
- *The dog barked at Fritz.*

Such work helps students better recognize the difference between how a sentence would look as influenced by their home language and how it looks according to English grammar.

Aspect

In addition to tense, verbs have another interesting characteristic called *aspect*.[4] Aspect provides information about the duration or ongoing nature of an action. In Standard English, it normally is conveyed by two verb constructions, the *progressive verb form* and the *perfect verb form*.

Sentences 26 and 27 show progressive verb forms:

26. Fred *was washing* his car.
27. Fritz *is reading* a book.

The progressive, as 26 and 27 indicate, consists of a tensed form of the verb *be* and a verb that has *-ing* attached (the *-ing* suffix is called the *present participle* marker), as indicated:

be (marked for tense) *verb* + *ing*

Sentences 28 and 29 show perfect verb forms:

28. Macarena *has visited* Buggsy before.
29. Fred and Fritz *had eaten* too many tacos.

---

[4]Black English Vernacular and Standard English have different ways of dealing with tense and aspect, a topic examined in chapter 7.

The perfect, as these sentences illustrate, consists of a tensed form of the verb *have* and a verb that has *-ed* or *-en* attached (the *-ed* and *-en* suffixes are called *past participle* markers), as indicated below:

have (marked for tense) *verb + ed/en*

Teaching Tip

The past participle in English is irregular owing to the influence of other languages over the centuries. Some verbs take the -ed suffix, some the -en suffix, as just illustrated. The verb "do" takes neither, instead ending in -ne, as in "She had done her homework." Students are easily confused by explanations of the past participle, with good reason. Adding to the problem is that many dialects of American English use the participial form of the verb as the simple past, as in "?I seen her before." Spending significant amounts of time on the grammatical explanation seems to have little effect on students' language patterns. Working with contrastive pairs offers a more useful approach:

- *?I been working on the paper.*
- *I have been working on the paper.*

Teachers can use students' own writing or can record and then transcribe students' speech to develop contrastive pairs, which gives a sense of authenticity that is conducive to better learning.

Transitive and Intransitive Verbs

There are several different kinds of verbs. Although we cannot examine all of them, we can look at some of the more important categories. Sentence 1—*Dogs bark*—has just a subject and a verb. Sentence 4—*Fritz hit the ball*—has a subject, a verb, and an object. The difference is related to the fact that *bark* and *hit* are different kinds of verbs.

Some verbs either require or can work with an object; *hit* is such a verb. We call these verbs *transitive verbs*. Other verbs, such as *bark,* cannot work with an object. If we put a noun phrase after *bark,* we have an ungrammatical sentence. Verbs that cannot be followed by a noun phrase are called *intransitive verbs*. This distinction is straightforward and does not normally cause students any confusion, but many verbs can function both transitively and intransitively, which can be very confusing. Consider the following:

30. Fred ate an apple.
31. Fred ate.
32. Macarena stopped the car.
33. Macarena stopped.
34. Fritz cooked the dinner.

35. Fritz cooked.

In each of these cases, the verb can function either transitively or intransitively.

To repeat:

- Transitive verbs are followed by an object.
- Intransitive verbs are not followed by an object.

Teaching Tip

Nonnative English speaking students, especially those from Asia, frequently confuse transitive and intransitive verbs. Below are some examples that illustrate the problem:

- **Yesterday, we graphed in class.*
- **They exhausted with too much hard work.*
- **The woman struggled the boy who wanted her purse.*
- **The taxi traveled us to the airport.*

Explaining to students that some verbs are transitive and some are intransitive doesn't help them much, although it is an important first step. Fortunately, the number of intransitive verbs in English is relatively small. An effective approach is to develop a list of the most commonly used intransitives that students can study. Most words not on the list will be transitive and will require a noun phrase object. Have students refer to the list during the editing phase of all writing activities, and they will demonstrate rapid improvement.

Usage Note

Perhaps one of the more widespread departures from standard usage involves the verbs *lay* and *lie*. *Lay* is a transitive verb, so it requires an object, as in *Please lay the book on the table. Lie,* on the other hand, is an intransitive verb and cannot take an object. Nevertheless, huge numbers of people use *lay* intransitively, as in sentence 36:

36. ?I'm going to lay down for a nap.

Standard usage is reflected in sentence 37:

37. I'm going to lie down for a nap.

Part of the confusion seems to be related to the fact that *lay* is the past tense of *lie*, whereas *laid* is the past tense of *lay*. Then there is the fact that *lie* also signifies a falsehood. Many people can't keep all these variations straight.

Teaching Tip

A few teachers try to solve the "lay/lie" problem by providing students with a memory aid: "Dogs lay down, but people lie down." This memory aid, of course, is wrong—the verb in both cases should be "lie." Some people argue that the intransitive use of "lay" has become so ubiquitous that it now is standard. This argument, however, fails to account for the fact that many people in influential positions continue to follow standard usage and judge the nonstandard usage negatively. Being able to apply the difference between "lay" and "lie" therefore has clear advantages because the intransitive "lay" is inappropriate in most situations, and it always is inappropriate in writing. Many teachers, for example, cringe whenever they see a student using "lay" intransitively, even though this usage has become so common that they cringe daily. The incorrect usage is ingrained in students' language patterns, making the task of shifting their usage to Standard English difficult. An effective activity involves teaching students the difference between "lie" and "lay" and then asking them, in teams, to listen to conversations in the cafeteria, the bus, on TV, and so on. Have them record every instance of incorrect and correct usage and then present an oral report on their findings. What was the frequency of incorrect and correct usage? Did usage differ in any way—by gender? age? socioeconomic status?

Incomplete Transitive and Incomplete Intransitive Verbs

A transitive verb requires a noun phrase to complete the predicate, but an intransitive verb does not. A subclass of transitive and intransitive verbs, however, requires another kind of construction to be complete. These special verbs are called *incomplete transitives* and *incomplete intransitives,* respectively. They require an additional element, a *prepositional phrase,* which is discussed in detail on pages 89 to 92. For example, consider the verbs *put* and *deal,* as illustrated in these sentences:

38. Mrs. DiMarco put the rent money *under her mattress.*
39. Buggsy dealt *with the problem.*

These sentences would be incomplete without the italicized constructions. Note that sometimes these verbs are called *prepositional verbs*.

Ditransitive Verbs: Direct and Indirect Objects

On pages 72 to 73, we saw that transitive verbs require an object. A special category of verbs, called *ditransitives,* usually appears with *two objects;* that is, the verb is followed by two noun phrases, as illustrated in sentences 40 and 41:

40. Fred sent *his mother* a card.
41. Buggsy asked *Fritz* a question.

Let's look carefully at these sentences. If we remove the noun phrases in bold, we have:

40a. Fred sent a card.
41a. Buggsy asked a question.

In these sentences, we can see that the noun phrases *a card* and *a question* are objects; they are acted upon by their verbs. In the original sentences, *his mother* and *Fritz* have a slightly different function: In 40, *his mother* accepted *a card,* and in 41 *Fritz* accepted *a question.*

We differentiate the two noun phrases following ditransitive verbs as follows: The noun phrase that is acted upon we refer to as a *direct object;* the noun phrase that accepts the direct object we call an *indirect object.* Thus, in 40 *a card* is the direct object and *his mother* is the indirect object. The sentences below are labeled to help illustrate the two constructions:

- Macarena gave Buggsy a kiss. (*a kiss* = direct object; *Buggsy* = indirect object)
- Fritz told Rita a story. (*a story* = direct object; *Rita* = indirect object)
- Buggsy wrote the gang a note. (*a note* = direct object; *the gang* = indirect object)
- Rita showed Fred her earrings. (*her earrings* = direct object; *Fred* = indirect object)

Ditransitive verbs raise some interesting questions and have been the subject of considerable study over the last several years (e.g., Kratzer, 1996; Langacker, 1999; McGinnis, 2002; Pylkkänen, 2002; Schmid, 2000). Do these verbs *require* two objects, or are there instances in which they can take only one, which means that they can *accept* two objects? In the case of *ask,* the answer clearly is that the verb can take a single object: *Buggsy asked Fritz a question* can become *Buggsy asked Fritz;* "a question" is implicit in the statement. For other ditransitive verbs, however, the answer is not so clear. In the case of *Fred sent Macarena a gift,* dropping the direct object may be grammatical, but it changes the sentence grammatically and semantically: *Fred sent Macarena.*

Dropping *a gift* maintains a grammatical sentence, but suddenly *Macarena* becomes the direct object rather than the indirect object, and the meaning is not even close to the original. An equally troubling example occurs with the ditransitive verb *buy:*

- Fred bought his mother a present.
- Fred bought his mother.

From this analysis, it appears that ditransitive verbs require two objects in most situations. The fact that there are some ditransitives, such as *ask,* that allow us to drop the direct object without changing the grammatical relations or the meaning of the sentence is coincidental and trivial.

Indirect Objects as Phrases. An interesting feature of indirect objects is that they can appear as a noun phrase or as a phrase that usually begins with the word *to* (a prepositional phrase). Thus, this single construction has two possible structures, as illustrated here:

40. Fred sent *his mother* a card.
40b. Fred sent a card to *his mother.*

In sentence 40b, *his mother* is the indirect object, even though it is part of a (prepositional) phrase. The following sentences offer further examples of these equivalent structures:

- Buggsy asked Fritz a question/Buggsy asked a question of Fritz
- Macarena gave Buggsy a kiss/Macarena gave a kiss to Buggsy
- Fritz told Rita a story/Fritz told a story to Rita
- Buggsy wrote the gang a note/Buggsy wrote a note to the gang
- Raul left Rita a present/Raul left a present for Rita
- Rita showed Fred her earrings/Rita showed her earrings to Fred

---

Teaching Tip

Native speakers of Spanish tend to structure indirect objects as prepositional phrases rather than as noun phrases. An effective way of building students' skills and expanding their sentence variety is to ask them to:

- *exchange papers.*
- *circle all instances of the word "to" that introduce an indirect object.*
- *revise sentences to turn the construction into a simple noun phrase.*

Note that "to" does not always introduce an indirect object. When followed by a verb, for example, it has a very different function.

Linking Verbs

Earlier, we saw that verbs describe an action or are existential. Sentence 2— *The tree was tall*—illustrates how the verb *was* expresses existence, or a state of being. We give such verbs a special classification: *linking verbs.* Linking verbs link a complement to the subject of a sentence. All forms of *be* can function as linking verbs, as can all sensory verbs, such as *taste, smell, feel, look,* and *sound.* Other linking verbs include *seems, prove, grow,* and *become* (*got* also can function as a linking verb when it is used in the sense of *become,* as in *Fred got tired*). Note, however, that some of these verbs, specifically *smell, feel, sound, prove,* and *grow,* also can function as regular verbs, as in *Fred smelled the flowers.*

Linking verbs can be followed by only three types of constructions: (a) noun phrases, (b) adjective phrases, and (c) prepositional phrases. The latter constructions are discussed on pages 78 and 89, respectively.

Gerunds

One of the interesting things about language is its flexibility. Words that we normally think of as existing in a certain category can easily function in another category. Many verbs, for example, can function as nouns, usually just by adding the suffix *-ing,* as in *running, jumping, driving,* and so forth. When verbs function as nouns, we call them *gerunds.* As noted on page 59, another (perhaps more useful) name is *nominals.*

APPLYING KEY IDEAS

An important part of mastering grammar lies in the ability to observe how people use language and then to compare it to a conventional standard. Listening to others helps one "listen" to one's own language. Spend some time listening to others speak, in the school cafeteria, on TV, on the bus, or some other place where you can be unobtrusive. Focus on two topics that were examined earlier—case and reflexive pronouns—using a notebook to record instances of nonstandard usage. Meet later with your class to discuss what you learned from this activity.

MODIFIERS

As indicated earlier, we can say that sentences essentially are composed of nouns and verbs and that nearly everything else provides information about those nouns and verbs. The words and constructions that provide such information are classified broadly as *modifiers.* Modifiers are of two major types; those that supply information to nouns and those that supply information to verbs. We call these *adjectival* and *adverbial* modifiers, respectively. These terms describe function, not form. Nouns, for example, can function adjectivally.

The complete picture is more complex than this overview may suggest. Modifiers also may supply information to other modifiers and to sentences or clauses, but their function nevertheless remains adjectival or adverbial.

Adjectival Modifiers

Adjectival modifiers supply information, usually sensory, to noun phrases. The most common type of adjectival modifier is the *simple adjective*. Consider these sentences:

42. Macarena bought a *red* dress.
43. The *new* book made her career.
44. His *wooden* speech put the crowd to sleep.

Each of these simple adjectives supplies information to its associated noun: The dress was *red;* the book was *new;* the speech was *wooden.*

As indicated earlier, many words can function as modifiers, and when they do they commonly function as adjectivals. Consider sentence 45:

45. Macarena bought an evening gown.

Evening is a noun, but in sentence 45 it functions as an adjectival.

Predicate Adjectives.   Simple adjectives come before the nouns they modify. However, there are two special adjectives that do not. The first kind is one that we've already seen in sentence 2: *The tree was tall.* The word *tall* is an adjective, and it supplies information to *tree,* but it follows the linking verb *was.* Because this construction has a special relation with the linking verb and is an adjective, we give it a specific name: *predicate adjective.* Predicate adjectives can only follow linking verbs.

Now we're in a better position to understand the difference between *ball* in *Fritz hit the ball* and *tall* in *The tree was tall.* Both complete the predicate, but *ball* is a noun functioning as an object, whereas *tall* is a predicate adjective functioning as a complement. Sentences 46 through 48 illustrate additional predicate adjectives:

46. Fritz felt *tired.*
47. The pizza tasted *funny.*
48. Fred was *disgusted.*

Adjective Complements.   The second type of special adjective is called an *adjective complement,* which is illustrated in sentence 49:

49. Macarena painted the town *red.*

Notice that the adjective *red* completes the predicate, but it doesn't immediately follow the verb. Moreover, *painted* is not a linking verb.

Adverbial Modifiers

Adverbial modifiers supply information to verbs, adjectivals, other adverbials, clauses, and sentences. They are versatile. Adverbials are not sensory; rather they provide six different types of information:

time, place, manner, degree, cause, concession

Like adjectivals, adverbials consist of *simple adverbs* as well as entire constructions that function adverbially. The following examples illustrate adverbials that provide the six types of information just listed. Note that adverbials of degree modify adjectivals, or they may modify other adverbials:

Time: They arrived *late.*

Place: We stopped *there* for a rest.

Manner: Fred opened the box *slowly.*

Degree: Macarena felt *very* tired. She opened the box *quite* rapidly.

Cause: We ate *because we were hungry.*

Concession: *Although she didn't like broccoli,* she ate it.

In the last two examples, we see illustrations of longer constructions (clauses) functioning as adverbials: *Because we were hungry* and *Although she didn't like broccoli* are *subordinate clauses,* which we'll examine shortly (page 86). Another important adverbial construction is the prepositional phrase, which we'll examine on pages 89–92.

Head Words

Modification in English is flexible, particularly with adverbials, which can appear in different places in a sentence. Earlier, we briefly examined an important principle of modification: No matter where a modifier appears, it is linked to one word in the sentence more closely than it is to other words. For example, in *The new book made her career,* the adjective *new* is linked to *book.* In *Fred opened the box slowly,* the adverb *slowly* is linked to *opened.* The word to which a modifier is linked is called a *head word.* Head words become important when modifiers are more complex than simple adjectives and adverbs, as in the sentence below from Ernest Hemingway:

- Manuel swung with the charge, sweeping the muleta ahead of the bull, feet firm, the sword a point of light under the arcs.

The modifiers here, which we discuss a bit later, are primarily verbal constructions, and their head word is *swung*.

The concept of head words is useful not only because it helps us when we need to talk about modifiers and what they modify but also because of another feature of modification, which sometimes is referred to as the *proximity principle:* Modifiers always should be as close to their head words as possible. Violation of this principle can result is what is termed a misplaced modifier, as in the sentence below:

- *?Walking across the window, I saw a fly.*

We certainly know that the *fly* was doing the walking here, not the subject *I,* but the placement of this modifier suggests the contrary. *Fly* is the head word for the verb construction *walking across the window,* but the link is unclear because the physical distance between them in the sentence is too great. Misplaced modifiers of this sort are very common in the writing of young students. Fortunately, such students easily understand the notion of head words and the proximity principle after a little instruction.

Teaching Tip

The Hemingway sentence is interesting because it illustrates an important feature of narrative-descriptive writing. Notice that the independent clause is rather short and not very rich in details. The description comes in the form of the phrasal modifiers attached to the clause: "sweeping the muleta ahead of the bull, feet firm, the sword a point of light under the arcs." Christensen (1967) called such sentences "cumulative" because of the way they are built up through a process of adding details. When students have opportunities to practice producing cumulative sentences, they show significant improvement in their writing skills. Use a piece of narrative-descriptive writing as a model for analysis to show students how details are built up on the base of the independent clause. Then ask them to observe a repetitive process, such as cars passing through an intersection, people moving forward in a queue, or water going down a sink drain. Have them describe the process in no more than two cumulative sentences. The goal is to produce cumulative sentences rich in detail.

Usage Note

Large numbers of people have difficulty with the modifiers *good* and *well*. Part of the problem is that *good* always is an adjective, whereas *well* can function as either an adjective or an adverb. In nonstandard usage *good* appears as both an adjective and an adverb, and *well* appears only in limited ways. The example sentences that follow illustrate the most common nonstandard usage of *good:*

50. ?I did good on the test.
51. ?You played good.

Standard usage is quite clear on this point—*well* is strongly preferred in these instances, as in sentences 50a and 51a:

50a. I did well on the test.
51a. You played well.

Another situation arises with the verb *feel*. When describing how they are feeling, most people say that they feel good, as in sentence 52:

52. I feel good.

However, formal standard usage differentiates between *I feel good* and *I feel well*. *Well* nearly always refers to one's state of health; only in the most unusual circumstances would *feel* appear as a regular verb signifying that one has a sense of touch that is working properly. Thus, *I feel well* indicates that one is healthy. More to the point, it indicates that, after some particular illness or disease, one has regained previous health. A person recovered from the flu, for example, might say *I feel well*. *I feel good,* on the other hand, can refer to one's general state of well-being, as in the famous James Brown song, *I Feel Good (Like I Knew That I Would)*. This state of well-being can be either physiological or psychological or both. With respect to one's health, however, *I feel good* does not mean, in formal standard usage, that one has regained previous health; it means that one is feeling better at the moment of the utterance than in the past but that the illness or disease is still present. On this account, one might say, after a few days in bed with the flu, *I feel good today,* meaning that one feels relatively better than the day before.

Equally problematic is the situation associated with the question, *How are you today?* If one responds in a way that signifies general well-being, then the appropriate response is *I am good,* although the inherent ambiguity here is interesting. It could mean that one is virtuous, which certainly is a state of being, but perhaps one more often desired than attained. If, however, one responds in a way that signifies health, the appropriate response is *I am well.* In the United States, such exchanges are nearly always for social recognition rather than for serious inquiry into one's health, so we rarely hear the response *I am well.* In Britain, the situation is different, and the response, *Very well, thank you,* is common.

The linking verb *feel* is associated with another problem that we observe in the language people use, a problem that can be humorous the first couple of times one thinks about it. When people learn of someone's hardship or accident, it is natural for them to want to express their sadness, sympathy, or remorse, but doing so can be problematic. There are two possibilities:

53. I heard about the accident. I feel badly.
53a. I heard about the accident. I feel bad.

But look carefully at the construction. *Feel* is a linking verb when referring to one's state of being, so it must be followed by an adjective. *Bad* is an adjective, but *badly* is not—it's an adverb. Consequently, *badly* does not make any sense, really, because it does not refer to a state of being. In fact, if we took sentence 53 literally, it would mean that the speaker has lost his or her tactile perception: When touching something, the speaker simply cannot feel it. This is not a state or condition that people experience very often, and it certainly isn't related to remorse. Thus, *I feel bad* reflects standard usage when expressing remorse or when describing one's health. *I feel badly* is, of course, grammatical, but only in the context of tactile sensitivity; and in this case, *feel* is not functioning as a linking verb.

We can differentiate those who use *I feel bad* or *I feel badly* by their level of education. However, the results are not what one might expect. Generally, people who have less education will apply standard usage and state *I feel bad.* Those with education, including well-educated PhDs and MDs, are much more likely to use *I feel badly.* Reality thus thwarts our expectations.

FUNCTION WORDS

A characteristic of subjects and predicates and most of the words that make up subjects and predicates is that they convey meaning, or what sometimes is referred to as *semantic content*. Indeed, we can say that meaning is a primary characteristic, given that language is by nature full of meaning and signification. For example, the word *ball* has an identifiable meaning, as does the word *tall*. People may disagree on the specific meaning of each word, but the disagreements are not major because everyone accepts their general signification. Function words, on the other hand, do not have meaning as a primary characteristic. They commonly connect or mark parts of sentences, and their semantic content is secondary. Function words can be classified into several discrete types, and the sections that follow examine four categories: *determiners, conjunctions, prepositions,* and *particles*.

Determiners

The category of determiners is broad and is made up of several subclasses of words, all of which interact with nouns in some way. In fact, determiners always come before nouns, although not necessarily immediately before. Determiners signal the presence of certain kinds of nouns, which is one reason that in some analyses determiners are designated as adjectives. But as mentioned earlier, the semantic content of determiners is secondary rather than primary; thus, they are sufficiently different from simple adjectives to warrant a separate classification.

At this point, we consider just one type of determiner, *articles*. Later in the text, we examine other types.

Articles.   There are two types of articles in English, *definite* and *indefinite:*

Definite: the

Indefinite: a, an

Nouns are either count nouns or noncount nouns, and all singular count nouns require an article unless it has a number (a quantifier) or a possessive pronoun in front of it. Definite articles signal that a noun is specific, often tangible, or that it is identifiable. Indefinite articles, on the other hand, signal that a noun is nonspecific, often intangible, or that it is not uniquely identifiable.[5] Consider these sentences:

---

[5] An exception occurs whenever we are referring to an entire class of objects or beings. Consider, for example, *The dolphin is a mammal, not a fish.*

54. *The* car was wrecked.
55. We could hear *a* man's voice coming up *the* stairwell.
56. After our ordeal, we had to search for *an* alibi.

Teaching Tip

Nonnative speakers of English have a difficult time with articles, especially if their first language is Asian. Japanese, for example, does not have articles, so native Japanese speakers tend to leave them out when writing English. An effective activity to help ELL students with articles is to have them team up with a partner (a native English speaker, if possible). Students should read the first three paragraphs of each other's papers, underlining all nouns. Then have them check for articles using the criteria listed for definite and indefinite articles.

Conjunctions

A characteristic of language is that it allows people to take small linguistic units and combine them into larger ones, in an additive fashion. Sometimes the units are equal, in which case they are coordinated; other times they are unequal, in which case some units are subordinated to others. *Conjunctions* are function words that make many of these combinations possible, and there are two major types: *coordinating* and *subordinating*.

Coordinating Conjunctions. Coordinating conjunctions, shown here, join equal linguistic units:

and, but, for, nor, or, yet, so

The following sentences illustrate coordinating conjunctions joining individual words/phrases:

57. Fritz *and* Macarena joined the party.
58. Buggsy drove to the casino *and* bet $100 on the upcoming race.

In sentence 57, the conjunction joins the two nouns, *Fritz* and *Macarena*. In sentence 58, the conjunction joins two verb phrases, *drove to the casino* and *bet $100 on the upcoming race*.

Coordinating conjunctions also join equal clauses, as shown here, producing what is referred to as a *compound sentence:*

59. Fred opened the door, *but* Macarena wouldn't come inside.

60. Macarena could feel the ocean breeze against her face, *so* she preferred to stay outside.
61. Fritz asked Macarena to go to Catalina, *and* Fred asked her to go to San Francisco.

Usage Note

Coordinating conjunctions frequently confuse writers when it comes to punctuation. For example, when a coordinating conjunction joins two clauses, as in sentences 59 through 61, many student writers leave out the comma that comes before the conjunction. It is important to understand that punctuation is a matter of convention, which means that people generally have agreed that it should be done a certain way. In this case, the convention maintains that writers need that comma. Without it, the sentence is called a run-on.

Equally problematic, however, is a tendency of many writers, even professional ones, to use a comma to separate two phrases—especially verb phrases—that have been joined with a coordinating conjunction. This tendency manifests itself whenever the conjoined phrases start to get long. Consider this sentence:

62. ?The governor asked the legislature to reconsider the bill that had failed during the previous session, *and* convened a special task force to evaluate its ramifications if passed.

This sentence has a compound verb phrase in the predicate. If we reduce it to its basic structure, with the verbs in italics, the sentence reads:

62a. The governor *asked* the legislature [something] and *convened* a special task force.

Clearly, a comma between the two verbs is inappropriate. In fact, the comma in sentence 62 is the equivalent of sentence 63, which even inexperienced writers do not produce:

63. ?The cat jumped, and played.

The motivation to put a comma in sentences like sentence 62 may be based on an unconscious fear that the long, compound predicate will be hard to process, but this fear is unfounded. Moreover, separating the two parts of the predicate with the comma is bound to make some readers think negatively about the writer because it is such an obvious violation of existing conventions.

Teaching Tip

Writers can connect independent clauses erroneously in three ways: (a) with a coordinating conjunction only, (b) with a comma but no conjunction, or (c) with nothing at all. Composition specialists have different terms to describe these three possibilities. As noted, the first case is a run-on sentence; the second case is a comma splice; and the third case is a fused sentence. For reasons that remain quite mysterious, large numbers of teachers tell students that they should put commas wherever there is a "pause" in the sentence. **This advice is totally wrong.** *English has natural rhythms and related pauses that have nothing at all to do with punctuation. Before students can master comma use, they need to understand clauses and phrases. They then must learn to recognize when they have put two independent clauses together with a coordinating conjunction. An effective technique is to conduct editing workshops on drafts of papers. Circulate among students and help them identify compound sentences and show them where the comma goes. Ask some students to put sample sentences on the board and explain them to the class.*

Subordinating Conjunctions.   Whereas coordinating conjunctions link equal elements, *subordinating conjunctions* link unequal elements. More specifically, they link a dependent clause to an independent clause. Because this type of dependent clause begins with a subordinating conjunction, we refer to it as a *subordinate clause*. A subordinate clause is a dependent clause that begins with a subordinating conjunction.

More Common Subordinating Conjunctions		
because	if	as
until	since	whereas
although	though	while
unless	before	once
after	as if	when
whenever	as soon as	even if
in order that		even though
so that		

The sentences that follow show subordinating conjunctions connecting subordinate clauses to independent clauses:

64. *Since he came home,* Fred hasn't turned off the TV once.
65. Buggsy was thrilled *when Rita de Luna walked into the casino.*
66. One of Buggsy's goons had ushered her to the table *before she could say a word.*

67. *While the band played "Moonlight Serenade,"* Buggsy whispered sweet nothings in Rita's ear.
68. Rita was afraid to move *because she had heard of Buggsy's reputation*.

Subordinate Clauses Are Adverbials. Subordinate clauses always function as adverbial modifiers, and the information they provide usually is related to conditionality, causality/reason, time, concession, or contrast. Because subordinate clauses are adverbials, they tend to supply information to a verb phrase, but they also can supply information to an entire clause, as in sentences 64 and 67. When they do, we say that they are *sentence-level* modifiers.

APPLYING KEY IDEAS

Directions: This activity is designed to help you assess how well you've mastered the information in the previous section related to form and function. Identify the form of each word in the sentences that follow. Next, use parentheses to mark the major constituents and then identify their function.

EXAMPLE: (The surfers) (arrived at the beach just after sunrise).
-article -noun -verb -prep -art -noun -adverbial -prep -noun

1. Fritz saw the ocean from his apartment in Venice Beach.
2. On the boardwalk, the skaters moved in unnatural rhythms.
3. Macarena made a reservation at China Club for dinner.
4. Fred thought about the hot salsa band and the exotic food.
5. Fred polished his shoes until he could see himself in them.
6. Macarena put on her red dress because it was Fred's favorite.
7. She also put on her pearl choker, even though it was a gift from Fritz.
8. Slowly, Macarena brushed her long hair as she looked in the mirror.
9. Three conga drummers appeared on the boardwalk, and they thumped the skins with taped fingers.
10. Fritz put down his racing form because the drumming was really loud.

Usage Note

Function words have some semantic content, and the semantic content of subordinating conjunctions is related to the type of information they supply to the constructions they modify. For example, in sentence 64—*Since he came home, Fred hasn't turned off the TV once*—the subordinate clause supplies information of time to the independent clause. In sentence 68—*Rita was afraid to move because she had heard of Buggsy's reputation*—the subordinate clause supplies information of causality. Formal standard usage requires a match between the semantic content of the subordinating conjunction and the modification provided by the subordinate clause.

The lack of a match has become very widespread, however. Not only in conversation but also in published texts, it is common to find incongruence with respect to time, causality, and contrast. Most people use a temporal subordinator where a causal and/or contrastive subordinator is required. Consider these sentences:

69. ?The President gave the order *since he is commander-in-chief.*
70. ?Rita de Luna wanted to leave, *while Buggsy wanted her to stay.*

In sentence 69, the relation between the two clauses is one of reason, not time, so standard usage requires the following:

69a. The President gave the order *because* he is commander-in-chief.

In sentence 70, the relation between the two clauses is contrastive, not temporal, so formal standard usage requires the following:

70a. Rita de Luna wanted to leave, *whereas* Buggsy wanted her to stay.

In addition to these concerns, there is another instance of nonstandard usage that has become remarkably widespread. Consider the following scenario: At a school board meeting, a local principal is explaining why her school needs to have Internet access:

• Of course, you want to know why our students need access to the Internet. *The reason is because everyone says that it's important.*

If we look carefully at the italicized sentence, we see that the main part consists of a noun-phrase subject, the linking verb *is,* and a subordinate clause that begins with the subordinating conjunction *because.* However, linking verbs cannot be followed by subordinate clauses. As noted on page 77, they can be followed only by a noun phrase, a predicate adjective, and a prepositional phrase. Given the grammar and usage conventions we have outlined here, any use of *the reason is because* must be deemed not only nonstandard but also ungrammatical. The grammatical form would be:

- Of course, you want to know why our students need access to the Internet. The reason is *that* everyone says that it's important.

APPLYING KEY IDEAS

Directions: This activity has two parts, both intended to provide an opportunity to apply information from the previous discussion to your own language.

First, listen carefully to the language around you—conversations, class lectures, news reports, and so forth. Over a 2-day period, keep a tally of the number of times you hear someone using one of the nonstandard or ungrammatical features discussed previously, such as *I feel badly, I did good,* and *The reason is because.* Discuss your tally with others in your class, perhaps examining the situations in which you observed the nonstandard usage and considering whether there are any connections.

For the second part of the activity, examine a paper you wrote recently, focusing on your use of subordinating conjunctions. Does the semantic content of your subordinating conjunctions match the relation you intended to establish between the dependent and independent clauses? If not, change the subordinating conjunction appropriately.

Prepositions

A *preposition* generally works with a noun phrase, and together they compose a *prepositional phrase.* (When a noun phrase is connected to a preposition, it often is called the *object* of the preposition.) The preposition links its noun phrase to either a verb phrase or another noun phrase, which means that the prepositional phrase functions either *adverbially or adjectivally.* Sentences 71 through 73 illustrate both types. Note that in sentence 73 the prepositional phrase functions as a sentence-level modifier:

71. The woman *with the red hair* drove a Porsche.
72. Fritz walked *down the street.*
73. *In the morning,* Fred always has wild hair.

The list of English prepositions is quite long, but some of the more common are listed below:

Common Prepositions

aboard	about	above	across	after
against	along	amid	among	around
as	at	before	behind	below
beneath	beside	besides	between	beyond
but	by	concerning	considering	despite
down	during	except	excepting	excluding
following	for	from	in	inside
into	like	minus	near	of
off	on	onto	opposite	outside
over	past	per	plus	regarding
round	save	since	than	through
to	toward	towards	under	underneath
unlike	until	up	upon	versus
via	with	within	without	

Usage Note

Nearly everyone is told in grade school that they must never end a sentence with a preposition. They aren't told why they must not do this, but they nevertheless are penalized in one way or another if they do. This prohibition is an example of the prescriptive nature of traditional grammar. It also is an example of a prohibition that does not fit the way the English language actually works. Certain types of sentences can quite easily *and quite correctly* end with a preposition.

One of the more obvious examples are questions, such as the following:

74. Won't you come *in?*

English grammar allows us to truncate the prepositional phrase in some instances, and this is one of them. There is only one other way to ask this question without ending it with a preposition, and that is to include the noun phrase object that has been dropped, giving us:

74a. Won't you come *in my house?*

A similar situation exists with sentences like 75:

75. Buggsy and his goons walked *in.*

Some might be tempted to argue that the word *in* in these sentences isn't a preposition but rather is an adverb, but that analysis seems off the mark. Prepositions are function words, so unlike adverbs their semantic content is secondary, often subtle. The semantic content of *in* is quite different from the semantic content of words that, although able to function as prepositions, more readily function as adverbs. We always come in *something;* we always walk in *something.* This point becomes clearer if we consider the opposite of being *in something,* which is to be *outside something,* as in sentence 76:

76. Buggsy and his goons walked *outside.*[6]

Outside is one of those words that can function as either a preposition or an adverb, but in the case of sentence 76, the semantic content is clear and specific because *outside* means *outdoors.* In chapter 5, we look more closely at this question of ending a sentence with a preposition, and we discuss a grammar rule that produces such sentences.

Usage Note

The word *like* is listed as a preposition, and in standard usage it introduces a prepositional phrase similar to sentence 77:

77. There was no one quite *like Macarena.*

Huge numbers of people, however, use *like* as a subordinating conjunction, as in sentences 78 and 79:

78. ?Mrs. DiMarco talked *like she knew something about science.*
79. ?If Fred had taken the money to Buggsy *like he should have,* he wouldn't have to hide from Buggsy's goons.

This usage is questionable. In formal standard usage, only a subordinating conjunction is appropriate in such constructions, as in sentences 78a and 79a:

78a. Mrs. DiMarco talked *as though* she knew something about science.
79a. If Fred had taken the money to Buggsy *as* he should have, he wouldn't have to hide from Buggsy's goons.

---

[6]One could argue that *in* means *indoors,* but replacing *in* with *indoors* changes the meaning of sentences 74 and 75, which suggests that this argument isn't sound.

It is important to note that the use of *like* as a subordinating conjunction has become so ubiquitous that it appears in the speech of even the most fastidious speakers. As a result, many people now apply the formal standard only when writing or when participating in very formal speaking situations.

Teaching Tip

As noted on page 20, nearly all young people use the word "like" repeatedly when speaking, and the expression "goes like" has in most instances replaced the word "said." We observe them using the expression "goes like" instead of "said," as in:

- *And then Macarena goes like, "I'm not going to dinner with you."*

In addition, "like" is used as a filler, as in:

- *And, like, I went to my room, like, and turned on some music, like, and then, like, the phone rang, and it was, like, Fritz, and he, like, ...*

These patterns of speech lead most educated people to judge the speakers as ignorant, which isn't good. There are some effective ways to help students reduce their use of "like." An in-class activity involves role playing:

1. Divide the class into groups of three to five. One person in each group role plays a professional employer while another person plays a job candidate whom the "employer" will interview. The groups should spend about 10 minutes choosing professions and jobs before they begin. Each person will rotate the roles; while the "employer" and the "job candidate" are talking, the other group members observe and record any inappropriate uses of "like." After everyone has taken a turn, students should talk about what they learned.

2. Divide the class into teams of three to five for a competition. Each team is to observe conversations on and around campus and record the inappropriate uses of "like" that they hear over a 2-day period. They then give a presentation of their findings. The team with the highest number of observations gets a free homework day.

3. Hold an election for three to five class monitors whose responsibility is to record the number of times individual students use "like" inappropriately in class over the course of a week. The monitors report their results to the entire class, and the student with the lowest frequency receives an award.

Particles.   Particles look like prepositions, and they resemble adverbials because they are linked to verbs, as in sentences 80 and 81:

80. Fritz looked *up* the number.
81. Macarena put *on* her shoes.

However, they are different from prepositions and adverbials with respect to how they can move in a sentence. Prepositions, for example, cannot move, but particles can. Sentences 80 and 81 also could be written as:

80a. Fritz looked the number up.
81a. Macarena put her shoes on.

English allows particles to move behind the object noun phrase. But when we move a preposition, we produce an ungrammatical sentence, as in:

82. Mrs. DiMarco stepped into her garden.
82a. *Mrs. DiMarco stepped her garden into.

The question of movement also explains why particles are not true adverbials. Most adverbials can move about in a sentence, as sentence 83 illustrates:

83. Macarena walked *slowly* to her car.
83a. Macarena *slowly* walked to her car.
83b. *Slowly,* Macarena walked to her car.

Particles, however, can move only behind the NP object. One possible exception may involve sentences like this:

Fritz picked up the book that Macarena had dropped.

If we move the particle behind the NP object, we have:

Fritz picked the book up that Macarena had dropped.

Some grammars, however, have developed rules that move the particle to the end of the dependent clause, and from time to time we may hear people doing so in their speech, producing:

*Fritz picked the book that Macarena had dropped up.

Sentences of this type, even when they are produced by grammar rules, are ungrammatical.

Usage Note

Sometimes people who assert that ending a sentence with a preposition creates an ungrammatical construction will offer as evidence an ungrammatical sentence that indeed ends with what appears to be a preposition. Such sentences commonly resemble sentence 84:

84. *Fritz put his shoes and then walked to the Qwikie Mart for a bottle of Wild Turkey on.

Sentences like this appeared with some regularity in style guides and writing manuals a couple of decades ago that were produced by people who lacked training in linguistics. Fortunately, they aren't common today. There is no question that sentence 84 is ungrammatical, but the problem is not that it ends in a preposition. *On* here is a particle, not a preposition, and it has been moved incorrectly. If we put the word *on* behind either *put* or *shoes,* the sentence is perfectly correct.

Phrasal Modification

On page 80, we looked at a sentence from Ernest Hemingway:

* Manuel swung with the charge, sweeping the muleta ahead of the bull, feet firm, the sword a point of light under the arcs.

This sentence is of interest because of the kinds of modifiers it contains. They are known generally as *phrasal modifiers*. If we analyze this sentence, we see that it contains a dependent clause and three phrasal modifiers:

Dependent Clause: Manuel swung with the charge

Modifier 1: sweeping the muleta ahead of the bull

Modifier 2: feet firm

Modifier 3: the sword a point of light under the arcs

We can say that at least modifiers 1 and 3 have their own head words, *sweeping* and the *sword,* respectively, which define the nature of the constructions. That is, the words that follow *sweeping* and the *sword* cluster around these head words. On this basis, we can say further that modifier 1 is a verb phrase (because *sweeping* is a verb) and that modifier 3 is a noun phrase (because the *sword* is a noun phrase). Thus, verbs and nouns compose two types of phrasal modifiers.

Modifier 2 is different because it has a noun that is followed by an adjective. In fact, it is representative of a type of phrasal modifier that has two related forms. The first form we see in modifier 2; the second form we see in the following: "Fred, *his head pounding,* took two aspirin and lay down."

The italics set off the phrasal modifier, which in this case is composed of a noun phrase and a verb. This type of modifier, in its two forms—noun phrase plus adjective and noun phrase plus verb—is called a *nominative absolute.* The verb phrase, the noun phrase, and the nominative absolute are three of the major kinds of phrasal modifiers. The fourth major kind is the prepositional phrase, which is explored in more detail in the next chapter.

Note that verb phrases can be either progressive participles *(-ing)* or past participles *(-ed)*.

Phrasal modifiers are used primarily in narrative-descriptive writing to provide details and images. In addition, phrasal modifiers can appear in three positions relative to the independent clause: in the initial position, the medial position, and the final position. Medial phrasal modifiers split the independent clause, separating the subject and the predicate, as in *Macarena, her eyes wild, confronted the waiter.* Most phrasal modifiers, however, are in the final position. Consider these sentences:

- I danced with excitement, *winding myself around my nana's legs, balling my hands in her apron, tugging at her dress, and stepping on her toes.* (Final position)
- The prisoners stumbled forward, *their ankles chained, their hands tied, sweat pouring down their faces and collecting into small pools at the base of the neck.* (Final position)
- The wind blew in from the desert, *a cold, dry wind that smelled faintly of sage and juniper,* and the moon rose overhead, *illuminating the courtyard and the three men talking in the night.* (Final position)
- *With Fred's cologne exuding from her pores in a thick vapor,* Macarena circulated among the cigar smokers in the hope that the stench adhering to her hair and clothes would at least confuse Fritz when she met him later that night. (Initial position)
- Fritz, *confused and somewhat nauseated by the various aromas coming from Macarena's skin and clothes,* suggested that she shower before dinner. (Medial position)

The phrasal modifiers in the first sentence are all verb phrases; in the second, they are all nominative absolutes; in the third sentence, there is a noun phrase and a verb phrase; in the fourth sentence, the modifier is a nominative absolute (introduced by a preposition); the last sentence has one verb-phrase modifier.

As noted previously, the chief advocate of phrasal modification was Francis Christensen, whose work on the rhetoric of the sentence was very influential from the late 1960s through the mid-1970s. In some respects Christensen's work was part of an effort to use grammar as a means of improving writing through what was known as *sentence combining.* Although several studies showed that students who engaged in sentence combining gained better control over sentence structure and produced more mature writing (Combs, 1977; Daiker, Kerek, & Morenberg, 1978; Howie, 1979; Pedersen, 1978), the approach had all but disappeared from teaching by the mid-1980s.

One reason was that a few studies indicated that the gains in student writing produced by sentence combining disappeared over time (Callaghan, 1978; Green, 1973; Sullivan, 1978). Another, more compelling, reason was that composition theory had shifted pedagogy from bottom-up methods to top-down. The new focus was on process and producing whole essays. Also, at about this same time, there was a dramatic shift toward personal experience writing, a shift that seems to have been motivated, in part, by a desire among educators to avoid the inevitable sorting associated with increased competition (see Williams, 2003a). There really isn't much a teacher can evaluate in a personal experience essay, for we can't realistically claim that one person's experiences are somehow better than another's. We can address issues of style, of course, but style is poorly understood and seldom taught. Moreover, stylistic features cluster in sentences and paragraphs, the very structures that receive little attention in the process-oriented classroom.

More recently, Connors (2000) suggested that dismissal of work at the sentence level may have been hasty and that the techniques of phrasal modification and sentence combining can provide valuable composing tools. I would add that, if nothing else, these techniques can help students make their writing more varied and interesting very quickly. It may well be the case that our implementation of process pedagogy led us to throw the baby out with the bath water, as it were.

4

Phrase Structure Grammar

FROM THE UNIVERSAL TO THE PARTICULAR

Until the 19th century, Latin grammar was deemed universally applicable to all languages, not just English and related European tongues. Those who were interested in studying grammar devoted a great deal of their attention to what are known as "linguistic universals"—features of grammar and language that transcend individual languages. All languages, for example, have subjects and predicates, and all have some way of referencing the time of actions in sentences. Within the context of modern grammar, the concept of linguistic universals also is concerned with the knowledge that a person has of language in general. This knowledge is deemed to be the result of certain innate characteristics of being human rather than of education or learning.

Linguistic universals were an important part of traditional grammar and served as a rationale for teaching. The study of English was a means to an end. Students studied English grammar in preparation for studying Latin grammar. It was understood that instruction in Latin could proceed more easily when children mastered terminology and concepts in their own language. But the enterprise was not without its problems. We have already looked briefly at the issue of tense. Latin and its associated languages have three tenses: past, present, and future. English, on the other hand, has only two: past and present. Nevertheless, many scholars opted to consider *will* + *verb* as the future tense in English because doing so appeared to be intuitively correct and logical. Indeed, it does not occur to many people that a language might have fewer than three tenses, although the perceived complexities of language cause these same people to shrug their shoulders in resignation at the prospect that a language might have more than three. Other inconsistencies simply were ignored as being irrel-evant to the larger goal of preparing students for Latin.

Although American schools have not taught Latin for decades, traditional grammar continues to try to match English grammar to Latin. Virtually all current handbooks, for example, propose that English has at least three tenses. Most take an inexplicable additional step: Rather than exploring as-pect, they instead treat progressive and perfect forms as tenses. They describe the *past progressive tense,* the *present progressive tense,* the *future progres-sive tense,* and so on. In these accounts, English has anywhere from 9 to 16 tenses, depending on the text.

Views on traditional grammar began to change toward the end of the 19th century, and much of the motivation for this change was the result of interest in American Indian tribal languages. Native Americans largely had been ignored after the great Indian wars, but they became the focus of much scholarly atten-tion when anthropologists began perceiving that the distinctive characteristics of these indigenous people were vanishing. An intensive preservation program started, and researchers such as Franz Boas began efforts to record the details of the tribal cultures, particularly their languages.

A few early missionaries had produced some records of these languages, but they were not systematic and lacked the rigor necessary to preserve the languages for the future. In addition, these missionaries used traditional grammar in their efforts, with less than satisfactory results. In his introduction to the *Handbook of American Indian Languages,* Boas (1911) lamented the fact that the descriptions were distorted by the attempt to impose traditional grammar on languages for which it was inappropriate. Trying to get these languages to fit traditional gram-mar was the linguistic equivalent of forcing a round peg into a square hole.

Tense again provides an interesting illustration. Many Indian languages have only one tense, usually the present, yet they were described as though they have three tenses, like Latin. In some cases, to ensure that the description was congruent with the Latin model, those describing the languages would produce a construction that did not naturally occur among native speakers. These were instances in which the grammar drove the language to such an extent that the finished description did not reflect the way people used the language. As more data were collected, the number of such incompatibilities grew, and researchers were at a loss. When confronted with different dialects of the same language, they could not decide which was "correct" because there was no standard by which to make a judgment. There were no texts, and the number of native speakers was shrinking rapidly, making it difficult to locate an informant who could offer advice. Eventually, scholars like Boas concluded that the goal of traditional grammar, prescription based on a literary model, was inadequate.

Now known as *structuralists,* these scholars, led by Boas and later by Leonard Bloomfield, worked for several years to develop a new grammar, one that did not make the same assumptions about linguistic universals that were inherent in traditional grammar. They called this grammar *Immediate Constituent Analysis* (ICA), a term that was so awkward that, in 1957, when Noam Chomsky dubbed ICA "phrase-structure grammar" the name stuck.

The differences between phrase-structure grammar and traditional grammar are many, but for our purposes we only need to focus on a few distinctive features. One of the more important was that the new grammar subordinated many of the notions of linguistic universals and opted instead to advocate the idea that every language is unique, with its own structure and its own grammar. Universals were considered in a relatively abstract way: All languages have subjects, all languages have ways of counting and thus making plurals, and so on. This reorientation reflected a fundamental shift in the way American linguists saw the study of grammar, a shift associated with different philosophies and worldviews. Traditional grammar was based largely on *rationalism,* which proposes that human knowledge is not based on the senses or experience. Rationalism can be traced back to Plato, who argued that the world of experiences is merely a shadow of a transcendental reality that can be known only through the powers of the intellect, guided by philosophy. The senses are incapable of revealing more than a distorted semblance of reality, an idea that Plato developed with memorable effect in *The Republic* through his allegory of the cave.

Transcendentalism can provide a workable model of reality with respect to certain concepts, such as geometric figures and justice. A circle, for example, is defined mathematically as a plane figure composed of a series of points equidistant from a center point. Drawing such a figure, however, is impossible owing to the problems associated with exact measurement. Thus, a perfect circle exists only in the mind. One likewise can propose that true justice exists only in the mind because the mundane reality of our court system is that it readily sacrifices justice for the sake of expediency. Nevertheless, in both cases the transcendental model is sufficiently close to reality to make a comparison possible. Thinking about a perfect circle can lead to the production of a circle that is a very close approximation of the mental model.

This approach does not work with language. The structuralists found that transcendentalism was so far removed from their experiences with actual language that a comparison was *not* possible. Just *thinking* about grammatical forms never would allow someone to develop a correct description of the tense system in Cherokee. Such a description required data collection, analysis, interpretation, and rule formation. It required, in other words, an empirical approach to language. The orientation of the structuralists therefore was the antithesis of their predecessors, for whereas rationalism proposes that all knowledge comes from reflection rather than from the senses, empiricism proposes that knowledge comes from the senses rather than from reflection.

Linked to this view was an equally important shift in the grammar away from prescription to *description*. Matters of correctness were replaced with what Bloomfield (1933) referred to as *acceptability,* which is determined on the basis of context. Thus, an utterance or a written statement might be grammatical but unacceptable. On this account, grammaticality judgments are linked to attested utterances, not to a literary norm. An immediate consequence of this view is that grammaticality becomes largely a matter of word order, not usage conventions. Consider the following sentences:

- ?He don't got no money.
- He doesn't have any money.
- *Doesn't money any he have.

The first two sentences are grammatical in this view because both conform to the subject-verb-object (SVO) word order of English. The third sentence is ungrammatical because it does not conform to that word order. The first sentence is nonstandard, however, so in those situations that call for Standard English it will be deemed unacceptable. It is reasonable to assume that the same would apply to the second sentence, that in those situations that call for nonstandard English—for example, a conversation in the home of a nonstandard speaker—this sentence would be unacceptable. There are occasions in which that assumption is correct, but we cannot say that it always is correct or even mostly correct. In general, nonstandard speakers are not critical of standard speakers, even in those situations in which nonstandard English is the norm. Standard speakers, on the other hand, generally are critical of nonstandard speakers in all situations and seldom will accept nonstandard English, regardless of the context.

The goal, then, of phrase-structure grammar is to describe how people use language. Grammatical sentences are those that conform to the standard word order of English, SVO or subject-verb-complement (SVC), which is the second major sentence pattern in English. It does not take a prescriptive stance regarding language use but instead assesses language on the basis of acceptability, or what in previous chapters was referred to as appropriateness.

The emphasis on description has led to widespread misunderstanding of the goals and principles of phrase-structure grammar. The popular perception is that the grammar takes an "anything goes" approach to language. The distinction between grammaticality and acceptability, which is the distinction between grammar and usage, clearly does not endorse such an approach. But the long-standing association between grammar and logic, as well as the pejorative connotations of the expression, "ungrammatical," make it hard for many to embrace the idea that nonstandard English can be just as grammatical and logical as Standard. The message inherent in phrase-structure grammar is that it is quite difficult for native speakers of a language to produce ungrammatical sentences. This message, as we shall see, has significant implications for teaching grammar and writing.

APPLYING KEY IDEAS

Observe how you change your language on the basis of context. Chances are that your language is more formal in the classroom than it is at home or in the school cafeteria. Using a small recorder, tape your conversations in two contrasting settings and then analyze your speech in a couple of paragraphs that explain how it differs by context. Look at word choice, sentence length and structure, and degree of repetition. Does your language vary by context? If so, what does this tell you about appropriateness conditions and acceptability?

PHRASE-STRUCTURE RULES

The emphasis on description in phrase-structure grammar is important in many ways, but one of the more salient is its effect on the notion of a grammar rule. In traditional grammar, rules are essentially inviolable, and we are asked to force language to conform to the rules. In phrase-structure grammar, the situation is different. The term "rule" is used very loosely to describe the observed grammatical patterns that exist in a given language. Consequently, when we use the term "rule" in phrase-structure grammar, we are not referring to an inviolable statement about language; instead, we are referring to a pattern of constructions that are characteristic of and that describe a given language. Another way of expressing this point is to say that phrase-structure grammar does not have a generative component. The "rules" we use do not *produce* sentences; they merely *describe* them. As a result, the "rules" change whenever we encounter a real-world utterance that the "rules" do not describe.

A key to understanding phrase-structure grammar therefore lies in being able to look at a string of words and determine how to describe the string using the grammar. That is one of the tasks of this chapter. We have already noted that grammatical analysis focuses on language at the sentence level; in phrase-structure grammar, this focus is made highly explicit through the kinds of questions it tries to answer and through the shorthand notation it uses for sentence analysis. We can begin examining both issues by considering that phrase-structure grammar recognizes that a sentence (S) has two primary components, a noun phrase (NP) and a verb phrase (VP). The level of grammatical analysis, therefore, proceeds on the basis of phrases. The first grammar "rule" in phrase-structure analysis reflects this basic characteristic:

S → NP VP

This expression is read as follows: "S is rewritten as NP VP." This rule is the starting point of all grammatical analyses in phrase-structure grammar. Keep in mind that this statement is not a rule for generating sentences; it simply describes the fact that English sentences that we can observe on a daily basis follow this basic pattern. Notice that phrase-structure grammar focuses on form, not function. In the stated rule, there is no reference to subject or predicate; instead, it is understood that the NP is the subject and that the VP is the predicate.

Let's examine how this rule can describe a sentence that we have seen before:

1. Dogs bark.

As we've already noted, *Dogs* is a noun phrase, and *bark* is a verb phrase. Thus, we can use phrase-structure notation to describe the grammatical structure of the sentences as follows:

S → NP VP

This rule describes the makeup of the sentence, but it is not sufficiently specific because it does not fully describe the noun phrase or the verb phrase. We can look at the sentence and determine the composition of these phrases, which in turn allows us to write additional rules for NP and VP. In this case, the NP is composed of a single noun (N), and the VP is composed of a single verb (V):

NP → N

VP → V

To complete the description, we need to assign words to N and V, which results in the following:

N → dogs

V → bark

Notice how each line of this analysis represents a specific assignment of features designed to reveal the structure of the various parts of this particular sentence. The sentence may consist of a noun phrase and a verb phrase, but what are these phrases composed of? Each is composed of an individual word, a noun and a verb, respectively. The final step is to describe the noun and the verb, to list the actual words that make up the sentence. This set of phrase-structure rules is referred to as a *grammar of the sentence.* The process of producing this grammar reflects the procedures that American linguists used in the 19th century to describe and record tribal languages. It builds a lexicon—a list of words—while showing how those words fit together to make grammatical sentences.

The sentence grammar for sentence 1 is pretty simple, but it contains within itself the power to describe quite complex sentences. The key lies in an important feature of language that phrase-structure grammar utilizes: *recursion.* With respect to language, recursion conveys the fact that complex expressions can be analyzed in terms of their simpler components. In addition, it bases analysis on *knowledge of the expected outcome.* That is, any analysis of a sentence begins with the completed sentence, not with an abstraction, and not with some unknown endpoint. It is like solving a math problem while knowing the answer in advance. *The goal is not to discover the answer but to understand the steps leading to it.*

The advantages these features lend to analysis become clearer if we look at a series of increasingly complex sentences and adjust the initial rule in ways that allow us to describe each of them grammatically:

2. Fred bought a suit.

The analysis begins with the first phrase-structure rule:

S → NP VP

Notice, again, that we are not attempting to show how the sentence ought to fit together but rather how it does. On this account, our phrase-structure analysis must describe the existing sentence while generalizing in ways that also allow us to describe sentence 1.

First, sentences 1 and 2 reflect differences in the verb phrase—one has an object and the other does not. We have to conclude that NP is an optional element in the verb phrase. Second, sentences 1 and 2 reflect differences in the noun phrase. The object NP in sentence 2 has a determiner (det), the indefinite article (art) *a*, whereas there were no determiners in sentence 1, and, indeed, there is no determiner in the subject NP of sentence 2. We therefore have to conclude that determiners are optional elements. Phrase-structure grammar uses a convention for optional elements: It places them in parentheses. With these factors in mind, we can adjust the earlier rules so that they describe both sentences, as shown here:

S → NP VP

NP → (det) N

VP → V (NP)

det → art

N → Fred, suit

V → bought

art → a

This sentence grammar is more complex than the previous one because we are writing a grammar that is generalizable to sentences 1 and 2, with the exception of the individual words assigned. Now consider another, more complex, example:

3. Maria wore an expensive evening gown.

This sentence is interesting because it adds adjectivals to our basic NP VP combination, and one of them is a noun, *evening*. We therefore must adjust the phrase-structure rules so that they will describe all three of our sentences, which means adding a rule for the adjective phrase (AdjP) that describes both types of adjectivals:

S → NP VP

NP → (det) (AdjP) N

VP → V (NP)

det → art

$$\text{AdjP} \rightarrow \begin{Bmatrix} \text{adj} \\ \text{NP} \end{Bmatrix}$$

N → Maria, evening, gown

V → wore

art → an

adj → expensive

The rule for AdjP introduces another convention—brackets. Brackets indicate that one of the elements, adj or NP, must be chosen.

Let's take this opportunity to generalize a bit. The rule for AdjP describes all adjectivals in a noun phrase, but it does not describe predicate adjectives, which we discussed in chapter 3. The sentence, *The tree was tall,* illustrates a basic sentence pattern, with *tall* functioning as a predicate adjective. Having discussed adjectivals in the noun phrase, it is a good idea to extend our analysis and adjust our rules here so that they will describe all instances of AdjP. We can do this by making a simple modification to our rule for VP:

VP → V (NP) (AdjP)

Adjusting the rule for the verb phrase raises an interesting issue with respect to verbs—the status of particles. We examined particles in chapter 3, but now we can look at them more closely. While doing so, let's consider another construction that can appear in both the verb phrase and the noun phrase—the prepositional phrase. Consider these sentences:

4. The goons with bow ties looked up the number for Pizza Hut.
5. Buggsy put the gun on the table.

The set of phrase-structure rules we have developed so far works to describe only parts of these sentences. Unlike sentences 1 through 3, sentence 4 has two prepositional phrases (PP) as parts of two noun phrases, and it has the verb particle *up* (prt). Sentence 5 has a prepositional phrase as part of the verb phrase. These structures were not in the previous example sentences, which means that we must treat them as optional elements. Adjusting the rules should be easy at this point: We must provide for optional prepositional phrases in both NP and VP, and we must allow two possibilities for V, one being a *verb + particle* combination. With these adjustments, we can describe sentences 1 through 5 and many others:

S → NP VP

NP → (det) (AdjP) (PP) N

VP → V (NP) (AdjP) (PP)

$$\text{AdjP} \rightarrow \begin{Bmatrix} \text{adj} \\ \text{NP} \end{Bmatrix}$$

$$\text{PP} \rightarrow \text{prep NP}$$

$$\text{V} \rightarrow \begin{Bmatrix} \text{V} \\ \text{V} + \text{prt} \end{Bmatrix}$$

N → goons, bow ties, number, Pizza Hut, Buggsy, gun, table

V → looked + prt, put

det → the

prep → with, for, on

prt → up

These rules have value beyond their ability to describe sentences 1 through 5. They also help us understand that, as sentences become more complex, the grammar must become more flexible if it is to describe a variety of structures. NP and VP, for example, may have several elements, but they are all optional except for the core features, N and V, respectively. Perhaps the larger goal of phrase-structure grammar is becoming clear. Individual sentence grammars are revealing, but the process of producing a new set of rules for all the possible individual sentences in English (an infinite number) is not practical. Moreover, it does not provide a coherent picture of the whole language. The goal, therefore, is to examine a wide range of sentences to develop a set of highly generalizable statements that describe most (but not necessarily all) of the grammatical sentences that speakers of the language normally produce.

APPLYING KEY IDEAS

Directions: Write separate phrase-structure rules for each of the following sentences:

1. A bug danced across my palm.
2. The cold wind blew from the distant lake.
3. An old man asked for a drink at the bar.
4. Buggsy put on a coat and walked into the desert.
5. Fritz really liked Macarena.

TREE DIAGRAMS

Grammar is about sentences—the form of the words and their functions in sentences. Consequently, analyzing individual sentences is a major part of grammatical study. Such analysis can provide a great deal of information about language. In the 19th century, Alonzo Reed and Brainerd Kellogg developed a way to diagram sentences in an effort to make grammatical analysis more revealing and meaningful. Many schools continue to use Reed-Kellogg diagrams today, more than a hundred years later. As the examples that follow suggest, the Reed-Kellogg approach to diagramming sentences gets very complicated very quickly. These diagrams have no labels for constituents, so it is not easy to note at a glance what the constituents are. Understanding the structure of any sentence demands understanding the structure of the diagramming procedure, which is arbitrary and often counterintuitive.

Let's consider three simple sentences:

6. Fred is a good friend.
7. Running is good exercise.
8. Buggsy believed that he was a handsome dog of a man.

Looking at sentences 6 and 7, we can see the counterintuitive nature of Reed-Kellogg diagrams. Any analysis of a sentence must provide information about form, but it also should describe clearly the relations of the various components. The lack of labels in the Reed-Kellogg approach is a big handicap in this regard. It forces Reed-Kellogg diagrams to adopt different graphic structures for words that have identical functions but different forms. All but exceptional students have a hard time figuring out how the different graphic structures reflect their corresponding grammatical relations. In sentence 6, for example, *Fred* is a noun functioning as the subject,

Sentence 4.6: Fred is a good friend. (Reed-Kellogg diagram)

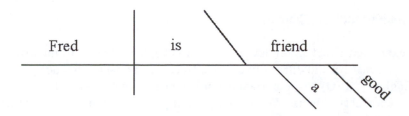

Sentence 4.7: Running is good exercise. (Reed-Kellogg diagram)

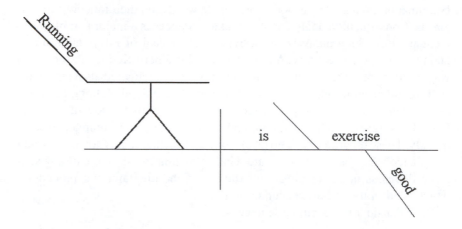

whereas in sentence 7, the subject *Running* is a gerund (a verb functioning as a noun) functioning as a subject—but the diagrams are significantly different. We should expect subjects to have a similar diagrammatic structure in every situation, but that isn't the case with Reed-Kellogg diagrams. Sentence 8 is seriously complex but grammatically it is very similar to sentence 6, which is really not evident from the diagrams.

A more revealing and instructional method of analysis is the *tree diagram,* in which all the components are labeled and in which all the grammatical relations are easily recognizable. Compare the tree diagrams on pages 110 and 111 with their corresponding Reed-Kellogg diagrams. Notice how the labels and consistent structure allow us to recognize the constituents easily. The rest of this chapter contains quite a few diagrams and even more phrase structure rules. The aim is not to introduce analyses simply for the sake of analysis but to aid in the understanding of some of the more significant grammatical structures in English. The diagrams and the rules allow deeper insight into the structure of language.

Direct and Indirect Objects

We examined direct and indirect objects in chapter 3 as part of the discussion of transitive and ditransitive verbs. Because the basic sentence pattern in English is SVO, it is important to consider early on how phrase-structure grammar treats objects. We already have a phrase-structure rule that describes objects:

Sentence 4.8: Buggsy believed that he was a handsome dog of a man. (Reed-Kellogg diagram)

Sentence 4.6: Fred is a good friend. (Tree diagram)

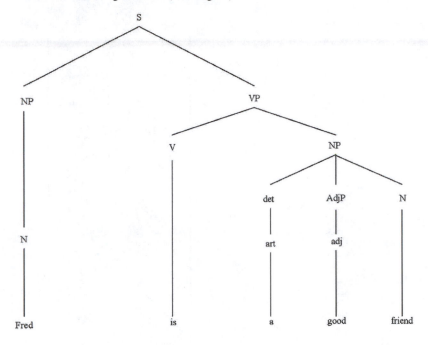

Sentence 4.7: Running is good exercise. (Tree diagram)

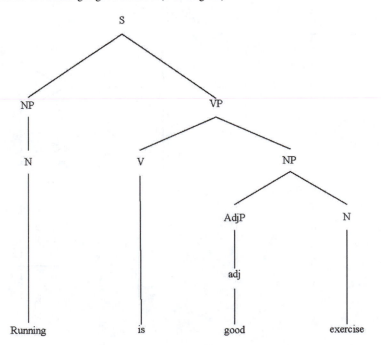

Sentence 4.8: Buggsy believed that he was a handsome dog of a man. (Tree diagram)

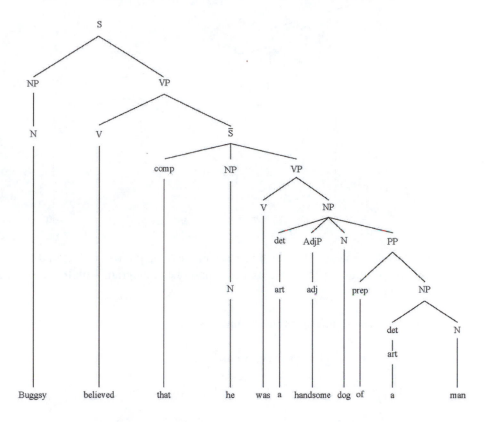

VP → V (NP) (AdjP) (PP)

The only thing we have to keep in mind with these rules is that, for indirect objects that appear as a noun phrase rather than as a prepositional phrase, we add another noun phrase to the analysis. Consider this sentence:

9. Fritz sent his grandmother a gift.

This sentence has a verb phrase of the form V NP NP. The corresponding diagram is on page 112.

Sentence 4.9: Fritz sent his grandmother a gift.

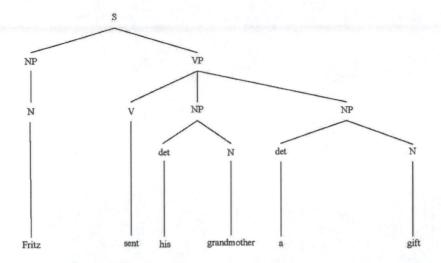

Now consider sentence 10, which is an example of an indirect object in the form of a prepositional phrase. Compare its associated diagram with the diagram for sentence 9.

10. Buggsy asked a question of the commissioner.

Sentence 4.10: Buggsy asked a question of the commissioner.

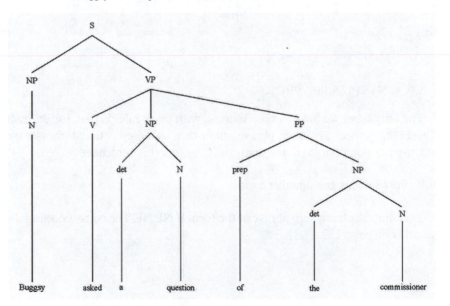

Prepositional Phrases

Prepositional phrases (PP) are interesting structures because they are so versatile. They can function as indirect objects, and they also can function as adverbial modifiers and as adjectival modifiers. As adverbials, they can function as sentence-level modifiers, which means that they can modify an entire clause. In chapter 3, we discussed phrasal modifiers and noted that the prepositional phrase is one of the major types. As indicated in that discussion, prepositional phrases can appear in the initial, medial, or final positions. When they appear in the initial positions, prepositional phrases are sentence-level modifiers. Sentences 11 through 15 illustrate the various positions and forms that prepositional phrases can take:

11. The goons put yellow flowers on the table. (adverbial)
12. Macarena, with a smile, accepted the invitation. (adverbial)
13. The woman with the red hair drives a Porsche. (adjectival)
14. In the morning, Buggsy went home. (sentence level, adverbial)

In addition, prepositional phrases can function as complements to certain kinds of verbs, as in sentence 15:

15. Fred stepped onto the stool. (verb complement, adverbial)

Usage Note

Before the advent of printing, handwritten books were valued as much as works of art as storehouses of information. They were beautifully illustrated, and the monks who produced them took great pride in the quality of their calligraphy. Anyone who views some of these books in a museum will notice that the calligraphy is so uniform as to rival mechanical printing. As literacy spread and became more utilitarian during the 15th and 16th centuries, there arose a demand for more readable and less expensive works. Punctuation emerged as a means of making books more readable, as did a significant reduction in the amount of artwork. Paragraphs, which were unknown in the ancient world, also became a means of helping readers process texts.

The lesson we learn from this brief discussion is that punctuation is largely a matter of convention rather than of rule. Indeed, different conventions govern punctuation in several contexts. Journalists, for example, follow the Associated Press convention when using commas with items in a series and do not put a comma before the conjunction joining the last item;

those who follow the MLA and the APA conventions, on the other hand, do put the comma before the conjunction.

With regard to prepositional phrases, there are two conventions governing punctuation of phrases in the initial position. One holds that writers should use length as the basis for deciding whether to set the modifier off with a comma. In this convention, short structures are not set off, whereas long ones are. Although this approach is perfectly acceptable, it creates problems for teachers whose students want as much consistency as possible.

Another convention holds that all modifying structures at the beginning of sentences should be set off with a comma. Many teachers have adopted this convention because it is easier to teach, or at least it is easier for students to accept. They do not have to think about length.

Ambiguity

Language is inherently ambiguous, but certain prepositional phrase constructions are quite obviously so. Under normal circumstances, we use context to disambiguate such constructions, but it is possible to provide a grammatical analysis that also disambiguates. Consider the following sentences:

16. Fred built the bench in the garage.
17. Macarena put the shoes in the box in the closet.

All ambiguous sentences have two possible meanings.[1] In sentence 16, one meaning could be that the act of building the bench could have taken place in the garage. The second meaning could be that the act of building could have occurred anywhere other than the garage, but the bench is in the garage now. In sentence 17, the shoes already could be in the box, and Macarena put those particular boxed shoes in the closet. The other meaning could be that the empty box already could be in the closet, and Macarena put the shoes in that box.

We can use grammatical analysis to disambiguate sentences like 16 and 17 because each possibility has a different phrase-structure, as illustrated in the diagrams on pages 115 and 116.

COORDINATION

Coordination is one of the more common features of language, and phrase-structure grammar provides a rule that is generally applicable to all coordinated

---

[1]Although the possibility exists for more than two meanings, examples are so rare that none could be found for this text.

Sentence 4.16: Fred built the bench in the garage.

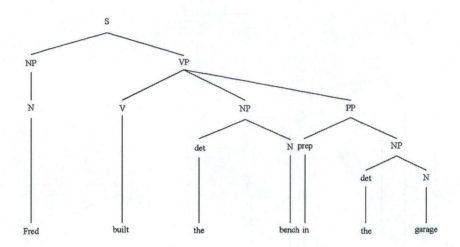

OR

Sentence 4.17: Macarena put the shoes in the box in the closet.

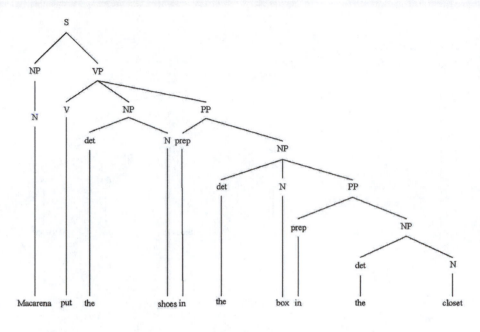

OR

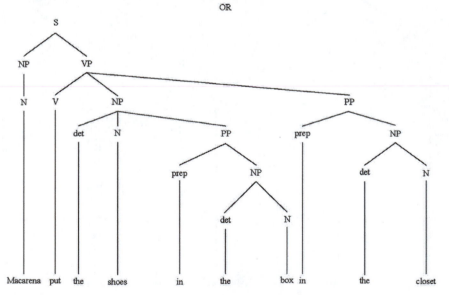

structures. It is called the *Coordinate XP* rule, where X is a variable identifying any element, such as noun or verb, and P is phrase. Coordinating conjunctions are designated by CC. This rule supplies two pieces of information. First, any phrase can be conjoined to another phrase of the same form. For example, any two noun phrases can be linked using a coordinating conjunction. Second, the two conjoined phrases function as a single unit that has the character of the individual phrases. In other words, two noun phrases joined by a coordinating conjunction function as a single noun phrase. The rule is shown as:

XP → XP CC XP

We can see how the XP rule works in sentences 18 through 20. In 18, the subject is *Fred and Fritz,* which exists as a single unit and can be represented by XP. But the subject consists of the two noun phrases: *Fred* and *Fritz.*

18. Fred and Fritz loved Cheerios.

The sentence grammar for 18 would be:

S → NP CC NP VP

NP → N

VP → V NP

Because language is inherently recursive, we can combine any number of similar phrases in a single unit, as shown in sentence 19:

19. Macarena danced, laughed, and sang at the party.

We would describe the grammatical structure of 19 as follows:

S → NP VP

NP → (det) N

VP → VP VP CC VP PP

PP → prep NP

Compound Sentences

The Coordinate XP rule also applies to entire clauses, giving us a way of describing the grammatical structure of *compound sentences*. A compound sentence is one that has two independent clauses. The analysis proceeds in exactly the same way as we saw earlier, but rather than repeating phrases, the rule repeats sentences.

Consider sentence 20:

20. A goon shot the ATM, so Buggsy made an easy withdrawal.

Because each clause has the structure of a sentence, by convention our grammar would begin with:

$S \rightarrow S_1 \, CC \, S_2$

What this means is simply that the sentence (S) consists of two clauses (S_1 and S_2). The grammatical analysis for 20 then would proceed like those shown earlier:

$S_1 \rightarrow NP \, VP$

$S_2 \rightarrow NP \, VP$

$NP \rightarrow (det) \, (AdjP) \, N$

$VP \rightarrow V \, NP$

$AdjP \rightarrow adj$

Teaching Tip

Tree diagrams can help students better understand the nature of compound sentences. If we diagram sentence 20, for example, the tree clearly shows how the sentence is composed of two equal Ss, or clauses. When students understand the structure of compounds, they more readily understand how to punctuate them correctly.

Sentence 20: A goon shot the ATM, so Buggsy made an easy withdrawal.

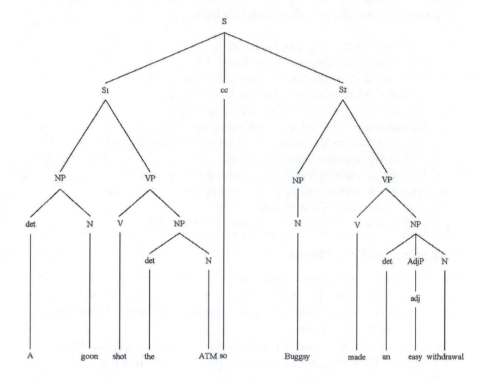

APPLYING KEY IDEAS

Directions: Draw tree diagrams for the following sentences. In the case of ambiguous sentences, disambiguate with two trees.

1. Macarena put the magazine on the table.
2. Fritz went to the races and bet on Lucky Lady.
3. Fred jogged to the boardwalk and watched the skaters.
4. Ophelia DiMarco and Raul drove to Rodeo Drive.
5. Fritz took the pictures with the camera in the den.
6. Macarena invited Fred for a swim, but he was busy.
7. Fritz sent roses to Macarena, and he bought her a lovely necklace.
8. Mrs. DiMarco baked a pie and a cake.
9. Without guilt or remorse, Buggsy enforced the contract.
10. Buggsy was on the road between Los Angeles and Las Vegas.
11. Raul cleaned the sofa in the living room.
12. Macarena and Fritz danced until dawn at China Club.

Expanding the Verb Phrase

Our description of verb phrases to this point has been rudimentary. It has not included any specification for tense, nor has it provided any means of describing future or aspect. To describe these features, phrase-structure grammar expands the analysis of the verb phrase.

Some minor changes to the phrase-structure rule for verb phrases are all that are necessary. Currently, our rule for verb phrases looks like this:

VP → V (NP) (AdjP) (PP)

It designates NP, AdjP, and PP as optional elements of the VP.

To describe tense, we change the rule to include an *auxiliary* (Aux) constituent that carries tense and other features to be discussed shortly:

VP → Aux V (NP) (AdjP) (PP)

Aux → tense

$$\text{tense} \rightarrow \left\{ \begin{array}{l} \text{past} \\ \text{present} \end{array} \right\}$$

(As noted earlier, the brackets around past/present indicate that one of the two must be chosen.)

One of the beauties of phrase-structure grammar is its versatility. Earlier, we modified our VP rule because we know that we have to be able to account for tense if we are going to describe sentences accurately. But what about adverbials? They are part of the VP, but so far we have not described grammatically how they appear in the language. Well, all we have to do is modify the VP rule again by adding an optional adverbial phrase:

VP → Aux V (NP) (AdvP) (AdjP) (PP)

On page 79, we differentiated simple adverbs from adverbials, noting that adverbs are single words and that adverbials are phrases and clauses—specifically, prepositional phrases and subordinate clauses—that function adverbially. Because phrase-structure rules do not provide explicit information about function, prepositional phrases and subordinate clauses are not included under the heading of AdjP. Consequently, if we expand the description of VP for adverbs, we have:

$$\text{AdvP} \rightarrow \begin{Bmatrix} \text{adv} \\ \text{NP} \end{Bmatrix}$$

This rule allows us to describe sentences like 21 and 22:

21. Quickly, she called her bank on the cell phone.
22. Macarena lost her checkbook yesterday.

Because adverbials and adjectivals frequently work together, we need one more adjustment to the VP to describe sentences like 23:

23. Buggsy bought his wife a very expensive emerald necklace.

Again, making the change to the rule is quite simple:

$$\text{AdjP} \rightarrow (\text{AdvP}) \begin{Bmatrix} \text{adv} \\ \text{NP} \end{Bmatrix}$$

At this point, the grammar rules are beginning to get more complicated, but diagrams can help us visualize how the rules work to describe sentence grammar. A diagram of sentence 23, for example, illustrates how the various components fit together.

Sentence 4.23: Buggsy bought his wife a very expensive emerald necklace.

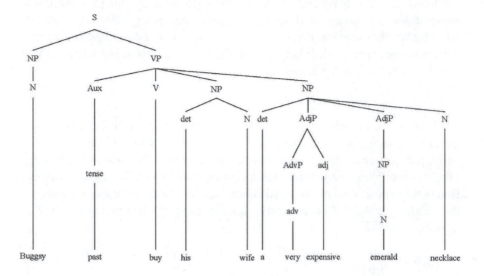

Mood. Although we won't examine this point in grammatical detail, verb phrases include a feature of verbs known as *mood.* Mood indicates the factuality or likelihood of the action or conditionality expressed by the verb, and it also can express politeness. Mood is interesting, in part, because we communicate this information in verbs without even thinking about it.

There are three moods in English:

- **Indicative**—used to state facts
  Example: Buggsy owned the casino.
- **Imperative**—used to express commands
  Example: Stop the car!
- **Subjunctive**—used to express matters contrary to fact, conditionality, hypotheticals, wishes, and politeness in making requests

The first two moods are fairly concrete, but the subjunctive mood is subtle and sometimes complicated because it applies under five different conditions. Contrary-to-fact statements always and expressions of conditionality sometimes require a dependent clause; this clause begins with the word *if* or *whether*—depending on the nature of the statement, for the words are not synonymous in formal Standard English.

Also, the subjunctive verb form is interesting. In some cases, such as contrary-to-fact statements, the verb form is in the past tense in the dependent as well as the independent clause. First- and third-person nouns and pronouns (*I, he, she*) take the second-person verb form. The following examples illustrate these unique features:

- **Subjunctive: *Contrary-to-Fact Statements***
  1. If Fred *were* just a bit younger, he *would apply* for the position.
  2. If I *were* you, I *would leave* town.
  3. They *acted* as though Buggsy *were watching*.
- **Subjunctive: *Conditional Statements***
  1. Fred *will leave* if Buggsy *comes* to the party.
  2. After eating his veggies, little Johnny *could have* his dessert.
  3. We *will gain* our reward, provided we *be* strong.
- **Subjunctive: *Hypothetical Acts***
  1. If Fred *bought* the new BMW, he *would be* completely broke.
  2. If he *were asked,* he *would serve*.
- **Subjunctive: *Expressing a Wish***
  1. Macarena *wished* she *were* rich.
  2. Fritz *recommended* that she *be* patient.
- **Subjunctive: *Politeness in Requests***
  1. *Would* you open the window?
  2. *Could* you close the door?

Usage Note

Linguists have noted a significant change in the use of the subjunctive in contrary-to-fact statements involving forms of *be*. In spoken English, there has been a shift in the verb form in the dependent clause to make it agree in number with its noun or pronoun (although this shift is apparent only in sentences with personal pronouns and names as subjects). As a result, the example sentences just cited increasingly are expressed as:

- If Fred *was* just a bit younger, he *would apply* for the position.
- If I *was* you, I *would leave* town.
- They *acted* as though Buggsy *was watching*.

The subjunctive marker is dropped in the verb in the dependent clause, but it is retained in the independent clause. Again, the question of what constitutes standard usage is important. Some people argue that standard usage is whatever the most people use. This argument is off the mark because it fails to take into account the influences of prestige and acceptability that generally govern standard usage. *Thus, standard usage is not, and never has been, the form used most widely; it is the form most widely accepted.* The subjunctive form is accepted by those who use formal Standard English and by those who do not, whereas the nonsubjunctive form is accepted only by those who use the nonstandard form. Standard usage of the subjunctive, for example, continues to appear in a great deal of writing, with the notable exception of popular journalism, as well as in the speech of many people.

Note that nonstandard usage does not differentiate between *if* and *whether* in contrary-to-fact clauses. As a result, these sentences are deemed equivalent:

- ?I don't know if it's going to snow.
- I don't know whether it's going to snow.

Standard usage, however, does make a distinction. *If* is used to introduce contrary-to-fact and conditional clauses, whereas *whether* is used to introduce clauses that express, implicitly or explicitly, alternative possibilities. Because there clearly are alternative possibilities to snow, the second sentence follows standard usage conventions, but the first one does not.

Some observers have suggested that the subjunctive is disappearing with respect to expressing politeness in making requests. The example requests cited earlier may be more commonly expressed today as commands with a tag question seeking agreement:

- Open the window, ok?
- Close the door, ok?

Identifying the causes for these changes must be a speculative endeavor, but the loss of subjunctive in contrary-to-fact and conditional statements may be related to a principle of behavioral efficiency. Generally, subjects and predicates agree with respect to number. In a wide variety of situations, English follows a pattern of using a singular verb form with singular subjects and a plural verb form with plural subjects, as in *I was tired* and *They were late.* The subjunctive alters this pattern. The lack of agreement seems—and is—contrary to the pattern that we find with most verbs. One therefore could argue that it is more efficient to eliminate the distinction and use the singular pattern of agreement in all situations.

With respect to the disappearance of the subjunctive to express politeness, many contemporary social commentators have remarked on the significant decrease in politeness in American society—or the increase in rudeness and outright hostility, depending on one's perspective—which might be a factor in the shift from requests to commands. The decrease in politeness, in turn, is seen as one reaction to the dramatic population increase that the United States has experienced during the last 30 years. As population becomes more dense, there is greater competition for resources and thus more hostility. The hostility, in turn, appears to be linked to the widely held view—which has erupted like the pox during the last 30 years—that others have no rights and are undeserving of respect or consideration. Social commentators point to a variety of behaviors, seldom observed a generation ago, as evidence for this assessment—the plague of drivers who cut off others in traffic, run red lights, and generally act as though they own the roads; the increase in littering that has piled rubbish ankle deep in so many cities; and the general surliness of service providers who have abandoned the traditional motto, "The Customer Is Always Right," for the unsavory alternative, "The Customer Is Always Wrong."

Teaching Tip

Students have difficulty with the subjunctive for two reasons. First, they aren't used to hearing it, so the form doesn't rest very firmly in their linguistic repertoire. Second, the form does, indeed, represent an unusual pattern, for it is contrary to the usual agreement between subject and verb. These difficulties require a systematic approach to instruction. One effective method is to begin by describing the nature of the subjunctive, how it is used and why, with plenty of examples. Then ask students to examine several paragraphs in their reading assignments and find at least three sentences that use the subjunctive; they should share these sentences with the class, explaining how the subjunctive is used in each case. Finally, have them work in pairs or small groups to observe conversations in the cafeteria, in other classes, or at the mall; the goal is to record any instances of the subjunctive in actual speech or any instances in which the subjunctive should have been used but was not. Student teams should share their findings with the class. What conclusions can they make on the basis of their study of texts and their observations of conversations?

Modals

Some features of mood, such as hypothetical permission, are expressed in words that are called *modals* (M). The modals are listed here:

will	all
may	must
can	

Historically, English modals came from a special class of verbs in Germanic, the ancestor of English and the other Germanic languages. Modals have always differed from ordinary verbs, to the point where they now belong to a special category of their own. Modals and verbs differ in the range of forms that they exhibit. English verbs appear in a number of distinct forms, whereas modals have a single, invariant form. For instance, modals never end in -*s*, even in sentences with third-person singular subjects.

To include the modal in our grammar, we simply expand the rule for auxiliary to account for tense markers (past and present) and modals, as shown:

Aux → tense (M)

$$
M \rightarrow \begin{Bmatrix} \text{will} \\ \text{shall} \\ \text{can} \\ \text{may} \\ \text{must} \end{Bmatrix}
$$

With this modification to our rules, we can describe sentences such as 24:

24. Fritz may get a promotion.

Analysis of this sentence is shown in the following tree diagram on the next page.

A question that often arises in the analysis of expanded verb phrases is why the tense marker is placed in front of the verb rather than after. The past participle suffix -ed/-en, after all, comes at the end of a verb, not at the beginning. The answer is that there is no simple way to capture schematically the relations among tense, modals, and verbs. Whenever a verb has a modal, the modal is tensed, not the verb. If our description put tense after the verb, we would solve nothing—we would still have the question of how tense jumps over the verb and attaches to the modal. The placement of tense at the head of the VP is a matter of convention; placing it elsewhere in the VP would not enhance the description.

What we learn here is that structural analyses are at best an approximate description of the language we actually use. If we wanted to account for the fact that the past participle appears at the end of verbs, we would have to develop a special

Sentence: 4.24: Fritz may get a promotion.

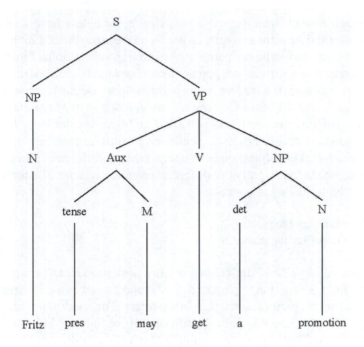

rule for attachment, which indeed is what linguists have done. Nevertheless, structural analyses reveal much about the nature of grammatical constructions.

Tense and Its Complexities

When we examine tense closely, it becomes apparent that the relation between tense and verbs is not a simple one. Tense does not merely indicate when an action took place, as evidenced in sentences such as *Macarena could visit her sick friend in the morning.* The verb *visit* is not tensed in this sentence; instead, the tense marker is attached to the modal. But although the modal is in the past tense, the action is to occur in the future. Many students have a hard time grasping this concept.

Usage Note

Although modals are function words, they nevertheless have a semantic content. *Can* and *may,* for example, do not mean the same thing. *Can* indicates ability, whereas *may* indicates permission as well as a conditional future. With regard to requesting permission, popular usage has largely eliminated *may* and replaced it with *can.* If a student wants permission to use the rest room, he or she invariably will ask, *Can I use the rest room* rather than *May I use the rest room.* In a department store, clerks will ask, *Can I help you,* not *May I help you.* Formal standard usage, however, continues to differentiate between these words, which makes helping students understand the difference a worthwhile goal. Because *may* can signify two different meanings, it can lead to ambiguity. Consider the following sentences:

25. Fritz can play the piano.
26. Fritz may play the piano.

Sentence 25 signifies Fritz's ability to play; sentence 26 can be understood as giving Fritz permission to play, or it can be understood as a comment about Fritz's playing the piano at some time in the future. The condition is uncertain. We easily can imagine this future conditional if we think of Fritz being at a party. Sentence 27 offers another example of *may* as a future conditional:

27. Buggsy may take a trip to Las Vegas next week.

It is worth noting that the past tense form of *may* is *might.* These words differ in that *might* signifies a more uncertain or doubtful future than does *may.* Thus, the likelihood of Buggsy taking a trip is more uncertain in sentence 28 than it is in sentence 27:

28. Buggsy might take a trip to Las Vegas next week.

Like many other usage distinctions, this one seems to be disappearing. Even speakers and writers of formal Standard English rarely differentiate the two forms. However, anyone interested in using language as precisely as possible will, indeed, differentiate them.

The difference between *will* and *shall* is far more complicated, and it, too, has essentially disappeared in American usage. The traditional distinction maintains that *shall* is used to indicate the simple future in the first person, as in *I shall go to the movies. Shall* cannot be used in the second and third persons, however, but instead must be replaced by *will,* as in *They will end the strike soon.* The use of *will* in the first person does not express simple future but instead signifies a promised action, as in *I will give you the loan.* The use of *shall* in the second and third persons signifies a command, as in *You shall stop seeing that horrible woman immediately.* Currently, there are only two instances of widespread use of *shall* in American English, even among Standard speakers: in legal documents and in questions, as in *Shall we go now?*

Do Support

In English, the word *do* is used to emphasize a statement, as in these examples:

29. Fred *does* like the veal.
30. Macarena *did* deposit the check into her account.

Sentence 4.30: Macarena *did* deposit the check into her account.

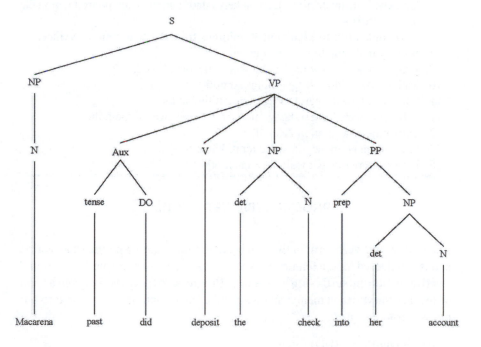

When *do* is used for emphasis, it is referred to as *do support*. *Do* is analyzed as part of the auxiliary. In Standard English, *do* cannot appear with another modal, although it can in Black English Vernacular. We therefore need to change our rule for the auxiliary once again:

Aux → tense (M) (DO)

A diagram of sentence 30 illustrates what our current analysis would look like.

APPLYING KEY IDEAS

Directions: Analyze the following sentences, identifying each of their components.

1. Fred and Macarena drove to the beach.
2. Fritz called Macarena several times.
3. Rita de Luna did return the telephone call.
4. Fritz polished the lenses of the telescope and considered the possibilities.
5. They would be at that special spot near Malibu.
6. Quickly, Fritz made himself a chicken salad sandwich and poured lemonade into the thermos.
7. Fritz could drive to Malibu in 40 minutes from the apartment in Venice.
8. Buggsy must employ a dozen goons.
9. If Buggsy were fully retired, he would become bored.
10. Mrs. DiMarco does forget things sometimes.
11. Someday, he will regret those poor eating habits.
12. If Buggsy were honest, he would turn himself over to the police.
13. They might vacation in Acapulco.
14. She can spend money in some remarkable ways.
15. Fred and Fritz do get jealous of each other.

PROGRESSIVE VERB FORMS

The progressive verb form in English indicates the ongoing nature of an action and is considered to be a feature of aspect. Progressives are formed with *be* and a verb to which the suffix *-ing* is attached. Progressive (prog) is analyzed as part of the auxiliary, which means that we need to make another adjustment to our phrase-structure rule:

Aux → tense (M) (DO) (prog)

prog → be -ing

This new rule allows us to analyze sentences like the following:

31. Macarena was *dancing* at China Club.
32. The band members were *playing* a hot salsa.
33. They are *thinking* about the next break.

Progressive Verb Forms and Predicate Adjectives

English presents an analytical problem with sentences like the following:

34. Raul was running.
35. His toe was throbbing.

The structure of these sentences seems to be very similar, and, in fact, it may seem reasonable to analyze them both as having progressive form verb phrases. Such an analysis, however, is not accurate. Sentence 34 indeed has a progressive form verb phrase, but sentence 35 does not; instead, the VP consists of a linking verb and a predicate adjective. The tree diagrams for these sentences clearly illustrate the difference between the two sentences.

Sentence 4.34: Raul was running.

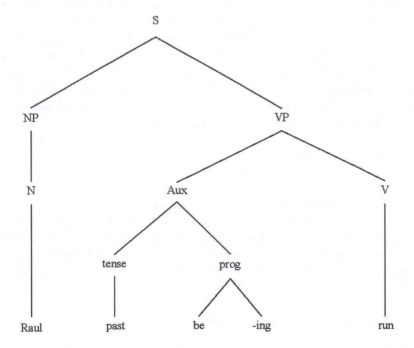

Sentence 4.35: His toe was throbbing.

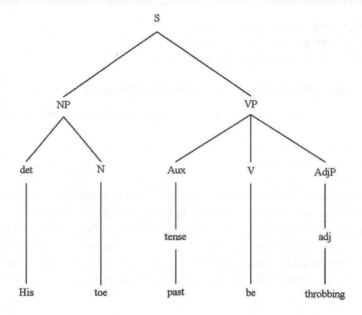

The key to understanding the difference lies in recognizing the distinct roles the two subjects have in these sentences. In sentence 34, the subject is an agent performing an action. In sentence 35, the subject is not an agent, so it does not perform an action, which means that *throbbing* cannot describe an action in this case because no action is performed. Instead, *throbbing* provides existential information. On this account, we can say that progressive forms always have an agentive subject. Whenever the subject is not an agent, the verb phrase consists of a linking verb and predicate adjective. This analysis is supported by the structures of sentences like the following:

- Mrs. DiMarco was boring.
- Mrs. DiMarco was boring Raul.

In the first example, Mrs. DiMarco is not an agentive subject, whereas in the second she is. The difference in function not only results in different grammatical analyses but also, as we should expect, in different meanings. Further support comes from the fact that words like *throbbing* also can function as simple adjectives, as in *She had a throbbing headache.* Following are some additional examples for illustration:

- Macarena *was jogging* along the beach. (progressive verb form)

- The waves *were glistening.* (predicate adjective)
- Buggsy *was watching* from the deck of his beach house. (progressive verb form)
- He found that the sight of all the happy people *was tiring.* (predicate adjective)

PERFECT VERB FORMS

The perfect verb form in English consists of *have* and a verb to which the past participle suffix *-ed/-en* has been attached. It signifies more than one temporal relation.

- **The past perfect,** for example, indicates that one event occurred before another event.
- **The present perfect** indicates that an event has recurred or that it already has occurred.
- **The future perfect** indicates that an event will have occurred by the time that another event will be happening.

These three possibilities, respectively, are illustrated in the following sentences:

36. Fred *had eaten* at Spago many times before that fateful day. (past perfect)
37. Macarena *has looked* everywhere for the diskette. (present perfect)
38. Fritz *will have driven* 150 miles before dark. (future perfect)

Like the progressive, the perfect verb form is analyzed as part of the auxiliary; we abbreviate it here as *perf* . Making the necessary adjustment to the phrase-structure rule results in:

Aux → tense (M) (DO) (prog) (perf)

Perf → have -ed/-en

POSSESSIVES

English forms the possessive using pronouns or a noun and a possessive (poss) marker, as in *her book* or *Maria's book.* Possessives are considered to be in the category of determiners. To this point, our discussion of determiners has included only articles, but now we need to expand our notion of this grammatical category. We can describe the nature of possessives by using an expression such as the following:

$$\text{det} \rightarrow \begin{Bmatrix} \text{pro} \\ \text{NP + poss} \\ \text{art} \end{Bmatrix}$$

poss → 's

This analysis shows that a determiner is a pronoun, a noun plus possessive marker, or an article. We can use sentence 39 to analyze the underlying nature of noun possessives:

39. Fred's shirt had a hole in it.

Most grammatical analyses pay little attention to possessive pronouns for good reason. The problem lies with pronouns. Designating the possessive *her* as *she + poss* seems counterintuitive because there is no evidence that *her* exists as anything other than an independent pronoun. We form the possessive noun by attaching the possessive marker to the noun. Possessive pronouns, however, exist as independent lexical items and are not formed at all—they already exist in the lexicon. Initially, it may seem strange to classify possessive NPs and pronouns as determiners, but they nevertheless do resemble articles. For example, we do not form *an* by adding *n* to *a;* the two forms exist independently. The same holds true for possessive pronouns. Consequently, most analyses exclude possessive pronouns from the domain of the NP and place them in the domain of determiner.

RESTRICTIVE AND NONRESTRICTIVE MODIFICATION

Let's consider the following sentences:

40. The goon with a gun in his hand stood guard at the entrance.
41. The goon, with a gun in his hand, stood guard at the entrance.
42. Buggsy's girlfriend Rita loved Porsches.
43. Buggsy's girlfriend, Rita, loved Porsches.

These sentences are very similar, but at the same time they are quite different. We first notice that the modifiers—*with a gun in his hand* and *Rita*—are functioning adjectivally to provide information to the noun phrases *The goon* and *Buggsy's girlfriend,* respectively.[2] In sentence 40, we understand that there

---

[2]*Rita* also renames the NP. Nouns that function in this way are often called *noun phrase appositives.*

are several goons and that one of them has a gun in his hand. In 41, there is only one goon, and he just happens to have a gun in his hand. A similar situation exists in sentences 42 and 43: In 42, we understand that Buggsy has more than one girlfriend and that the one named Rita loved Porsches; in 43, Buggsy has one girlfriend, she loved Porsches, and her name just happens to be Rita.

What differentiates the sentences in each case is the nature of the modifiers. Note that the PP *with a gun in his hand* and the NP *Rita* in sentences 40 and 42, respectively, are not set off with punctuation, whereas in 41 and 43 they are. Moreover, the PP in sentence 40 *defines* the goon, distinguishing him from others. The same can be said of the NP *Rita* in sentence 42. In sentences 41 and 43, on the other hand, the modifiers are set off with commas, and they simply supply *additional* information, not defining information. We use the terms *restrictive* and *nonrestrictive* modification to differentiate the two types of structures. Restrictive modifiers provide defining information and are not punctuated. Nonrestrictive modifiers provide nondefining information and are punctuated.

Teaching Tip

Restrictive and nonrestrictive modification is one of the more confusing topics in writing classes. By the time students reach high school, for example, a majority will use nonrestrictive modification when they should use restrictive, and vice versa. We see this most frequently with regard to the titles of literary works, with students regularly producing sentences such as:

- *?Steinbeck's novel, The Grapes of Wrath, was inspired by the wave of socialism that swept America in the 1930s.*

The problem here is that Steinbeck wrote several novels, not just one. Because the title is punctuated as a nonrestrictive modifier, the writer communicates that he or she believes otherwise—not a good position to be in if writing for an audience that knows anything at all about John Steinbeck. The correct form is:

- *Steinbeck's novel The Grapes of Wrath was inspired by the wave of socialism that swept America in the 1930s.*

Most students have a hard time remembering the terms "restrictive" and "nonrestrictive," so in many cases it is easier to focus on the role of punctuation. When there is no punctuation around the modifier—when it functions restrictively, in other words—the modifier is defining one among many. When there is punctuation around the modifier—when it functions nonrestrictively—the modifier is nondefining, just supplying additional information, and there is only one. Of course, one needs a certain amount of knowledge in some situations to make this distinction. If a student doesn't know anything about Steinbeck, determining the correct punctuation is a real problem. But solving the problem offers opportunities for learning.

SUBORDINATE CLAUSES

We discussed subordinate clauses (SC) on pages 86 to 89 and noted that they always begin with a subordinating conjunction. When a sentence contains a subordinate clause (or any other type of dependent clause) it is called a *complex sentence*. (A sentence with coordinated independent clauses and at least one dependent clause is called a *compound-complex sentence.*) Some of the more common subordinating conjunctions were listed previously and are shown again here for convenience:

because	if	as
until	since	whereas
although	though	while
unless	so that	once
after	before	when
whenever	as if	even if
in order that	as soon as	even though

Subordinate clauses function as adverbials; thus, they modify a verb phrase or an entire clause. In the latter case, they are sentence-level modifiers. The difference is related to the restrictive or nonrestrictive nature of the modifier. Let's examine these two possibilities:

44. Fred drove to Las Vegas because he liked the desert air.
45. Macarena exercised until she was exhausted.
46. Although he was uncultivated, Buggsy liked opera.
47. Fritz wore a sweater, even though the evening was warm.
48. Raul, because he was young, showed the confidence of youth.

In sentences 44 and 45, the SC is a restrictive modifier, which means that it supplies necessary or defining information to a verb phrase. In sentences 46 through 47, however, the subordinate clause is a nonrestrictive modifier in the initial, final, and medial positions, respectively. Nonrestrictive subordinate clauses are sentence-level modifiers. However, some subordinate clauses at the beginning of a sentence may not be punctuated if the writer is using the length convention for initial modifiers. Such initial subordinate clauses nevertheless are deemed nonrestrictive. They have to be because as adverbials they must modify either a VP or an S. In the initial position, they can modify only an S.

With certain verbs, subordinate clauses can function as complements, as in:

49. We wondered *whether the fish were fresh.*
50. They could not decide *whether the trip was worth the cost.*

In an ideal world, we would be able to write a phrase-structure rule that describes all these structures and that also captures the fact that a subordinate clause functions adverbially as part of the verb phrase or as a sentence-level modifier. But there is no way to provide such information in the rule, so we must be satisfied with a rule that just describes the structure; only diagrams can illustrate how the SC functions. Several possibilities exist for rules, but the simplest seems to be one similar to the XP rule we used for coordination. If we think of a dependent clause as $\bar{S}$ (read bar-S), our rule would be:

$$XP \rightarrow XP\ \bar{S}$$

$$\bar{S} \rightarrow Sconj\ NP\ VP$$

The first expression states that any phrase, XP, can be rewritten as that phrase plus $\bar{S}$. $\bar{S}$, in turn, can be rewritten as a subordinating conjunction (Sconj), a noun phrase, and a verb phrase. Stated another way, any XP may have a $\bar{S}$ attached to it. As in the rule for coordination, XP can represent either a clause or a phrase. We must explain outside the rule, as a constraint, that $\bar{S}$ attaches either to S or VP. We can do this because the grammar is concerned primarily with describing existing sentences. If structuralists had given the grammar a generative component—that is, if it were more concerned with how people generate sentences with subordinate clauses—they might have attempted to develop an expression that addresses the question of placement. Without this concern, the issue is moot because placement is given in the utterance being described.

We want a rule that is very generalizable, of course, so shortly in this chapter we expand the definition of $\bar{S}$ to include other types of dependent clauses, which means that $\bar{S}$ attaches to various types of phrases.

A couple of diagrams can make it easier to understand the nature of SC modification. Consider these diagrams for sentences 45 and 46:

Sentence 4.45: Macarena exercised until she was exhausted.

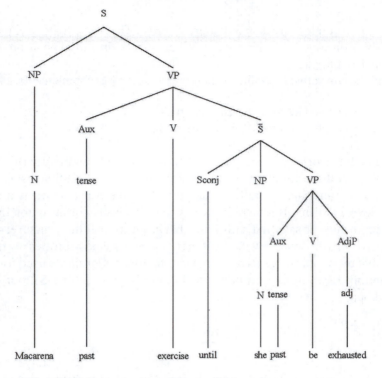

Sentence 4.46: Although he was uncultivated, Buggsy liked opera.

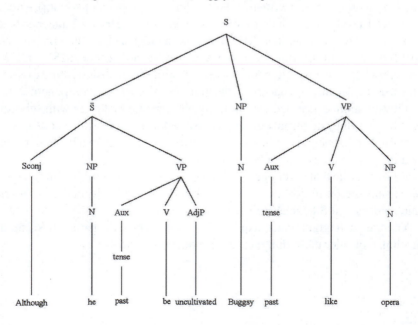

COMPLEMENT CLAUSES

Earlier we looked at a common problem in nonstandard English that involves a subordinate clause and a linking verb:

- *The reason is because it's important.

We noted that subordinate clauses cannot follow linking verbs; only noun constructions, adjective constructions, and prepositional phrases can do so. With respect to this example sentence, Standard English therefore calls for:

- The reason is *that it's important.*

When discussing this construction previously, there was no analysis of the italicized portion of the sentence. We now have the grammatical tools and vocabulary to look at it more closely. The construction is a *complex noun construction* known as a *complement clause.*

Complement clauses are quite versatile. They can function as subjects, objects, noun complements, verb complements (as previously shown), and adjective complements. The following sentences illustrate these possibilities:

51. *That Macarena liked Buggsy* surprised everyone. (subject)
52. Raul knew *that he should get* a job. (object)
53. Mrs. DiMarco scoffed at the idea *that she should remarry.* (NP complement)
54. The problem was *that Buggsy's wife could be mean.* (VP complement)
55. Macarena was sad *that she had missed the concert.* (AdjP complement)
56. Raul knew nothing except *that he loved Maria.* (object of preposition)

A complement clause always has a subject and a predicate, and it begins with the complementizing conjunction (comp) *that.* In the case of complement clauses functioning as objects, however, we have the option of deleting the complementizer, which results in sentences like 52a:

52a. Raul knew *he should get a job.*

(When sentences like 52a are analyzed on a tree diagram, the null symbol [Ø] takes the place of the complementizer.)

We can describe this construction by again adjusting the relevant phrase-structure rule. We simply need to add a complementizer to our $\overline{S}$ rule:

$$\overline{S} \rightarrow \begin{Bmatrix} Sconj \\ comp \end{Bmatrix} NP\ VP$$

$$comp \rightarrow \begin{Bmatrix} that \\ \varnothing \end{Bmatrix}$$

The following diagrams illustrate how to analyze the kinds of sentences represented by 51, 52, and 52a:

Sentence 4.51: *That Macarena liked Buggsy* surprised everyone. (subject)

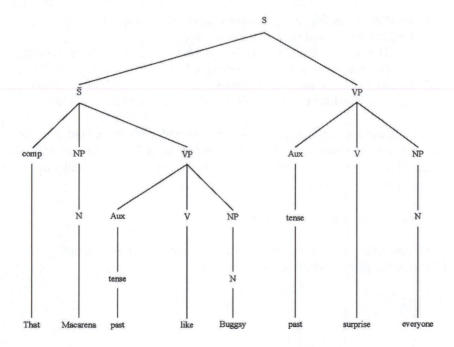

Sentence 4.52: Raul knew *that he should get* a job. (object)

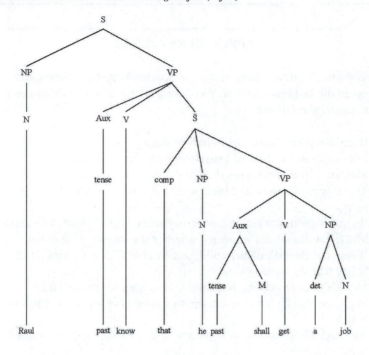

Sentence 4.52a: Raul knew *he should get a job.*

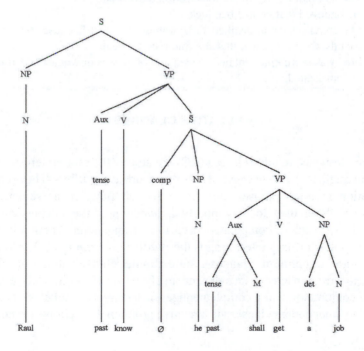

APPLYING KEY IDEAS

Directions: Analyze these sentences to check your understanding of the concepts in the last few sections. You may want to draw tree diagrams to show the grammatical relations.

1. Buggsy's goons had come from New Jersey.
2. Fritz realized that he could have forgotten the meeting.
3. Macarena liked Fritz, even though she hated his apartment.
4. That Buggsy flirted with Macarena and Rita de Luna shocked the host of the party.
5. Buggsy's goons got nice tans after they arrived in L.A. from the East Coast.
6. Macarena sometimes wondered whether she should settle down.
7. When she thought of her childhood in cold Chicago, Mrs. DiMarco was happy that she lived in L.A.
8. Mrs. DiMarco's nephew had lost his way after his parents died.
9. She knew that he ran with a dangerous crowd but was unsure that she could help him.
10. Although Fritz had had little success with women, he thought that he was a ladykiller.
11. The fact that he was obnoxious troubled everyone.
12. He believed that he had bad luck.
13. Macarena's friends disliked Fritz immensely, and because they were her friends, they suggested that she find a better beau.
14. Fred was more kind, but he brooded and often was downcast because he felt unappreciated.

RELATIVE CLAUSES

In many respects, relative clauses (RC) are among the more interesting structures in English, in part because of how they work as modifiers. They supply information to noun phrases, but they also can function as sentence-level modifiers. When they do, they modify the *meaning* of the independent clause rather than a syntactic component—a curious arrangement. Another factor that makes relative clauses interesting is the *relative pronoun* (RP). We have seen how other dependent clauses—subordinate clauses and complement clauses—are connected to an independent clause via a linking word (a subordinating conjunction and a complementizer, respectively). Relative clauses are linked to independent clauses via a relative pronoun, but relative pronouns are more than just linking words. They are like regular pronouns in that they replace a duplicate noun phrase in a sentence. In addition, they function as either the subject or the object of the relative clause. Thus, they can perform three syntactic functions in a sentence, whereas subordinators and complementizers can perform only one.

The more common relative pronouns are shown here:

who	whom	that
which	whose	where
when	why	

A relative clause must always begin with a relative pronoun because it needs to be linked to the independent clause. We can see the linking function in the following sample sentences:

57. Buggsy bought the house *that* had belonged to Liberace.
58. The boy *who* drove the van played the blues.
59. The book *that* Fritz borrowed lacked an index.

It is always important to understand that any sentence with a dependent clause has undergone a process of combining that joins two (or more) clauses into a single sentence. In the case of relative clauses, the relative pronoun replaces a noun phrase duplicated in the two clauses. Sentences 57 through 59, for example, are made up of the following clauses.

57a. Buggsy bought *the house. The house* had belonged to Liberace.
58a. *The boy* played the blues. *The boy* drove the van.
59a. *The book* lacked an index. Fritz borrowed *the book*.

If we attempted to combine these clauses without using a relative pronoun, the results would be ungrammatical:

57b. *Buggsy bought the house the house had belonged to Liberace.
58b. *The boy played the blues the boy drove the van.
59b. *The book lacked an index Fritz borrowed the book.

Relative Pronoun Shift

The multiple functions that relative pronouns play in sentences create a certain degree of confusion for many students. Especially problematic are sentences like 59, in which the relative pronoun replaces an object noun phrase. Sentence 59a clearly shows that *the book* functions as the object noun phrase in the second clause (Fritz borrowed *the book*). The confusion arises from the fact that objects follow nouns. Students know this intuitively. It represents a basic feature of English word order.

But the relative pronoun must link the RC to the independent clause. As a result, when we convert *the book* to a relative pronoun, we must shift the pronoun from its position behind the verb to a new position in front of the subject, thereby violating the standard SVO word order. This violation makes it difficult for large numbers of native English speakers to recognize that the word *that* in sentence 59 is an object. This problem is most noticeable with regard to the relative pronouns *who* and *whom*. We use *who* when we relativize subjects; we use *whom* when we relativize objects. They have different cases. Nearly every native English speaker finds it difficult to use the correct form, even those who generally have little trouble using the correct case for other pronouns.

Teaching Tip

An effective way to help students understand the difference between subject and object relative pronouns is to take sentences and break them into two separate clauses, as shown for sentences 57 through 59. For sentences with a relativized object NP, walk them through the process of relativization step by step. Get them to recognize the object NP in the target clause, have them change the NP to a relative pronoun, and then emphasize the need to have a linking element that combines the two clauses. After some practice, shift the activity to reading assignments. Have students work in teams to find relative clauses in their reading, and then have them explain the structure on the board. Because the real test of mastery lies in how students can use relative clauses in their writing, have them identify relative clauses in one of their writing assignments.

Usage Note

The difference between *who* and *whom* is related to case, which we examined on pages 61–64. *Who* always functions as the subject of a relative clause, so it is in the nominative case. *Whom,* on the other hand, always functions as an object, either of the verb of the relative clause or of a preposition, so it is in the objective case. Consider the following sentences:

- The man *who owned the BMW* worked at a bank.
- The man *whom I knew* worked at a bank.

The structure of these relative clauses is quite different. *Who* functions as the subject of *owned* in the first case, and *I* functions as the subject of *knew* in the second. *Whom* is the object of *knew,* even though it appears at the beginning of the clause. Most people do not pay much attention to this difference, especially when speaking: They have not had sufficient exposure to formal standard usage for it to have become internalized, so applying the *who/whom* distinction requires conscious application of grammatical knowledge that many either do not possess or have not fully grasped. Even those with this knowledge commonly fail to apply it because the flow of the conversation interferes with application or because they fear that using *whom* will make them sound elitist.

When the relative pronoun is an object, it is possible to drop it from the sentence *(The man I knew worked at a bank),* which helps a bit. People do this naturally, so they do not have to learn anything new. More problematic, perhaps, are instances in which the relative pronoun functions as the object of a preposition: "Ask not for whom the bell tolls...." Some speakers will use the nominative case in such constructions *(for who the bell tolls),* but many others simply avoid using these constructions entirely.

The most common method of avoidance is to use the pronoun *that.* This method is so common, in fact, that many people now believe that these words are interchangeable:

- ?The boy *that* found the wallet turned it in at the police station.
- The boy *who* found the wallet turned it in at the police station.

These relative pronouns are not interchangeable in formal Standard English. Formal standard usage provides that *who* is used for people and *that* is used for everything else. This convention used to be followed with some consistency, as evidenced by the fact that not even nonstandard speakers use these pronouns interchangeably in sentences like the following:

- The lamp *that* is on the table cost $300.
- *The lamp *who* is on the table cost $300.

This interesting example raises the question of why English has two relative pronouns that are so similar. Both words have Old English roots, so the answer does not lie in English's famous ability to absorb words from other languages. Most likely, these pronouns reflect a time when English was more concerned about distinctions, much in the way that Spanish is concerned about identifying gender: *La muchacha es linda* (The girl is pretty) versus *El muchacho es lindo* (The boy is cute). In any event, we appear to be witnessing a shift in English to a single form—*that*—for use in all situations. If this shift continues, both *who* and *whom* eventually may disappear from contemporary English. Meanwhile, students need to be aware that many people still do differentiate between *that* and *who/whom,* and they should be prepared to adjust their language according to the situation they find themselves in.

Relative Clauses and Modification Type

Like certain other modifiers, relative clauses can function restrictively or nonrestrictively. Restrictive relative clauses supply defining or necessary information, so they are not set off with punctuation. Nonrestrictive relative clauses, on the other hand, supply additional or nonessential information; thus, they are set off with punctuation. The nonrestrictive subordinate clauses we have examined to this point have been adverbials, and they always have been sentence-level modifiers. Nonrestrictive relative clauses are different in this respect because sometimes they are sentence-level modifiers and sometimes they are not. Consider the following:

60. The book, *which was a first edition,* had a gold-inlaid cover.
61. Fred vacationed in Mexico, *which disturbed his parents.*

In sentence 60, the relative clause, even though it is nonrestrictive, clearly modifies the noun phrase *The book.* In sentence 61, however, there is no single head word; instead, the relative clause is modifying the meaning of the independent clause. That meaning might be described as "the fact that Fred vacationed in Mexico." Because the entire clause is receiving the modification, we must consider the relative clause in sentence 61 to be a sentence-level modifier. Please note: Relative clauses that function as sentence-level modifiers always begin with the relative pronoun *which (in which* is a common exception), but not all relative clauses that begin with the relative pronoun *which* are sentence-level modifiers.

Following are some additional examples that show the difference between the two types of nonrestrictive modification:

62. Fritz enjoyed talking about his feelings, *which drove Macarena crazy.* (sentence modifier)
63. The Malibu house, *which Buggsy used simply for relaxation,* was damaged in the mud slide. (NP modifier)
64. Buggsy took up golf, *which troubled his wife.* (sentence modifier)
65. Mrs. DiMarco's properties, *which were extensive,* provided her with a very comfortable living. (NP modifier)
66. China Club always had an attractive crowd, *which appealed to Fritz.* (sentence modifier)

We saw earlier that when complement clauses function as objects, English allows deletion of the complementizer, as in *She knew that Fred was tired/She knew Fred was tired.* English also allows us to delete relative pronouns under the same conditions, as the following sentences illustrate:

67. The dress that Macarena wanted was expensive.
67a. The dress Macarena wanted was expensive.

The grammar of relative clauses requires a slight adjustment to our phrase-structure rules. Note that we must make NP optional to describe the fact that some relative clauses have a relative pronoun as the subject. RP, of course, signifies any relative pronoun:

$$\bar{S} \to \begin{Bmatrix} Sconj \\ comp \\ RP \end{Bmatrix} (NP)\ VP$$

Diagrams of a few of these sentences will illustrate the grammatical structure of sentences with relative clauses. The diagrams for nonrestrictive modifiers are especially interesting because they show the difference between sentence-level modification and NP modification:

Sentence 4.57: Buggsy bought the house *that* had belonged to Liberace.

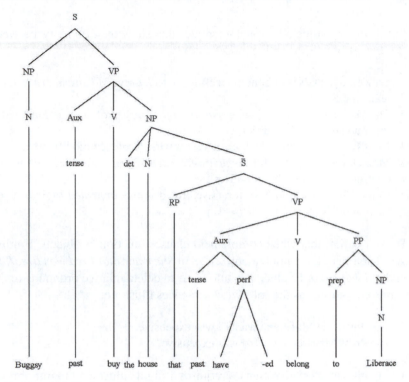

Sentence 4.59: The book *that* Fritz borrowed lacked an index.

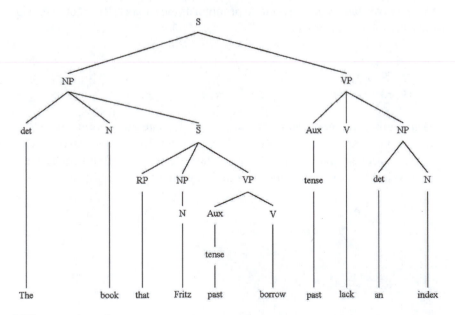

Sentence 4.60: The book, *which was a first edition,* had a gold-inlaid cover.

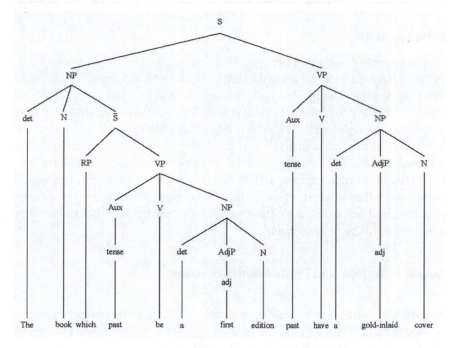

Sentence 4.61: Fred vacationed in Mexico, *which disturbed his parents.*

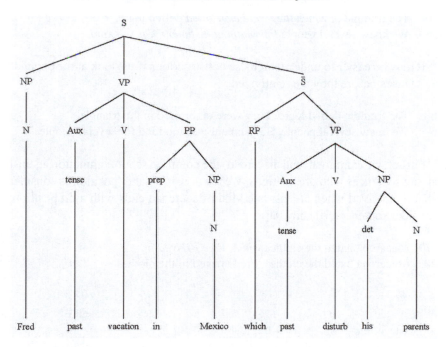

Usage Note

Most people treat the relative pronouns *that* and *which* as being identical. In fact, many teachers are known to tell students who ask about these words that they are interchangeable and that they should be used alternatively to add more variety to writing. Formal standard usage, however, differentiates them along a very clear line: *That* is used exclusively to introduce restrictive relative clauses, and *which* is used, generally, to introduce nonrestrictive relative clauses. The word "generally" is important because there are several types of relative clauses, and some involve the relative pronoun *which* even though they are restrictive, as in: "The deposition *in which* the answer appeared had been sealed by the court." This construction is examined in more detail in the next section.

Relative Clauses and Prepositional Phrases

Another interesting feature of relative clauses is that they often involve a prepositional phrase. When they do, the noun phrase in the prepositional phrase is a relative pronoun. Consider the following sentences:

68. The triangle *in which they were embroiled* defied logic.
69. We knew several people *for whom banishment was too kind.*

It may be easier to understand these constructions if we look at the dependent clauses before they are relativized:

68a. The triangle defied logic. They were embroiled in the triangle.
69a. We knew several people. Banishment was too kind for several people.

Earlier, we examined (and discarded) the common school injunction against ending sentences with prepositions. We are now in a better position to consider what is involved when at least one kind of sentence ends with a preposition. Consider sentences 70 and 70a:

70. Macarena hated the clothes *which Fred arrived in.*
70a. Macarena hated the clothes. Fred arrived in the clothes.

Sentence 70 is very similar to sentence 68 in that it involves a prepositional phrase with a relative pronoun in the NP. It differs, however, in that the prepositional phrase has been split; the relative pronoun is at the beginning of the relative clause, but the preposition still follows the verb. English allows this sort of construction.

Examining 70a suggests an important pattern for relatives. When we take a clause like *Fred arrived in the clothes,* where the NP that gets relativized is an object—either of the verb or of the preposition—we move the resulting relative pronoun to the front of the clause. We do not have to do this when we relativize a subject NP because it is already at the beginning of the clause. When the relativized NP is the object of a preposition, as in sentence 70, *we have the option of shifting the entire PP to the beginning of the clause or of shifting just the relative pronoun.* Exercising the second option results in sentences like 70, with a preposition at the end. This analysis offers a grammatical explanation for why the injunction against ending a sentence with a preposition is wrong.

A couple of small adjustments to our phrase-structure rules allow us to account for sentences with relative clauses that are part of a prepositional phrase:

$$\bar{S} \rightarrow \begin{Bmatrix} \text{Sconj} \\ \text{comp} \\ \text{RP} \\ \text{PP} \end{Bmatrix} \text{(NP) VP}$$

$$\text{PP} \rightarrow \text{prep} \begin{Bmatrix} \text{NP} \\ \text{RP} \\ \varnothing \end{Bmatrix}$$

These rules allow us to describe a relative clause with a PP when the object of the preposition is a relative pronoun. Note that the rules also indicate that a prepositional phrase with a relative-pronoun object outside the domain of a relative clause will be ungrammatical. The null marker fills the place of a shifted relative pronoun. As in some other cases, there is a feature here that we cannot write into the rule, and we must consider it outside the expression: The optional NP occurs only when the RP of a relative clause is functioning as the subject; otherwise the NP is obligatory.

A single diagram illustrates the role of relative pronouns in prepositional phrases:

Sentence 4.68: The triangle *in which they were embroiled* defied logic.

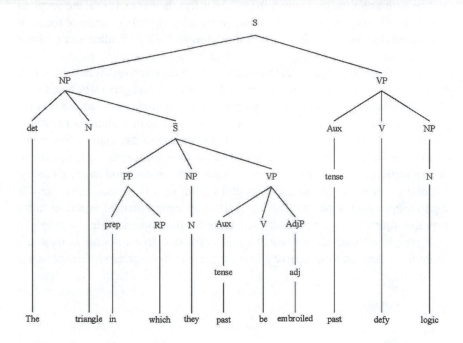

NEGATIVES

Although there are many ways to say *no* in English even when appearing to
say *yes,* grammatically we form the negative using *no, not,* and *never.* Technically, these words are adverbials, but phrase-structure grammar analyzes
them as negation markers in the Aux, as the following phrase-structure rule
shows:

Aux → tense (neg) (DO) (M) (prog) (perf)

$$neg \rightarrow \begin{Bmatrix} no \\ not \\ never \end{Bmatrix}$$

An interesting feature of the negative is that it triggers *Do Support* in the
verb phrase of simple active sentences. Consider these examples:

71. Fred kissed Macarena.
71a. Fred *did not* kiss Macarena.

Strangely enough, negation does not have this effect on progressive or perfect verb forms, as the following sentences illustrate:

72. Buggsy is inviting Michael Star to his next party.
72a. Buggsy is not inviting Michael Star to his next party.
73. Buggsy had left the waiter a huge tip.
73a. Buggsy had not left the waiter a huge tip.

APPLYING KEY IDEAS

Directions: Analyze these sentences, identifying their constituents.

1. The movie that Universal made on the USC campus disrupted classes.
2. Raul played the part of a man who won the lottery.
3. He liked the work, which thrilled his aunt.
4. Raul did not want the part.
5. Raul did not complain.
6. The actress who played his wife had amazing red hair.
7. The director whom Raul had met at a beach party gave him some acting lessons before filming.
8. Fritz, who knew Raul slightly, was jealous when he heard about the film.
9. Fritz was not happy with his career in banking because it lacked glamour.
10. He knew that Mrs. DiMarco had pawned the bracelet that he had given her for the rent.
11. The bracelet, which had been a gift for Macarena, looked like an heirloom.
12. Fritz thought that he could ask Buggsy for a loan that would buy back the bracelet, but he was afraid of the goons, who always looked mean.
13. Meanwhile, Fred had decided that Macarena, whom he loved, was the woman for him.
14. He did not have much money, but he went to Beverly Center for an engagement ring.
15. He knew a jeweler there who would give him a good price.
16. The ring that Fred wanted was very expensive, which did not surprise him.
17. Reluctantly, he turned his attention to a smaller ring that had been marked down.
18. The jeweler Fred knew was not working that day, which was a disappointment.
19. A young woman who had eyes as blue as the Pacific helped him at the counter.
20. She told him that some girl was really lucky, which made Fred blush.
21. Suddenly, he wondered whether he should ask Macarena about marriage before buying the ring.

22. The young woman, whose name was Maria, told him that most women do not like surprises of this kind.
23. At that moment, Raul, who had a date with Maria, walked into the store, which interrupted the moment.
24. Maria remembered the day when she met Raul.
25. Fred could not think of a reason why he had not talked to Macarena about his dream.

NONFINITE VERB FORMS

Up to this point, all the verb constructions we have worked with have included tensed, or what are called *finite,* verbs. Some of the more interesting grammatical constructions, however, involve untensed, or *nonfinite,* verbs. There are two major types of untensed verb forms: *infinitive* and *bare infinitive* (inf). The infinitive involves *to + verb,* whereas the bare infinitive lacks the word *to.* These constructions are significantly different from any we have looked at so far, and analyzing them requires a level of abstraction that is quite a bit higher than what we have needed in the other sections. For reasons that are beyond the scope of this book, nonfinite verb constructions are deemed to be clauses, even though they do not look much like any clauses we have considered.

Nonfinite verb forms function as subjects, noun phrase complements, predicate complements, and adverbial modifiers, as illustrated in the following sentences:

74. *For him to invite Rod Harris* is crazy. (subject)
75. Mrs. DiMarco had a job *for him to do.* (NP complement)

The word *for,* which normally would be a preposition, is functioning as a complementizer in both 74 and 75.

76. Macarena wanted *to hold the baby.* (predicate complement)

The bare infinitive verb form, illustrated in sentence 77, also functions as a predicate complement:

77. Raul's mother made him *eat his vegetables.* (predicate complement)

As an adverbial modifier, infinitive verb forms are sentence-level modifiers, as in sentences 78 and 79:

78. *To appear calm,* Fred smiled. (adverbial)

79. Macarena, *to stay awake,* made a pot of coffee. (adverbial)

We also have instances in which nonfinite verb forms appear with negative markers, as in:

80. Macarena answered slowly, *not to be coy but to be clear.*

Our phrase-structure rules require some significant adjustment if we are to describe these structures; we must change the rule for $\overline{\text{S}}$, write a new VP rule, and change the rules for Aux and comp:

$$\overline{\text{S}} \rightarrow \left(\left\{ \begin{array}{l} \text{Sconj} \\ \text{comp} \\ \text{RP} \\ \varnothing \end{array} \right\} \right) (\text{NP}) \left\{ \begin{array}{l} \text{VP} \\ \overline{\text{VP}} \end{array} \right\}$$

$$\overline{\text{VP}} \rightarrow \text{Aux (inf) V (NP) (AdjP) (AdvP) (PP)}$$

$$\text{Aux} \rightarrow \left(\left\{ \begin{array}{l} \varnothing \\ \text{(tense)(neg)(do)} \\ \text{(m)(prog)(perf)} \end{array} \right\} \right)$$

$$\text{comp} \rightarrow \left\{ \begin{array}{l} \text{that} \\ \text{for} \\ \varnothing \end{array} \right\}$$

What does all this mean? Well, when we modified the $\overline{\text{S}}$ rule, we put parentheses around the dependent clause markers; this indicates that the marker now is optional. We have to do the same thing for NP to describe the fact that our nonfinite verb clauses do not have a visible object. Then we need to add a new constituent, $\overline{\text{VP}}$, which we call bar-VP. The $\overline{\text{VP}}$ will be the core of the new clause.

The second line of the modified rules indicates that the new clause has a verb with an optional infinitive marker (inf) and optional NP, AdjP, AdvP, and PP. To describe negatives, we also must adjust the expression for Aux, transforming it so that all constituents are optional (we must include a null marker also). The last step is to allow *comp* to include *for* as well as *that.*

With this fairly good set of phrase-structure rules, we have the ability to analyze a wide variety of sentences. Many of those we just covered have a very interesting structure when we look at their diagrams as illustrated in 4.78 – 4.80.

Sentence 4.78: *To appear calm,* Fred smiled. (adverbial)

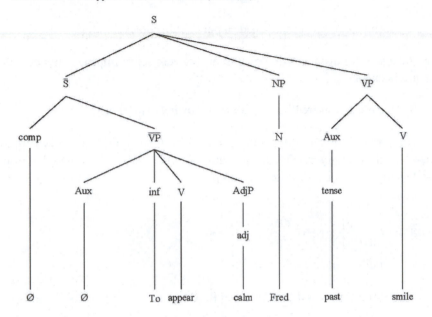

Sentence 4.79: Macarena, *to stay awake,* made a pot of coffee. (adverbial)

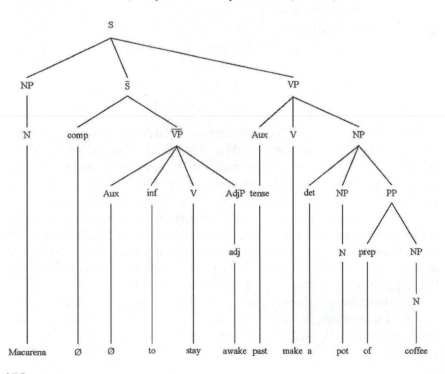

Sentence 4.80: Macarena answered slowly, *not to be coy but to be clear.*

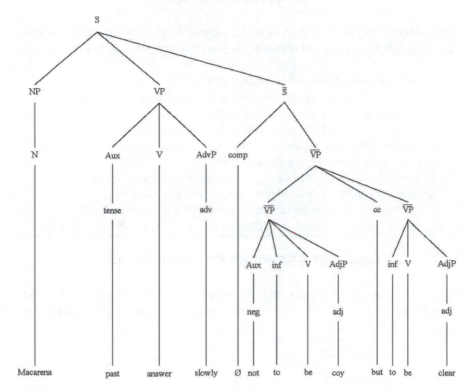

As with some of our other rules, the grammar requires us to add restrictions that cannot be written into the expressions. For example, the dependent clause marker is only optional in the context of S̄, and NP in the S̄ is optional only in the presence of VP̄. Bare infinitives only appear with certain kinds of verbs, such as *make,* and tense is optional only in a VP̄.

The necessity of adding these extra-rule restrictions is clearly a problem for phrase-structure grammar. The grammar would be more elegant, perhaps, if we could write the rules in such a way as to include these restrictions, but no one has figured out how to do that. As we approach the end of this chapter, it may be tempting to anticipate the next by intuiting that transformational-generative grammar solves the problem of restrictions. In this case, however, intuition would be wrong.

APPLYING KEY IDEAS

Directions: Analyze these sentences, identifying their constituents. Select five and diagram them using the phrase-structure rules presented in this chapter.

1. Fred wanted to talk to Macarena about marriage.
2. For him to buy an engagement ring at this point would be foolish.
3. Fred decided to discuss the matter with his priest.
4. Her fondness for the two boys made Macarena tell them a lie.
5. Buggsy told his goons that he had a message for them to deliver.
6. Raul asked Maria to go with him to the dance.
7. Macarena was delighted to get the invitation to Buggsy's next party.
8. To tell the truth, she was impressed with Buggsy's money.
9. For her to turn down the invitation would have been unthinkable.
10. She decided to tell Fred and Fritz that she wanted to visit her sick aunt.

SUMMARY OF PHRASE-STRUCTURE RULES

Before we go on to consider transformational-generative grammar in the next chapter, let's take a moment to review the final versions of the phrase-structure rules we've developed:

1. $XP \rightarrow XP \; CC \; XP$

2. $XP \rightarrow XP \; \overline{S}$

3. $S \rightarrow NP \; VP$

4. $NP \rightarrow (det) \; (AdjP) \; N \; (PP)$

5. $VP \rightarrow Aux \; V \; (NP) \; (AdjP) \; (AdvP) \; (PP)$

6. $V \rightarrow \begin{Bmatrix} V \\ V + prt \end{Bmatrix}$

7. $prt \rightarrow particle$

8. $AdvP \rightarrow \begin{Bmatrix} adv \\ NP \end{Bmatrix}$

9. $det \rightarrow \begin{Bmatrix} pro \\ NP + poss \\ art \end{Bmatrix}$

10.   pro → possessive pronoun

11.   poss → 's

12.   tense → $\begin{Bmatrix} \text{past} \\ \text{present} \end{Bmatrix}$

13.   neg → $\begin{Bmatrix} \text{no} \\ \text{not} \\ \text{never} \end{Bmatrix}$

14.   AdjP → $\begin{Bmatrix} \text{adj} \\ \text{NP} \end{Bmatrix}$ (AdvP) (PP)

15.   M → $\begin{Bmatrix} \text{will} \\ \text{shall} \\ \text{must} \\ \text{may} \\ \text{can} \end{Bmatrix}$

16.   prog → be -ing

17.   perf → have -ed/-en

18.   PP → prep $\begin{Bmatrix} \text{NP} \\ \text{RP} \\ \varnothing \end{Bmatrix}$

19. $\overline{\text{S}}$ → $\left(\begin{Bmatrix} \text{Sconj} \\ \text{comp} \\ \text{RP} \\ \varnothing \end{Bmatrix} \right)$ (NP) $\begin{Bmatrix} \text{VP} \\ \overline{\text{VP}} \end{Bmatrix}$

20. $\overline{\overline{\text{VP}}}$ → Aux (inf) V (NP (AdjP) (AdvP) (PP)

21.   comp → $\begin{Bmatrix} \text{that} \\ \text{for} \\ \varnothing \end{Bmatrix}$

22.   Aux → $\begin{Bmatrix} \varnothing \\ \text{(tense) (neg) (DO) (prog) perf)} \end{Bmatrix}$

APPLYING KEY IDEAS

Directions: Analyze the following sentences, identifying their constituents. Select five and diagram them using the phrase-structure rules presented in this chapter.

1. Mrs. DiMarco's nephew was Raul, who had a crush on Maria.
2. Maria worked in a jewelry store, but she did volunteer work at a hospital.
3. Raul dreamed of being a movie star.
4. When Macarena accepted Buggsy's invitation to the party, she did not know that Fred and Fritz would be there.
5. The party was at Buggsy's house in Beverly Hills, which Liberace had owned.
6. Macarena was impressed when she saw the celebrities at the party, and she was thrilled when Michael Star shook her hand.
7. Buggsy, who was drinking too much champagne, pulled Macarena into a dark corner and whispered sweet nothings in her ear.
8. He promised to take her to Mexico if he could get his wife to go to Paris for a holiday.
9. Macarena knew that she really wanted to take the trip.
10. Later, Macarena was stunned as Fred and Fritz walked into the party.
11. She set her drink down and walked over to her guys with an angry expression on her face.
12. Fred looked guilty because he remembered the party in Malibu when the paramedics had taken Buggsy away.
13. They gave Macarena a kiss, and she decided to mingle.
14. By accident, she stumbled upon Buggsy and Rita de Luna, who was wearing a white spandex jumpsuit that barely covered her anywhere.
15. Macarena could not believe her eyes, because Buggsy was trying to whisper sweet nothings into Rita's ear.
16. Rita, although aware of Buggsy's status, seemed uninterested.
17. Macarena slipped away, but Michael Star grabbed her and pulled her to the dance floor, where he started to boogie.
18. Suddenly, three goons lifted Michael up and carried him outside.
19. Macarena began to think that Buggsy might be rather selfish and possessive.
20. In that moment, she worried about Fred and Fritz because Buggsy would send the goons after them.
21. She also felt flattered that Buggsy wanted her, but the matter of Rita de Luna presented a big problem.
22. Macarena picked up another drink and thought about solutions as the music played.
23. She saw Fred and Fritz across the room, where they were talking intensely with Senator River Run and four young women.
24. Because she watched the news, Macarena knew that the women were Brazilian quadruplets who had discovered a cure for baldness in the Amazon jungle.

5

Noam Chomsky and Grammar

THE CHOMSKY REVOLUTION

Academics hate theoretical vacuums. Clearly, one existed with respect to phrase-structure grammar, which, although effective at describing languages, did not have a theoretical component. Structuralists were interested primarily in application, not theory. In the mid-1950s, a young linguist named Noam Chomsky set out to fill the theoretical vacuum by challenging most of the dominant assumptions underlying phrase-structure grammar.

Examining Chomsky's approach to grammar and its influence requires that we step away somewhat from the pragmatic. In the decade between the mid-1960s and mid-1970s, Chomsky's ideas about language and grammar had a significant influence on composition pedagogy, providing the basis for sentence combining and studies of style and writing maturity in children and promising to give teachers valuable insight into composing, reading, and language errors and growth. This influence faded, however. Sentence combining did not survive the shift to process, which focuses on entire papers rather than individual sentences, and the promised insight never materialized (see Williams, 2003a, for a more complete discussion). Also, there is no denying that Chomsky's views on grammar and language are complex and abstract. This chapter and the next explore the principles and theories, as well as some of the linguistic influences, of his work. They necessarily are demanding.

Although trained as a structuralist, Chomsky was intrigued by the idea that grammar could reflect a *theory of language* and, in turn, a *theory of mind*. He explored this idea around 1955 in a mimeographed paper titled "The Logical Structure of Linguistic Theory," which formed the foundation for his first book,

Syntactic Structures (1957). In this book, Chomsky argued that phrase-structure grammar was inadequate, and he proposed an alternative that proved to be so powerful that it revolutionized linguistics.

Many books have explored the significance of *Syntactic Structures* and related works, and what follows must, necessarily, be just a short summary. *Syntactic Structures* argued that phrase-structure grammar could never be a viable intellectual enterprise, offered a new grammar to replace it, reasserted rationalism as the *sine qua non* of linguistics, and established language study firmly as a branch of psychology. It vitalized the emerging field of cognitive psychology, gave birth to a new area of language study called psycholinguistics, influenced philosophers working in the philosophy of language, and gave English teachers a new tool for helping students become better writers. Given such intellectual influence, Chomsky has been, with good reason, widely hailed as one of the more important thinkers of the 20th century. Among modern intellectuals cited by other writers, Chomsky ranks eigth (Harris, 1993, p. 79).

That Chomsky found phrase-structure grammar lacking is an understatement. But why? Chomsky had several criticisms of phrase-structure grammar; perhaps the two most important involved describing and explaining language. Phrase-structure grammar focused on *languages* rather than *language*. Structuralists studied a given language in order to record as many features of it as possible, building a corpus, or body, of utterances that formed the foundation of the grammar for that language. These utterances were sentences and expressions that native speakers actually used, what are called *attested utterances*. The corpus was made up only of attested utterances, and the grammar was constructed so that it described them.

Chomsky argued that this whole approach was misguided. Basing grammar on attested utterances cannot lead, he claimed, to an adequate description of a given language for the simple reason that it is based on a finite set of utterances/sentences, whereas any language is potentially infinite. From this perspective, no matter how large the corpus, it never can constitute a significant portion of the language.

A related problem is that the resulting grammar may describe the corpus, but it does not describe all the grammatical sentences of the language. It fails to account for the fact that language is inherently creative, with few sentences ever being repeated exactly from one situation to the next. That is, phrase-structure grammar can describe just attested utterances; it cannot describe the infinite number of grammatical sentences that may have been uttered before the corpus was compiled, that have yet to be uttered, or that never will be uttered but are potential utterances. Even though phrase-structure rules such as those we developed in the previous chapter are sufficiently general to describe a vast array of sentences, this array is insignificant in the context of an infinite number of *possible* sentences.

Sentence 1, which is quite a common sentence, illustrates this point:

1. The day was hot.

This sentence reasonably would appear in the corpus of English, as would sentence 1a:

1a. The day was very hot.

We might even imagine sentence 1b in the corpus, because it, too, is rather common:

1b. The day was very, very hot.

At some point, however, we reach the limit of the number of *very*s we can put in front of the adjective and still be congruent with attested utterances. It is unlikely that anyone has ever uttered this sentence with, say, 53 *very*s. Nevertheless, such a sentence would be grammatical. In fact, we can imagine sentence 1c quite easily (where n equals an infinite number of iterations of the word *very),* and we also understand that it is grammatical:

1c. The day was very ... n hot.

Chomsky correctly observed that phrase-structure grammar did not have the means to account for our ability to insert an infinite number of adverbial intensifiers *(very)* in front of the adjective and still have a grammatical sentence. He concluded that "it is obvious that the set of grammatical sentences cannot be identified with any particular corpus of utterances obtained by the linguist in his field work" (1957, p. 15). In other words, a given body of sentences cannot fully identify a grammar of the language.

Chomsky's second major criticism focused on our intuitive understanding that certain types of sentences have some underlying relation, even though they look quite different from each other. Actives and passive are the most significant examples of sentences that we intuitively sense are related. The most common type of sentence in English follows SVO word order, has an agent as the subject, and an object, as in sentence 2:

2. Macarena kissed Fritz. (active)

The passive form of this sentence reverses the order of subject and object, modifies the verb phrase, and adds the preposition *by,* converting the subject to an object of the preposition, as in sentence 3:

3. Fritz was kissed by Macarena. (passive)

Although these sentences do not look the same, Chomsky argued that they express the same meaning and that the passive form is based on the active form. Phrase-structure grammar does not address the connection between such sentences; in fact, it would assign different sentence grammars to them: Sentence 2:

S → NP VP

VP → V NP

Sentence 3:

NP be –en V PP

PP → prep NP

Prep → by

In Chomsky's view, this approach fails to explain what our intuition tells us is obvious: These sentences are closely related. Sentence 2 somehow has been transformed into sentence 3. However, the only way to get at that relation was with a grammar that examined the *history of sentences,* one that looked beneath the surface and into what we may think of as *mentalese*—language as it exists in the mind before it reaches its final form, before it is transformed. In other words, Chomsky was keenly interested in exploring how people *produce* language, and in this respect he was quite different from the structuralists.

Chomsky proposed that the ability to look into the history of a sentence gives a grammar a *generative component* that reveals something about language production—about how people connect strings of words into sentences—but it also, he argued, allows us to understand something about how the mind operates. On these grounds, Chomsky developed a grammar that claimed a cognitive orientation because it focused on the transformation of mentalese into actual language. His goal was to develop a theory of language that provided a theory of mind. His theory of language was inherent in his grammar, which he called *transformational-generative* (T-G) grammar.

Universal Grammar

The grammar that Chomsky (1957) developed consists of a complex set of trans-formation rules. The goal of developing a cognitive theory of language necessar-ily required that the rules apply to all languages, given that human cognition is the same regardless of language or culture. Chomsky (1995) therefore argued that the rules were linked to a *universal grammar*. We might be tempted immedi-ately to conclude that universal grammar is identical to the linguistic universals associated with traditional grammar, but this would be a mistake. There is a con-nection, but a tenuous one. Linguistic universals refer to a relatively narrow range of shared features across languages, such as the fact that all languages have sub-jects and predicates, kinship terms, and a means of indicating when actions oc-cur. Universal grammar is different. In Chomsky's (1995) words:

> The human brain provides an array of capacities that enter into the use and understanding of language (the *language faculty*); these seem to be in good part specialized for that function and a common human endow-ment over a very wide range of circumstances and conditions. One com-ponent of the language faculty is a generative procedure ... that generates *structural descriptions* (SDs), each a complex of properties, in-cluding those commonly called "semantic" and "phonetic." These SDs are the *expressions* of the language. The theory of a particular language is its grammar. The theory of languages and the expressions they gener-ate is *Universal Grammar* (UG); UG is a theory of the initial state ... of the relevant component of the language faculty. (p. 167)

To be fair, we need to remember that phrase-structure grammar grew out of attempts in the late 19th and early 20th centuries to preserve American Indian tribal languages. The goal was to preserve the body of the languages as they were spoken—it was not to develop a theory of language or grammar. In fact, phrase-structure grammarians like Bloomfield (1933) were wary of univer-sal-grammar claims because in the past they had resulted in distortions in the records of investigated languages. Nevertheless, Chomsky's critique resonated strongly among scholars, in part because the alternative he proposed was ele-gant, powerful, and offered exciting new lines of research.

Today, almost 50 years later, the grammar Chomsky proposed to replace phrase-structure is still vibrant and, indeed, remains a significant factor in American language study. However, it does not have the same allure that it once had. One reason is that, over the years, Chomsky revised the grammar numerous times, which should have been viewed as perfectly reasonable and in keeping with scientific principles but which nevertheless has often been

viewed as quirkiness. In addition, the revisions made the grammar more abstract and thus more difficult to understand for anyone without significant
training in linguistics.

This chapter cannot provide an in-depth analysis of the grammar and all of
its permutations; instead, it will offer an overview that traces some of the significant features of the grammar from the initial formulation in 1957, concluding
with an examination of Chomsky's latest version.

DEEP STRUCTURE AND SURFACE STRUCTURE

In *Syntactic Structures,* Chomsky (1957) hinted that grammatical operations
related to language production work in the background. We do not really see
them at work; we see only the consequences of their application on an underlying structure. In *Aspects of the Theory of Syntax* (1965), Chomsky developed
this proposal by resuscitating the prestructuralism idea that there is something
underneath language, some universal feature of the human mind, such as logic,
that determines the substance of utterances. This argument effectively addressed the problem presented by actives and passives. A passive sentence like
Fritz was kissed by Macarena will have its corresponding active, *Macarena
kissed Fritz* as an underlying structure. This structure is then transformed to the
passive through a grammatical transformation rule.

Chomsky identified a basic grammatical structure in *Syntactic Structures* that
he referred to as *kernel sentences.* Reflecting mentalese, or *logical form,* kernel
sentences were where words and meaning first appeared in the complex cognitive process that resulted in an utterance. However, the overall focus in *Syntactic
Structures* was syntax, not meaning. In fact, Chomsky indicated that meaning
was largely irrelevant, as he illustrated in the sentence, "Colorless green ideas
sleep furiously" (1957, p. 15).[1] It means nothing but is nevertheless grammatical.

As impressive as *Syntactic Structures* was, the idea that any theory of language could ignore meaning was difficult to accept. Chomsky (1965) responded to the criticism in *Aspects of the Theory of Syntax,* in which he
abandoned the notion of kernel sentences and identified the underlying constituents of sentences as *deep structure.* Deep structure was versatile: It contained
the meaning of an utterance and provided the basis for transformation rules that
turned deep structure into *surface structure,* which represented what we actually hear or read. Transformation rules, therefore, connected deep structure and
surface structure, meaning and syntax.

---

[1]Chomsky (1957) wrote: "the notion 'grammatical' cannot be identified with 'meaningful' or 'significant' in any semantic sense" (p. 15).

Central to the idea that transformation rules serve as a bridge between deep structure and surface structure was the notion that transformations do not alter meaning. If they did, it would be difficult to justify the rules. Not only would they interfere with understanding, but they also would fail to realize Chomsky's goal of developing a grammar that looks into the history of a sentence. Deep structure was a convenient means of countering an alternative and nagging argument: that meaning is in the surface structure, that the words we hear and read mean pretty much what the person who created them intended.

Understanding the consequences of this argument is important. If meaning is in the surface structure, there is no need for a mediating structure between mind and utterances. Transformation rules become irrelevant. However, it was clear that some transformations *did* change meaning. In the early version of the grammar, negatives are generated from an underlying affirmative through a transformation rule. That is, the negative transformation turns a positive statement into a negative one, as in these sentences:

4. Maria wanted to dance with Raul.
4a. Maria did not want to dance with Raul.

The deep structure of 4a is 4, and the meanings are clearly different. The question transformation results in a similar change, turning an assertion into a question. Sentences like these presented a big problem for T-G grammar. Just prior to the publication of *Aspects,* Lees (1962) and Klima (1964) proposed that such difficulties could be eliminated by specifying certain phrase-structure markers in the deep structure of sentences like 4a, which triggered transformation. These markers—governing, for example, negatives and questions—were hypothesized to reside in the deep structure of all utterances and were said to be activated by contextual cues. Once activated, they triggered the transformation. The result is that sentence 4a would not have sentence 4 as its deep structure but instead would have sentence 4b:

4b. neg Maria wanted to dance with Raul.

This approach solved the problem in a clever way, and Chomsky adopted it. But the solution was highly artificial and not very satisfactory. In fact, it created more problems than it solved. Markers for questions and negatives seem straightforward, but we have no way of determining what kind of markers would govern such sentences as the following, which also undergo a change in meaning as a result of transformation:[2]

---

[2]Taken from Lee (2001).

- To solve the crossword is difficult.
- The crossword is difficult to solve.

T-G grammar specifies that the second sentence is derived from the first through what is called the *object-raising* transformation. (*The crossword* functions as the subject in the second sentence but as an object in the first.) In the first sentence, the focus is on the process of solving the crossword, whereas in the second it is not. Thus, the meaning of the first sentence can be generic; in the second, it cannot.

Or consider the following:

- Fritz gave the flowers to Macarena.
- Fritz gave Macarena the flowers.
- Fred cleared the table for his mother.
- *Fred cleared his mother the table.

How would markers account for the fact that the transformation that derived the grammatical *Fritz gave Macarena the flowers* from *Fritz gave the flowers to Macarena* also produces the ungrammatical *Fred cleared his mother the table*?

Equally problematic is that psychological research on language processing could find no evidence of markers of any type in language. It also failed to find any evidence that meaning resides anywhere other than in the surface structure.[3] The rationalist response has been that such evidence counts for very little, but there also is no intuitive basis for specifying such markers in the deep structure. Thus, these problems remained unsolved.

APPLYING KEY IDEAS

1. Explain two differences between phrase-structure grammar and transformational grammar.
2. The idea that there are internalized rules for generating sentences might lead to an assumption regarding composition. What might this assumption be?
3. The question of whether the theoretical features of transformational grammar are important for teachers has been debated for many years. What do you think might be the central issues in the debate, and what is your position?

---

[3]The next chapter examines this assertion more closely through the concept of *construal*, which centers meaning in the surface structure of sentences but connects it to context and to readers/hearers. Stated most simply, what a speaker means when uttering a sentence very often is not what the hearer construes it to mean.

THE BASICS OF TRANSFORMATION RULES

For the time being, let's set aside the issue of meaning in a theory of language and grammar and turn to the transformation rules themselves. Transformation rules have undergone significant change over the years. Necessarily, this section serves merely as an introduction to some of the rules in Chomsky's early work. Later in the chapter, we consider the current approach to transformations. Thus, the goal here is to provide some understanding of the general principles of T-G grammar rather than an in-depth analysis.

In *Syntactic Structures* and *Aspects,* Chomsky (1957, 1965) proposed a variety of transformation rules, some obligatory and others optional. The rules themselves specify their status. Rather than examining all possible transformation rules, only a few are presented, those that govern some common constructions in English. Before turning to these rules, however, it is important to note that transformations are governed by certain conventions. Two of the more important are the *ordering convention* and the *cycle convention.* When a sentence has several transformations, they must be applied in keeping with the order of the rules. In addition, when a sentence has embedded clauses, we must begin applying the transformations in the clause at the lowest level and work our way up. This is the cycle convention. Failure to abide by these conventions when analyzing structure with T-G grammar may result in ungrammatical sentences. What we see in T-G grammar, therefore, is a *formalistic* model of language production that employs a set of rigid rules that must operate in an equally rigid sequence to produce grammatical sentences.

The Passive Transformation

The relation between actives and passives was an important part of Chomsky's (1957) critique of phrase-structure grammar, so it is fitting that we examine the rule that governs passives first. Only sentences with transitive verbs can be passivized, and we always have the option of keeping them in the active form, which means that the passive transformation is an optional rule.

Consider sentence 5:

5. Fred bought a ring.

If we change this sentence to the passive form, it becomes:

5a. A ring was bought by Fred.

In keeping with the early version of T-G grammar, sentence 5 represents the deep structure of 5a. The process of the transformation is as follows: First, the object NP (*a ring*) shifted to the subject position. Second, the preposition *by* appeared, and the deep-structure subject (*Fred*) became the object of the preposition. Third, *be* and the past participle suffix appeared in the auxiliary, turning the deep structure verb *buy* into a passive verb form.

The grammar rule represents these changes symbolically. In this rule, the symbol ⇒ means "is transformed into":

Passive Transformation Rule.

NP_1 Aux V NP_2 (Fred bought a ring)

⇒

NP_2 Aux + be -ed/en V by + NP_1 (A ring was bought by Fred)

With respect to sentence 5:

NP_1 = Fred

NP_2 = a ring

V = bought

T-G grammar is predicated on examining the history of a given sentence, and the most effective way of doing so is through tree diagrams, which allow us to examine the deep structure and its corresponding surface structure. The process, however, is different from phrase-structure analysis because it requires a minimum of two trees, one for the deep structure and one for the surface structure. For more complicated sentences, there are more trees, each one reflecting a different transformation and a different stage in the history of the sentence. A convenient guideline is that the number of trees in a T-G analysis will consist of the number of transformations plus one. We can see how this process works by examining sentence 5a on the next page.

Passive Agent Deletion.   In many instances, we delete the agent in passive sentences, as in sentence 6:

6. The cake was eaten.

When the subject agent is not identified, we use an indefinite pronoun to fill the slot where it would appear in the deep structure, as in 6a:

6a. [Someone] ate the cake.

This deep structure, however, would result in the surface structure of sentence 6b:

Sentence 5.5a: A ring was bought by Fred.

Deep Structure

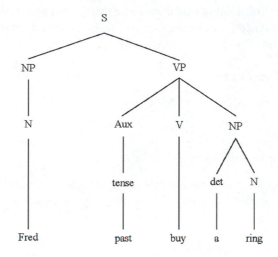

T-passive

Surface Structure

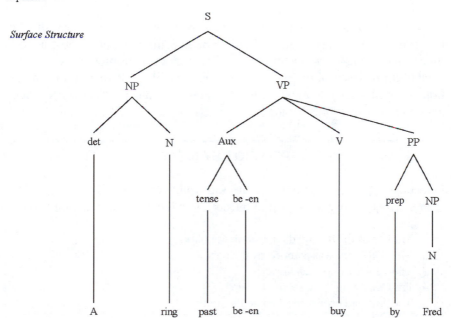

171

6b. The cake was eaten [by someone].

To account for sentence 6, T-G grammar proposes a deletion rule that eliminates the prepositional phrase containing the subject agent. We can say, therefore, that sentence 6 has undergone two transformations, passive and passive agent deletion. The deletion rule appears as:

Agent Deletion Rule.

NP_2 Aux + be -ed/en V by + NP_1

$\Rightarrow$

NP_2 Aux + be -ed/en V

In many cases, passive agent deletion applies when we don't know the agent of an action or when we do not want to identify an agent. Consider sentences 7 through 10:

7. The plot of the play was developed slowly.
8. The accident occurred when the driver's forward vision was obstructed.
9. The family was driven into bankruptcy.
10. Buggsy's favorite goon was attacked.

In sentence 7, we may not know whether the slow plot development should be attributed to the playwright or the director. In 8, the cause of the obstruction may be unknown, but we can imagine a scenario in which someone would not want to attribute causality, owing to the liability involved. Perhaps the obstruction occurred when the driver—a female, say—poked herself in the eye when applying mascara while driving.

APPLYING KEY IDEAS

Directions: Produce diagrams for the following sentences. Remember: T-G grammar requires two trees for any sentence that has undergone transformation.

1. Maria was thrilled by the music in the park.
2. Mrs. DiMarco was stunned by the news.
3. The door was opened slowly.
4. Fred was stung by a swarm of bees.
5. The nest had been stirred up deliberately.

Usage Note

Many writing teachers tell students not to use the passive in their work, and they urge students to focus on "active" rather than "passive" verbs. However, teachers usually do not link passive verbs to passive constructions but instead identify them as forms of *be,* which creates quite a bit of confusion. For example, students who write something like "The day was hot" might find their teacher identifying *was* as a passive verb—even though it is not in this case—and recommending a revision into something like "The sun broiled the earth." Of course, this revision entirely changes the meaning of the original, and in some contexts it will be inappropriate. The injunction against passives is meaningful in the belles-lettres tradition that has shaped the critical essay in literature, but it is misplaced in the broader context of writing outside that tradition.

In science and social science, the passive is a well-established and quite reasonable convention. It normally appears in the methods section of scientific papers, where researchers describe the procedures they used in their study and how they collected data. The convention is based on the worthwhile goal of providing an objective account of procedures, one that other researchers can use, if they like, to set up their own, similar study. This objectivity is largely a fiction because anyone reading a scientific paper knows that the authors were the ones who set up the study and collected the data. Nevertheless, the passive creates an air of objectivity by shifting focus away from the researchers as agents and toward the actions: "The data were collected via electrodes leading to three electromyograms." Moreover, contrary to what some claim, there is nothing insidious about the fiction of objectivity.

The widespread use of passive constructions outside the humanities indicates that blanket injunctions against them are misguided. It is the case, however, that the passive is inappropriate in many situations. Even in a scientific paper, the passive usually appears only in two sections—methods and results. In the introduction and conclusion sections, writers tend to use active constructions. In addition, most school-sponsored writing is journalistic in that it does not address a specific audience of insiders, as a scientific paper or even a lab report does. Journalistic writing by its very nature is written by outsiders for outsiders, and it follows conventions associated with the goals of clarity, conciseness, and generating audience interest. Any writing with these goals will not use passives with much frequency. Quite simply, it is easier for people to process sentences in the active voice with a readily identifiable subject.

Because the passive allows us to delete subject agents, many people use it to avoid assigning responsibility or blame. Sentence 8 on page 172, for example, came from an automaker's report on faulty hood latches in a certain line of cars. The driver's forward vision was obstructed by *the hood* (subject agent deleted) of his car, which unlatched at 60 miles an hour and wrapped itself around the windshield. The report writers could not include the subject agent without assigning responsibility and potential liability to the company, which they avoided for obvious reasons. Using the passive, with agent deleted, allowed them to describe the circumstances of the accident without attaching blame, which was left to a court to determine.

Industry and government are the primary but not the sole sources of such evasiveness. Passives appear spontaneously in the speech and writing of people who strive, for one reason or another, to be circumspect. The usage question regarding passive constructions, consequently, revolves around situation.

APPLYING KEY IDEAS

Directions: Examine a paper you've written for another class and see whether you can find any passive constructions. If you find some, determine whether they are appropriate to that context, given the previous discussion. If they are not appropriate, rewrite them in active form.

RELATIVE CLAUSE FORMATION

Relative clauses generally function as modifiers that supply information about nouns. In addition, they generally allow us to avoid repeating a noun. Consider the following sentences:

11. The message, *which Macarena had left near the flowers,* baffled Fred.
12. The wallet *that held Macarena's money* was in the trunk.
13. The woman *whom I love* has red hair.

Each of these sentences contains an independent clause and a relative clause. Each relative clause is introduced by a relative pronoun. The respective clauses are shown here:

11a. the message baffled Fred/*which* Macarena had left near the flowers
12a. the wallet was in the trunk/*that* held Macarena's money
13a. the woman has red hair/*whom* I love

Being able to identify the underlying clauses in a sentence that has a relative clause is an important part of understanding the grammar. On this account, if we consider the deep structure of each sentence, we need to look at the underlying noun phrases that get replaced during relativization. Doing so results in the clause pairs as shown:

11b. the message baffled Fred/Macarena had left *the message* near the flowers
12b. the wallet was in the trunk/*the wallet* held Macarena's money
13b. the woman has red hair/I love *the woman*

Teaching Tip

Students often find relative clauses confusing. Examining the underlying structure of sentences like those cited helps students recognize the duplicate NPs that must be changed to relative pronouns. It also provides a foundation for discussing sentence combining. Many students tend to write short, choppy sentences of the sort that we would have if we punctuated the clauses in 11b through 13b as independent clauses:

* *The message baffled Fred. Macarena had left the message near the flowers.*
* *The wallet was in the trunk. The wallet held Macarena's money.*
* *The woman has red hair. I love the woman.*

Showing students how to join these clauses through relativization is a quick and easy way to help them improve their writing. Indeed, as mentioned previously, T-G grammar provided the foundation for sentence combining, a very effective method for teaching students how to increase their sentence variety.

In T-G grammar, relative clauses are generated with the following rule:

Relative Clause Rule

$NP_{1\ S}[Y\ NP_2\ Z]_S$

$\Rightarrow$

$NP_{1\ S}[\text{wh-pro}\ Y\ Z]_S$

$$\text{wh-pro} \rightarrow \begin{Bmatrix} RP \\ prep + RP \end{Bmatrix}$$

This rule looks more complicated than it is. Y and Z are variables that T-G grammar uses to account for constituents that do not affect the transformation. The important factors are that NP_1 must equal NP_2 and that there is a clause, represented by S and the brackets, that branches off NP_1. The transformation takes NP_2 and turns it into a relative pronoun, which is designated as *wh-pro* because so many relative pronouns begin with the letters *wh*. In the event that NP_2 is the subject of the clause, the variable Y will be empty. In the event that NP_2 is the object, Y will be everything in front of the object.

The diagrams 5.11 through 5.13 illustrate how the transformation works.

Sentence 5.11: The message, *which Macarena had left near the flowers,* baffled Fred.

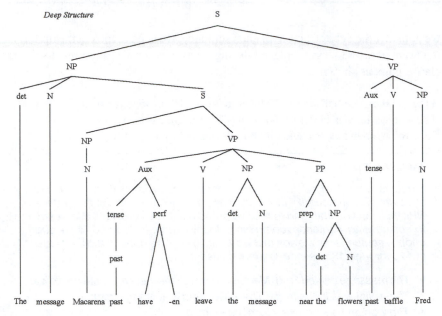

Deep Structure

Sentence 5.11: The message, *which Macarena had left near the flowers,* baffled Fred. (*continued*)

T-relative

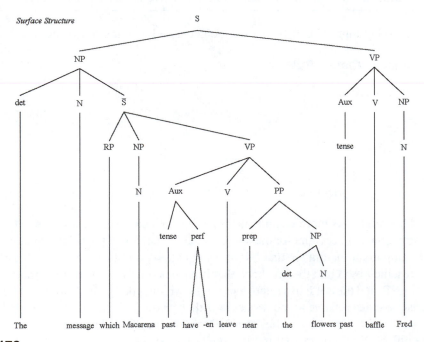

Surface Structure

Sentence 5.12: The wallet *that held Macarena's money* was in the trunk.

Deep Structure

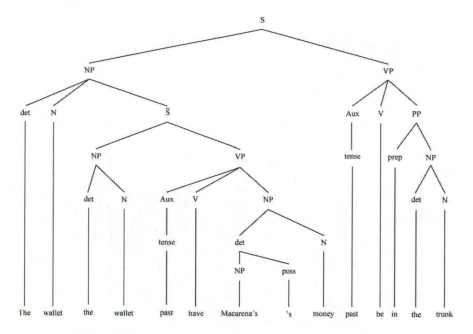

Sentence 5.12: The wallet *that held Macarena's money* was in the trunk. (*continued*)

T-relative

Surface Structure

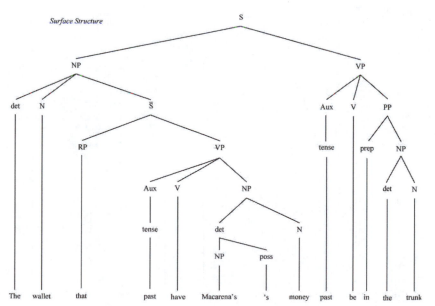

Sentence 5.13: The woman *whom I love* has red hair.

Deep Structure

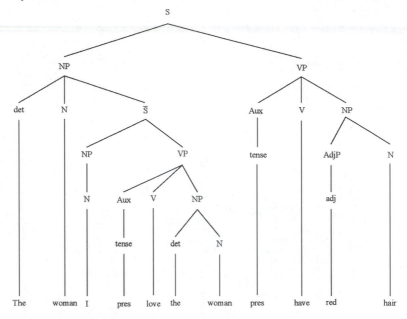

Sentence 5.13: The woman *whom I love* has red hair. (*continued*)

T-relative

Surface Structure

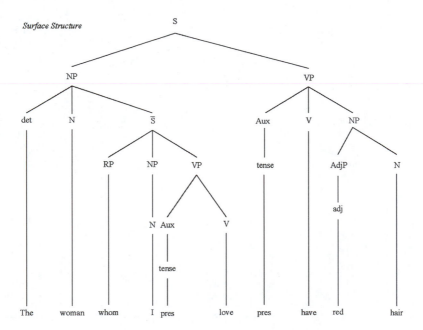

APPLYING KEY IDEAS

Directions: Identify the deep structure for each of the following sentences:

1. Macarena was the woman who danced on the bar at China Club.
2. The high heels that she was wearing almost slipped on the slick surface.
3. A bartender who knew her grabbed Macarena's arm.
4. The patrons who were seated at the bar laughed at her in good fun.
5. Macarena dropped the drink that she had in her hand.

Relativizing Noun Phrases in Prepositional Phrases

The relative clause rule recognizes that sometimes a duplicate NP appears as the object of a preposition, and we have to relativize it, as in sentence 14. This procedure raises some interesting grammatical questions:

14. Fred loved the house *in which the couple lived.*

This sentence is made up of the following clauses:

- Fred loved the house/the couple lived in the house

We see immediately that our RC transformation rule has a problem. It shifts the entire PP. But in English we can choose to shift just the noun phrase, as in sentence 14a:

14a. Fred loved the house which the couple lived in.

The underlying structure for 14a is exactly the same as for sentence 14:

- Fred loved the house/the couple lived in the house

Relativizing initially produces:

- Fred loved the house/the couple lived in which

At this point, there must be some mechanism or operation that allows us to decide between shifting the entire PP or just the relative pronoun. Here the transformation rule fails us. There is no elegant way of rewriting the rule to provide the necessary mechanism, so we are forced to provide it externally with an ad hoc provision.

Usage Note

The usage note on page 150 mentioned that most people use the relative pronouns *which* and *that* interchangeably. Although these words are very similar, they are not exactly the same: *Which* generally is used in nonrestrictive relative clauses, whereas *that* is used in restrictive ones. There is another difference, however, as sentence 14a illustrates—*which* can function as the object of a preposition, but *that* cannot. As noted, T-G grammar suggests that there is an intermediate step that lies between sentences 14 and 14a, in which the underlying form is:

• Fred loved the house/the couple lived in which

Nevertheless, common usage treats *which* and *that* as being the same, with one result being that we observe people using sentence 14b more often than 14a:

14b. ?Fred loved the house that the couple lived in.

Even though this sentence is quite common, close analysis suggests that it may violate the rules of the grammar. Sentence 14b would have the following as an intermediate underlying form:

• Fred loved the house/the couple lived in that

Now notice what happens if we shift the entire prepositional phrase to the front of the relative clause:

• *Fred loved the house in that the couple lived.

Other Relative Pronouns

Perhaps even more interesting than sentences with relativization in a prepositional phrase are sentences like 15:

15. They drove to Big Sur, *where the sea otters play.*

The deep structure of this sentence would have to be something along the lines of 15a:

15a. they drove to Big Sur/the sea otters play at Big Sur

We can duplicate *Big Sur* in both clauses, but we cannot duplicate the prepositional phrase that governs this NP. It is possible to suggest that the preposition *at* is not necessary in the deep structure, that we can substitute a marker for the preposition (e.g., Z). The transformation then would delete this marker as it relativizes the NP. This approach seems ad hoc and counterintuitive, however. It is also incongruent with analysis of sentences like 14 (Fred loved the house in which the couple lived), where the preposition *in* is a real preposition in the deep structure as well as the surface structure. In sentence 14, the preposition cannot be deleted because doing so produces an ungrammatical construction:

- *Fred loved the house *which the couple lived.*

We therefore are forced to propose that the prepositional phrases in the deep structure for sentences like 15 simply do not match. To make this proposal more reasonable, we also would have to propose that relative clauses involving the relative pronoun *where* are different from those involving relative pronouns such as *which, who,* and *whom.* Once we accept these proposals, accounting for what happens to the preposition *at* is fairly straightforward: It is absorbed into the relative pronoun. However, on principle, we should expect relativization to be congruent across structures.

In addition, what are we to do with nonstandard or ungrammatical but nevertheless widely used constructions, such as:

- *Where is he at?

In this common sentence, *at* is redundant because it is implicit in the word *where.* Are we forced to conclude that the same principle applies in relative clauses of the type illustrated in sentence 15? On what basis?

Equally troubling are sentences such as 16 and 17:

16. The reason why Fred was late was unknown.
17. Fred bought a thong swimsuit, which horrified his mother.

We must analyze sentence 16 as consisting of the following clauses:

16a. The reason was unknown/Fred was late for the reason

As in sentence 15, we are forced to assume that relativization alters the entire prepositional phrase, not just the NP.

Sentence 17 is even more problematic because there is no antecedent for the relative pronoun. The relative pronoun does not duplicate a noun phrase in the independent clause; instead, it seems to replace the semantic content of the independent clause. We might analyze sentence 17 as consisting of the following clauses:

17a. Fred bought a thong swimsuit/the fact that Fred bought a thong swimsuit hor-
      rified his mother

The Slow Demise of T-G Grammar

These analyses are not particularly satisfying, and they presage what lies
ahead. From the beginning, T-G grammar proposed that its focus on the history
of sentences was a significant strength. But as the previous discussion suggests,
reconciling deep structure with surface structure presents numerous problems.
If we were to move further into the grammar, we would see that these problems
become more severe, forcing increasingly ad hoc—or even far-fetched—explanations of deep structure.

   As Chomsky initially formulated the grammar, there was a clear separation between syntax and semantics, yet sentences like 16 and 17 indicate that
this separation is artificial and unsatisfactory. The relative pronoun's chief
syntactic function in sentences is to link the dependent and independent
clauses. However, it also has a clear semantic component that cannot be described in the grammar. One result is that the transformation rule presented on
page 175 for relative clauses does not work for sentences 15 through 17. It is
possible to formulate additional rules to account for sentences 15 and 16, but
such rules would be contrary to the goal of T-G grammar to provide general
rather than specific rules. It is not possible to formulate an additional rule for
sentence 17 because transformation rules do not, and cannot, address issues
of semantic content. Consequently, we have to rely on intuition and guess-
work to analyze the deep structure of such sentences and we also must rely on
an ever-expanding set of ad hoc constraints to account for linguistic features
that cannot be expressed in transformation rules. Such a reliance is not desirable in T-G grammar, which from the beginning strove to eliminate guess-
work through a rigorous formulation of the grammar. It is one of several
problems with T-G grammar that has not been satisfactorily solved. Add to
this the fact that work in psychology and neuroscience failed to find any evidence for the existence of transformation rules (see Williams, 1998, for a
summary), and the basis for T-G grammar seems suspect.

THE MINIMALIST PROGRAM

Chomsky was aware of the noted problems fairly early, but he so vigorously opposed other linguists' efforts to solve them that the ensuing debate came to be
called "the linguistics wars" (Harris, 1993). The role of meaning in a theory of
language and grammar was at the heart of the debate. Many linguists argued
that a viable theory of language must be able to account for meaning. Chomsky,

on the other hand, steadfastly insisted that meaning was irrelevant. According to Harris, when linguists like Lakoff and Ross pressed the importance of developing a method to bring meaning into grammatical theory, Chomsky's response was vicious:

> [He] repudiated successful early work, proposed radical changes to the *Aspects* model, and opened ad hoc escape channels for those changes—all on the basis of quite meager evidence—with no more motivation, as far as anyone could see, than to cripple the work of his most productive colleague and of some of the most promising former students they shared. (p. 142)

Eventually, necessity forced Chomsky to revise T-G grammar, reducing the role of deep structure in determining meaning. Simultaneously, he increased the emphasis on universal grammar and strengthened his argument that language is an innate faculty of mind. Each revision made his conceptualization of grammar, ironically, more abstract and more removed from language itself. As Taylor (2002) noted, Chomsky postulated "entities and processes ... which have no overt manifestation in actual linguistic expressions" (p. 7). Thus, writing and language arts teachers are not likely to find much in the revisions that is useful in the classroom. *Principles and parameters theory*, proposed in 1993, represented a dramatic departure, in many respects, from the grammar developed in *Syntactic Structures* and *Aspects*. Over the next two years, Chomsky (1995) elaborated the theory and renamed it the *minimalist program* (MP). Currently, the MP reflects his most fully developed ideas about language and grammar, although various linguists, such as Kitahara (1997) have made minor modifications.

Understanding the MP in any detail requires a high degree of training in linguistics, and even a bare-bones exploration would be well outside the scope of this text. Nevertheless, a discussion of general principles is possible and can provide a sense of what the program is about. The minimalist program is not entirely new but should be considered a substantial revision of T-G grammar. That is, Chomsky retained some T-G features and eliminated others, while in some cases going in new directions. What follows is an overview.

The Language Faculty and Language Acquisition

The question of language acquisition is of special interest to those of us who teach reading and writing. By the time children enter school, they have mastered nearly all the grammatical features of their home language, and the question of whether these features are mutable is important because home language seldom is congruent with school language.

The study of acquisition has been shaped by two assertions that, if accurate, present significant logical problems for our understanding of language. First, children experience a finite number of sentences but are nevertheless able to develop the grammar tools to produce a theoretically infinite number of sentences. Second, much of the language children encounter is qualitatively defective. In other words, acquisition must proceed in the face of impoverished stimuli. To address the problem, T-G grammar proposed an innate "language acquisition device" that induces the specific grammar rules of the child's home language from limited and distorted data. By about age 3, and certainly no later than age 6, most of the rules are in place, and the child applies those rules consistently.

The MP offers a slightly different model. Chomsky (1995) noted that "language acquisition is interpreted as the process of fixing the parameters of the initial state in one of the permissible ways" (p. 6). This statement requires a bit of interpretation. It is based on the idea that each child is born with a language faculty that contains a universal grammar. Although Chomsky's argument that humans have an innate language faculty was first strongly expressed in *Aspects* (1965), the MP modifies it by emphasizing the notion that the language faculty operates on its own principles, which are distinct from other cognitive operations. As Johnson and Lappin (1997) indicated, Chomsky's language faculty "is, at root, a biological organ. Hence, the properties of UG [universal grammar] are biologically determined properties of mind" (p. 45).

More on Universal Grammar. Chomsky's (1995, 2000) discussion of universal grammar and the properties of the language faculty is neither concrete nor unambiguous. According to Chomsky (1995), "It is clear that ... a theory of the initial state [of universal grammar] must allow only limited variation: particular languages must be largely known in advance of experience" (p. 4). On this account, at birth, the universal grammar is in an *initial state of zero,* what we may think of as chaos with "borders." These borders contain the chaos of potential language-specific grammars and ensure that the range of grammars is not infinite, a necessary restriction owing to limitations on cognitive processing. The child's home language "fixes" the grammar of the specific language—for example, fixing SVO as the basic parameter if the home language is English or SOV if the home language is Japanese.

The term itself—*universal grammar*—may be unfortunate. There are about 5,000 distinct languages, yet their grammars are remarkably similar. On the face of it, we have no reason to expect this. Let's consider just one, albeit important, example.

In chapter 3, we examined head words and saw how phrases are attached to them to form modifiers. The idea of head words also applies to the basic structure of languages. In English's SVO pattern, the object follows the verb. This pattern is repeated in prepositional phrases: The object NP follows the preposition. In these instances, the verb and the preposition serve as head words for their NP objects. Moreover, we find this same pattern in many other languages. As a result, we call them "prepositional" languages, signifying that the head word is in the "pre," or initial, position.

When we look at Japanese, we find the opposite pattern, SOV. That is, head words *follow* the NP object. Thus, the English sentence *Fred drank sake* would be structured as *Fred sake drank* (*Fred-wa sake-o nonda*) in Japanese. We therefore call Japanese and other languages with this pattern "postpositional" languages. What's interesting is that about 95% of all human languages are either prepositional or postpositional.

The idea of universal grammar is partially based on this observation. Chomsky (1965, 1995) proposed that humans have only one grammar and that the amount of variation is severely limited. Acquisition involves setting the specific parameters that characterize the child's home language, such as whether it is prepositional or postpositional. The question that immediately arises is whether this feature of grammar is unique to language or whether it is a feature of human cognition in general. Although the current state of knowledge does not allow us to answer this question definitively, it is the case that cognitive operations are widely viewed as hierarchical (e.g., Bradshaw, Ford, Adams-Webber, & Boose, 1993; Grossberg, 1999; Pinker, 2002; Schilperoord, 1996).[4] Applying hierarchy to language means that there will be a tendency to put the most important part of any utterance or sentence at the beginning rather than at the end or in the middle. And this is just what we see: Most languages have a word order that puts the subject first. On this basis, it seems reasonable to suggest that if linguistic processes are not unique but rather are a specialized manifestation of general cognitive operations, the term "universal grammar" can be an obstacle to better understanding acquisition and language-specific grammars.

The language faculty is deemed to consist of four parts: the lexicon, logical form, phonetic form, and the computational system—all of which are governed

---

[4]Note, however, that Edmondson (2000) pointed out that hierarchy in cognitive operations may be an illusion based on the fact that all actions, even psychophysiological ones, are sequential. As he stated, "A significant byproduct of the effect of the sequential imperative on cognitive entities is the generation of structures which appear to be principles of organization—e.g., hierarchies—but which are in fact artifacts of behaviour" (p. 9).

by the universal grammar. According to Chomsky (1995, 2000), these four parts work together in fairly complex ways that allow us to produce language. Thus, language acquisition in the minimalist program consists of the following stages:

1. At birth the language faculty contains the universal grammar.
2. Birth immerses the infant in the home-language environment, which "fixes" the parameters of the universal grammar so they are consistent with the grammar of the home language.
3. Immersion also provides the child with a lexicon, a list of individual words with real-world correlates.
4. Language production consists of selecting words from the lexicon and putting them into logical and phonetic form.

The MP account of acquisition solves the problems associated with acquisition. If children are born with the core components of grammar, they will encounter little difficulty in induction from limited and distorted input. The reason is straightforward: The child already "knows" the language, so poverty of input will not be a detriment to acquisition; likewise, distorted input will be filtered out by the parameters of the universal grammar and will have no effect on acquisition.

The Computational System

The computational system is a key feature of the MP. Chomsky (1995) proposed that this system selects items from the lexicon and assigns them a logical and a phonetic form. The logical form contains meaning, and the phonetic form is a manifestation of sound correspondences. We can imagine how the process might work by considering a word like *bad,* which can mean bad or good, depending on context and inflection. The computational system would calculate the context, select the word *bad,* and assign the appropriate meaning. We should note, however, that although the logical form of words with semantic content is reasonably clear—we might consider it to be a concatenated series of propositions and attributes—it is not at all clear for function words that have significantly less semantic content.

In the model of language acquisition outlined here, the computational system, or something like it, is inevitable. If the language faculty indeed merely sorts through all available grammar patterns, minimal "learning" is involved. The real cognitive work of language production must consist of selecting the right words, with all their myriad attributes, and putting them in the correct form. Some kind of sorting and processing ability—if not mechanism—would be required to do this.

The computational system, however, is not a new idea. The majority of work in cognition is predicated on a computational model, so its application to language seems intuitive and commonsensical. In its simplest form, the computational model of cognition posits that we process information and generate ideas and language by putting small pieces of data together into larger ones. Sometimes this process is referred to as *compositionality*. A useful analogy is the way we form written words by combining the letters of the alphabet in principled ways. The word *run,* for example, is composed by combining the letters *r, u,* and *n.* We must note that "The idea that language processing involves combining small linguistic units to create larger ones ... [is so compelling that] few people have been able to escape its allure" (Williams, 1993, p. 545). We should not be surprised, therefore, to recognize in Chomsky's (1995) computational system a view of cognition that has dominated psychology for decades. What makes Chomsky's computational system remarkable is that it reflects what we call "strict compositionality." The product of composition is not only the form of words but also their meaning. The meaning of an individual sentence, on this account, consists of the combination of the individual words.

Competence and Performance

In all of his earlier work, Chomsky had proposed *competence* and *performance* as a means of accounting for the fact that people are prone to produce errors in language even when they have developed grammar rules that will produce only grammatical sentences. The MP retains the competence/performance distinction, but the terms have different meanings. Linguistic competence in the T-G model is the inherent ability of a native speaker to make correct judgments about whether an utterance is grammatical; performance is what we actually do grammatically with the language, given the fact that a range of environmental factors can upset our delicate competence. In the minimalist program, competence is more closely associated with Chomsky's (1995, 2000) view that the language faculty and universal grammar represent a "perfect" system for generating language. He stated, for example, that the language faculty "not only [is] unique but in some interesting sense [is] optimal" (1995, p. 9) and that "there are even indications that the language faculty may be close to 'perfect'" (2000, p. 9). This revision changed the notion of competence significantly, shifting it from grammaticality judgments to a constructive process based on biology. Competence on this account relates to humans in general as possessors of the language faculty, not to individuals.

Performance also took on a different meaning. On the one hand, Chomsky (1995) asserted that performance consists of having a language and the mental mechanisms necessary to produce that language. But in doing so, he recognized the limitations of this proposal and noted that a full explanation of "performance" would require "the development of performance theories, among them, theories of production and interpretation. Put generally, the problems are beyond reach" (p. 18). Thus, performance in the MP has a theoretical basis that must model how people generate and understand language, a task that Chomsky deemed beyond us.

The End of Transformation Rules

Perhaps the most striking feature of the minimalist program was the elimination of transformation rules and deep structure. As Chomsky (1995) noted, "D-Structure disappears, along with the problems it raised" (p. 189). The lexicon takes on a central role, assuming responsibility for many of the functions once performed by transformation rules. As Chomsky (1995) explained:

> The lexicon is a set of lexical elements, each an articulated system of features. It must specify, for each such element, the phonetic, semantic, and syntactic properties that are idiosyncratic to it, but nothing more.... The lexical entry of the verb *hit* must specify just enough of its properties to determine its sound, meaning, and syntactic roles through the operation of general principles, parameterized for the language in question. (pp. 130–131)

Stated another way, the computational system selects words from the lexicon and combines them into linguistic expressions in keeping with the various semantic and syntactic restrictions associated with each word.

This departure from T-G grammar must be considered carefully to gauge its effects. The minimalist program keeps meaning as a form of mentalese, but now meaning is deemed to reside in the individual words that make up the lexicon. The meaning of sentences arises from their particular combinations of words. Advantages appear immediately. No longer do we face the embarrassing situation of transformations that change meaning or that sometimes produce ungrammatical sentences. Syntax determines meaning, for the structural restrictions of words themselves will dictate whether a word functions as, say, a subject or a verb.

In the MP, the process of combination—or derivation, in keeping with T-G terminology—involves only four rules: *merge, agree, move,* and *spellout.* Let's consider a simple sentence and see how the process works:

18. Fred kissed Macarena.

The three words of this sentence exist in the lexicon, along with their associated features. For example, both *Fred* and *Macarena* are proper nouns and are singular; *kiss* is a transitive verb marked with the past tense. (These words have additional features, such as both proper nouns designate people, *Fred* is male and *Macarena* is female, *Macarena* is a Spanish name, men and women engage in an act called "kissing," and so on, but these features aren't particularly relevant at this point, although they will be in the next chapter, when we consider association networks.) The computational system selects these words and combines them using an operation called *merge,* creating a tense phrase consisting of a verb phrase with two nouns and a verb. To establish agreement between the verb and the agentive noun and to tense the verb, the computational system applies an operation called *agree*. Next, the agentive noun must be relocated to the head of the tense phrase. This process is accomplished through an operation called *move*. The final operation consists of what is referred to as a grammar/phonology interface rule called *spellout* that produces the target sentence. The MP maintains that these operations govern all sentences. The diagram on page 190 illustrates the steps in the derivation and serves as an aid to visualizing the process.

The End of Grammar?

In keeping with the emphasis on universal grammar, Chomsky (1995) proposed that all languages are the same, except for how they form words: "Variation of language is essentially morphological in character, including the critical question of which parts of a computation are overtly realized" (p. 7). This notion is in many respects similar to the traditional views on language that existed prior to the development of phrase-structure grammar, a point discussed in chapter 1.

Questions immediately arise from Chomsky's (1995) proposal. What about grammar? How can language variation be limited to morphology when, as in the case of Japanese and English, they have very different grammars? Chomsky's response may seem daring—he eliminated the concept of grammar, per se:

> The notion of construction, in the traditional sense, effectively disappears; it is perhaps useful for descriptive taxonomy but has no theoretical status. Thus, there are no such constructions as Verb Phrase, or interrogative and relative clause, or passive and raising constructions. Rather, there are just general principles that interact to form these descriptive artifacts. (pp. 25–26)

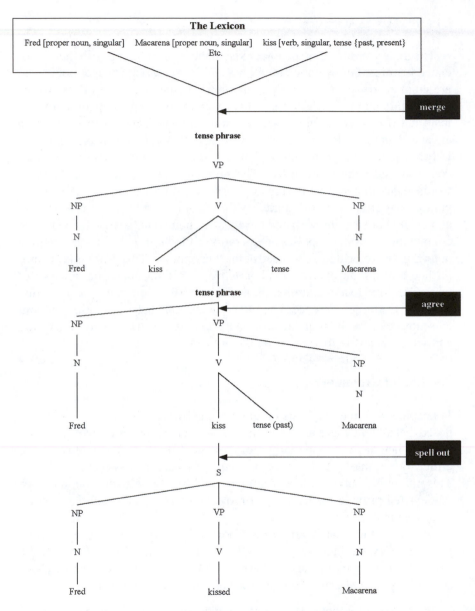

FIG. 5.1. The Minimalist Program Analysis of *Fred kissed Macarena.*

190

A CRITIQUE OF THE MINIMALIST PROGRAM

A full critique of the minimalist program would be lengthy, owing to the complexity of the theory. However, some discussion of key elements is possible. Without question, the MP's generalization of production rules and elimination of deep structure offer a significant improvement over transformational-generative grammar. T-G grammar rules struck many working in linguistics and cognitive science as being both too numerous and too complex to reflect actual language production. In addition, a range of studies found no evidence that meaning resided in the deep structure. By eliminating deep structure, the minimalist program overcomes the problem inherent in this T-G claim, as well as the claim that surface structure was merely a manifestation of syntax. If nothing else, common sense tells us that meaning permeates the entire language system, and the MP allows for this.

The exploration of universal grammar represents a clear step forward in linguistic analysis. Although the term may be misleading or even inappropriate (as discussed previously), there is no question that the MP identifies an important area for future research. Why do the world's languages show so little variation at the deepest level? Does the structure of language reveal operational limitations of the brain?

Other features of the minimalist program are a bit problematic. In *Syntactic Structures,* Chomsky (1957) argued that the crucial problem for phrase-structure grammar was its lack of either descriptive or explanatory adequacy. That is, phrase-structure grammar did not sufficiently describe or explain language. T-G grammar, he claimed, was superior because it was descriptively and explanatorily sound.

Time showed that these claims were inaccurate (see Harris, 1993). According to Chomsky (1995), the minimalist program eliminates the deficiencies of T-G grammar. He noted, for example, that "A theory of UG [universal grammar] is true if ... it correctly describes the initial state of the language faculty. In that case it will provide a descriptively adequate grammar.... A true theory of UG meets the condition of *explanatory adequacy*" (pp. 18–19). The problem, of course, is that we have no way of ascertaining whether a theory of universal grammar correctly describes the initial state of the language faculty—or even whether there *is* a language faculty as described in the MP. Moreover, the MP focuses so much on explanation that it neglects description. Stated another way, the MP aims narrowly to describe the cognitive operations related to language production and summarily dismisses the "descriptive taxonomy" of language. This taxonomy is not inconsequential, especially for teachers and others who must work with the structure of language. In addition, the description of cognitive operations necessarily is metaphorical; it does not convey a realistic account of actual mental activities, and given the total lack of empirical data from cognitive and neuroscience to support the description, one could easily conclude that it never can. Taylor (2002) noted in this context that "the theory has been driven by its own internal logic, not by any considerations deriving from independently established facts about human cognition" (p. 8).

The Language Faculty

Taylor's (2002) criticism is not trivial. That humans have a predisposition to develop and use language is not really debatable. Nor can we deny that this predisposition—like our bipedalism, for example—is innate. But is the language faculty a unique biological function, or is it an amalgam of cognitive processes that, over evolutionary time, have become integrated for language? We know that two areas of the brain, Broca's and Wernicke's, have significant responsibility for processing language. Damage to these areas of the left hemisphere interferes with language production and comprehension, respectively. However, it seems unlikely that they could house Chomsky's (1995) language faculty because these areas work in cooperation with others, such as the cerebral cortex, amygdala, hippocampus, cerebellum, and basal ganglia. Brain imaging has shown that writing in response to a simple oral prompt, for example, begins in the auditory cortex, which activates Wernicke's area, which in turn activates the angular gyrus.[5]

One could make the argument, perhaps, that the connections to other areas of the brain are ultimately insignificant, that the language faculty is nevertheless centered in Broca's area. The argument is problematic for several reasons. Chomsky (1995) suggested that the sole function of the language faculty is language processing. However, to date there is no evidence that any area of the brain has this sole function. Grodzinsky (2000) argued that Broca's area is not even responsible for syntax but rather is the "neural home to mechanisms" involved in moving phrases from one location to another (p. 4). Müller, Kleinhans, and Courchesne (2001) and Müller and Basho (2004) found that Broca's area is regularly involved in "nonlinguistic processes" associated with visuo- and audiomotor functions.

In addition, a large body of brain imaging research indicates that bilinguals have two distinct areas for language processing (Bhatnagar, Mandybur, Buckingham, & Andy, 2000; Dehaene, 1999; Fabbro, 2001;

---

[5]Such imaging studies are not without their own problems. As Fabbro (2001) pointed out, in a great deal of research "brain activation was studied with tasks that are too complex ... and whose linguistic and pragmatic nature is still scarcely known; these tasks generally simultaneously activate many linguistic, pragmatic, and affective structures, thus making it difficult to interpret data" (p. 216).

Hernandez, Martinez, & Kohnert, 2000; Illes et al., 1999; Kim, Relkin, Lee, & Hirsch, 1997; Paradis, 1999; Perani et al., 1998). This research suggests that the notion of a localized language faculty described by the minimalist program is not viable. Such a large lateral region of the cerebral cortex is involved in language processing that we cannot even state that the left hemisphere is the "language center" with much accuracy (Bhatnagar et al., 2000; Ojemann, 1983). As Fabbro (2001) reported, the right hemisphere "is crucially involved in the processing of pragmatic aspects of language use," especially during second-language learning (p. 214). Fabbro also noted that "when a second language is learned formally and mainly used at school, it apparently tends to be more widely represented in the cerebral cortex than the first language, whereas if it is acquired informally, as usually happens with the first language, it is more likely to involve subcortical structures (basal ganglia and cerebellum)" (p. 214).

These findings are supported by a variety of studies of children who at birth were diagnosed as having one diseased hemisphere that would lead to death if left alone. In some cases, the entire left hemisphere was removed, but these children nevertheless developed language function with only minor deficits (Day & Ulatowska, 1979; Dennis & Kohn, 1975; Dennis & Whitaker, 1976; Kohn, 1980). The right hemisphere "rewired" itself to assume responsibility for language processing.

Also worth noting is that neurological language function differs from person to person to a significant degree even among monolinguals. When people undergo surgery to remove brain tumors, the operation must be performed with the patient awake so that the medical team can map the locations of the various language areas by asking him or her to respond orally to questions. If the language faculty is a bodily organ, as Chomsky (1995, 2000) argued, it seems reasonable to expect it to be located pretty much in the same place for everyone. In this light, the assessment of the Society for Neuroscience takes on added significance: "The neural basis for language is not fully understood" (2002, p. 19).

Certainly, one could claim that a theory of grammar or a theory of language does not need to be congruent with the findings in medicine and neuroscience, but is any theory relevant that is lacking empirical validation? Consequently, Chomsky's (1995, 2000) claim for a centralized language function—a "biological organ," as he called it (2000, p. 117)—appears insupportable. Unless evidence to the contrary emerges through brain research, we are left to conclude that "language faculty" is, at best, a poor choice of words to describe an array of cognitive processes that together allow us to produce and process language.

Acquisition and Innateness

When discussing the MP's model of language acquisition, we saw that our understanding of how children acquire language is based on the claim that children develop language even though they experience impoverished input, qualitatively and quantitatively deficient. This claim is so powerful that it has shaped the majority of all research and thought associated with acquisition.

But just what is the basis for this claim? Relatively few studies have investigated this facet of language acquisition, and they report little evidence to support the poverty of stimulus model. Pullum (1996) and Sampson (1997), for example, found no indication that parental language was deficient in any respect. Newport, Gleitman, and Gleitman (1977) reported that "the speech of mothers to children is unswervingly well formed. Only one utterance out of 1,500 spoken to the children was a disfluency" (p. 89). Hendriks (2004) concluded after reviewing various studies that "the language input to the child seems to be neither 'degenerate' nor 'meager'" (p. 2). Perhaps this conclusion would be obvious to anyone who is a parent or who has observed parents, other adults, and children interacting, for even a casual assessment indicates that parents and other adults talk to children frequently and clearly. Indeed, a variety of research leads one to suspect that some sort of biological imperative is at work, motivating parents not only to immerse infants in language but also to modify intonation and rhythm to ensure that each utterance is articulated clearly (e.g., Fernald, 1994; Fernald, Swingley, & Pinto, 2001).

The difficulty here is subtle. The MP's universal grammar was proposed, in part, to solve the logical problem created by the poverty of stimulus assumption. If this assumption is false—or at least unsupported by the data—the rationale for universal grammar becomes questionable. Whether language is the product of universal cognitive processes rather than a specific faculty with a universal grammar again becomes an important issue.

In the next chapter, we look more closely at language acquisition, but at this point we should note that alternatives to Chomsky's formalist model do exist. Rumelhart and McClelland (1986), for example, suggested that language acquisition is linked to the human talent for pattern recognition, not to any innate device related to grammar. Grammar, from any perspective, is a pattern of word combinations. Chomsky's (1995) argument is that our ability to internalize this pattern and use it to produce language is not only specific but also distinct from all other pattern-recognition processes. In this view, language represents a perfect system fundamentally different from all other mental faculties (Chomsky, 2000).

Generally, human mental abilities are understood to have evolved through a process of natural selection. How the language faculty could develop in isolation from other mental faculties, therefore, is a bit of a mystery. Language is, as far as we know, a relatively recent phenomenon, having emerged between 100,000 and 40,000 years ago. Chomsky (1972), Gould (1991), and others argued on this basis that there was insufficient time for language to evolve as an adaptation through natural selection and thus is an *exaptation,* a term that describes the coopting of previously evolved functions to do new things. However, if Rumelhart and McClelland (1986) are correct, language not only developed through evolutionary processes but also is a specialized adaptation of the general cognitive function of pattern recognition. In this case, language is innate in the same sense that our abilities to recognize patterns and establish cause–effect relations are innate.

Calvin (2004), drawing on his work in neurobiology, made a compelling argument that the origin of language was associated with improved planning among early hominids. Planning involves structured thought, particularly with respect to cause–effect relations. For this reason, it was popular a few decades ago to propose that language developed as a result of organized hunting—"until it turned out that chimps had all the basic moves without using vocalizations. Now it is supposed that much of the everyday payoff for language has to do with socializing and sexual selection, where 'verbal grooming' and gossip become important players" (p. 50). In Calvin's view, the evolution of language is related to general cognitive development through an expanded neocortex, which began with *Homo erectus* 1.8 million years ago. The cognitive apparatus necessary for language would have significantly predated actual language, if Calvin is correct. Improved socialization and sexual selection had evolutionary consequences that tapped existing abilities.

The roots of Chomsky's (1995) view extend to Plato, who believed that a wide range of human behaviors and attributes were innate. Prior to the 17th century, virtue, morality, mathematical ability, even the concept of God, were thought to be innate. Failures in virtue or morality, and even disagreements about what constituted "the good," were explained on the basis of functional capacity. The virtuous person had a grasp of right and wrong and behaved appropriately, whereas his or her counterpart was deemed to be mentally defective in some way. If we consider language as an innate "perfect system," we are led ineluctably to the conclusion that the problems in language that we can observe on a daily basis—such as ungrammatical sentences in writing—are the result of a defective functional capacity. A perfectly functioning language faculty would not produce errors. This is difficult terrain. Can we legitimately conclude that the numerous errors we see in speech and writing, particularly that of our students, are the result of defective functional capacity? Would not such a conclusion lead inevitably to another—that many students simply cannot be taught?

APPLYING KEY IDEAS

Quietly observe adults interacting with infants and toddlers in two or three different contexts. Malls and grocery stores won't be good choices. As best you can, record how the adults use language with the children. What conclusions can you draw from your observations?

6

Cognitive Grammar

WHAT IS COGNITIVE GRAMMAR?

The previous chapter offered an overview of transformational generative grammar and the minimalist program, allowing us to examine some of their strengths and weaknesses. T-G grammar was characterized as "formalistic" because it employs a set of rigid rules that must operate in an equally rigid sequence to produce grammatical sentences. Although the MP is different in many respects, it, too, is formalistic: It has fewer rules, but they operate in much the same fashion as T-G rules.

The issue of formalism is important because it led several scholars to question whether T-G grammar or the minimalist program truly help us understand the nature of language. Recall that Chomsky revolutionized linguistics in 1957 by arguing that language study should reflect a theory of mind. As a result, all modern grammars are concerned with and influenced by studies of cognition to one degree or another. This characteristic is one of the more important factors that differentiate modern grammars from traditional grammar. Although Chomsky laid the groundwork for the connection between grammar and cognition, many would argue that he did not build on this foundation. Some would even argue that his approach is fundamentally flawed: Rather than exploring what the mind can tell us about language, his work has focused on what language can tell us about the mind. Such an approach may have made sense before technology gave us the means to increase our understanding of the brain's operations, but is it reasonable today, given the advanced state of science and technology? The answer to this question seems clear when we consider that the minimalist program describes a system of cognitive operations that appear to have little connection to how the brain actually works. On this account, various scholars do not consider Chomskian grammar to be cognitive (Taylor, 2002).

We also saw in chapter 5 that the question of meaning cannot be addressed adequately in a formalist grammar. Meaning, when considered at all, is understood to reside in mentalese, the lexicon, or the sentence. Neither T-G grammar nor the MP take into account that we use language to communicate with other people in a meaningful context. We might be able to claim that meaning resides in sentences if we limit our understanding to example sentences that lack a context, but we cannot do so if we are to consider actual language use. People frequently do not say what they mean, and they often construe statements in ways that are different from what was intended. It seems reasonable to propose that any viable study of language and grammar should take these factors into account.

These issues have troubled some linguists for years, motivating them to seek an alternative to Chomskian formalism. A significant step forward occurred in the 1980s when Ronald Langacker, a linguist, and David Rumelhart, a cognitive scientist, came into contact at the University of California, San Diego. What emerged in two important books by Langacker (1987, 1990) was *cognitive grammar.*

As with the discussion of transformational grammar and the minimalist program in the previous chapter, what follows necessarily is an overview rather than an in-depth analysis. This chapter aims merely to present some of the more important principles of cognitive grammar. It is crucial to note at the outset that cognitive grammar does not consist of a new set of grammar rules. Nor does it involve new sentence diagrams, new classifications, or new grammatical analyses. Instead, cognitive grammar involves a new way of looking at language and its relation to mind. The sections that follow examine what this means.

MODULARITY

Transformational-generative grammar and the minimalist program emphasize formal rules and treat language as a self-contained system that is largely unrelated to other cognitive operations and mental capacities. This approach is based on the idea that the brain is *modular,* divided into discrete processing units that function independently of one another. There is no doubt that the brain is modular to a significant degree. For example, the senses—sight, hearing, smell, and taste—operate as independent modular systems. Whether language also is modular, however, is controversial and uncertain (e.g., Barkow, Cosmides, & Tooby, 1992; Calabretta, Nolfi, Parisi, & Wagner, 2000; Carruthers & Chamberlain, 2000; Chomsky, 2000; Fodor, 1983).

Cognitive grammar accepts a limited view of modularity, proposing that language is intricately connected to other cognitive functions and is an important part of the social, cultural, biological, and psychological dimensions of human existence. Language processing is recognized as involving a complex interaction among different areas of the brain—the temporal lobe associated with receptive speech, the parietal lobe with writing, the frontal lobes with motor speech, and so forth. Consequently, language is deemed to be embedded in a variety of interconnected cognitive operations and is necessarily influenced by them. As mentioned in the previous chapter, we can see this interconnectivity through brain imaging, but we don't need to rely exclusively on technology here: We need only consider how a person's emotional state affects language.[1] Thus, cognitive grammar strives to explain language and its structure in terms of both brain function and communication. Lamb (1998), for example, noted that all cognitive activity, including language, consists of complex patterns of neural firing and inhibition, like switches turning on and off. Attempts to describe these patterns in terms of rules and transformations, Lamb noted, seem farfetched. He argued that the study of grammar and language should be linked to the study of neurocognitive processes. As we see later in this chapter, this approach lends itself to helping us understand some of the problems we encounter when teaching language.

DETERMINING MEANING

Recall that T-G grammar and the MP maintain that language is computational and compositional; a cognitive mechanism performs various language operations, such as inducing grammar rules and combining small linguistic units into larger ones. On this account, the language module is said to consist of *submodules* that are responsible for a range of different processes. Computation is related to the idea that language—specifically, grammar—is largely independent of language use. In T-G grammar, for example, the language acquisition device induces the rules of the grammar with minimal input; in the MP, universal grammar is innate, and input does nothing more than set certain parameters. Also, both T-G grammar and the MP deal with example sentences rather than utterances. Neither addresses the fact that such sentences lack a context that includes someone with an intention to communicate a message to someone with the ability to understand (or misunderstand) the message, and neither makes any attempt to examine units of discourse beyond the sentence.

The idea of independence is especially problematic for those of us who teach reading, writing, and speaking because it does not consider issues of rhetoric. Chomsky's approach to grammar always has been plagued by his ambiva-

---

[1]Emotions involve several areas of the brain, especially the limbic system and the frontal lobes.

lence and ambiguity regarding meaning. In *Syntactic Structures,* he noted that transformational grammar "was completely formal and non-semantic" (1957, p. 93). None of his work with grammar has considered language's rhetorical dimension. As teachers, we need to be able to draw on theory and research to inform our work with students. We need tools that allow us to understand more clearly how students use language, the nature of their errors, and how to help them become more proficient readers and writers.

Language as a Social Action: Metaphor and Symbol

Cognitive grammar, much like rhetoric, views language as a social action. Meaning, therefore, emerges out of language in a social context and is usage based. More often than not, the language we use is metaphorical and symbolic, for we rarely assign a literal meaning to our words.

This concept is not particularly difficult, but it creates significant problems for the idea of compositionality, at least in its strict sense. Let's take a simple word like *run*. Compositionality indicates that we form the word by combining its constituent parts: $r + u + n$. The result is the word *run,* but nothing in the process of composing the word or in the word itself tells us much about the word's meaning. Without a context, it can mean any number of things, as the following short list of possibilities illustrates:

1. the act of moving swiftly on foot so that both feet leave the ground during each stride
2. a score in baseball
3. a snag in a woman's stocking
4. a string of good luck
5. a scheduled or regular route
6. to move at a gallop on horseback
7. to retreat
8. to flee
9. to emit pus or mucus
10. to melt

On this basis, we see that *run* is both metaphor and symbol. Processing the meaning of *run* requires not only that we recognize its symbolism but also what it signifies. Signification, in turn, requires a speaker/writer with an intention to designate one thing in terms of another. Thus, we cannot separate the meaning of the word from the person who uses the word. Equally important, we cannot separate the meaning of the word from the audience.

The situation becomes more complex as soon as we move from individual words to entire expressions. We can say that someone is *cool,* and mean, most of the time, something other than a description of body temperature. We can say that someone is *hot* with a similar effect. Indeed, we can use both expressions to describe a single person, as in:

- Macarena is cool.
- Macarena is hot.

Interestingly, these statements are not contradictory but can be easily understood as complementary: Macarena's coolness may, in fact, make her hot, and vice versa. With these and countless other statements, the meaning cannot readily be calculated on the basis of the words themselves. Taylor (2002) expressed the problem neatly when he wrote: "complex expressions nearly always have a meaning that is more than, or even at variance with, the meaning that can be computed by combining the meanings of the component parts" (p. 13). The most well-known expressions of this type are idioms, such as *The goon kicked the bucket, Rita needs to come down off her high horse, Everything's turning up roses,* and so forth.

The metaphorical nature of language prompts many cognitive grammarians to argue not only that meaning does not reside in individual words but also that the meaning of individual words is *conceptual* rather than specific. Conceptual meaning relies on a network of associations for each word that radiate in numerous directions. The word *tree,* for example, designates a generic concept, or category, that serves as a *prototype*. In isolation, the word means very little. However, its network of associations radiates outward to palm trees, oak trees, maple trees, poplar trees, apple trees, and so on, allowing us to use *tree* in meaningful ways. Especially interesting is the fact that the human mind is so good at identifying and abstracting patterns that we can apply the term *tree* to categories that have nothing at all to do with natural organisms like apple trees. We accept the sentence diagrams in chapters 4 and 5 as *tree diagrams* even though they have only one feature in common with actual trees—a branching structure. On this account, we can say that the conceptual nature of meaning in cognitive grammar underscores language as a symbolic system.

This approach to meaning allows for a better understanding of the relation among cognition, grammar, and semantics. Function words, such as prepositions, provide interesting illustrations:

1. The book was on the table.
2. The book was under the table.

Sentences 1 and 2 are grammatically identical, consisting of a noun phrase, a linking verb, and a prepositional phrase. Their opposite meanings result from their conceptually different prepositions, not from their grammar. Our ability to formulate these sentences is based on our ability to establish logical propositions for the mental model of *the book* and *the table* through what Fauconnier and Turner (2002) called *conceptual blending*. Meaning in this case is not related to grammar but to the underlying logical propositions, which define the location of *the book* with respect to *the table*.

On this basis, cognitive grammar suggests that some language errors, as well as misunderstandings, are related to different experiences, backgrounds, or knowledge. The English prepositions *on* and *in,* for example, are notoriously difficult for nonnative speakers of English: We get *in* a car, but we get *on* a train, bus, and airplane. Many languages, such as Spanish, have a single preposition (*en*) that serves as both *on* and *in.* As a result, native Spanish speakers will not have different conceptual categories for these prepositions. Teaching the grammar of prepositions and prepositional phrases will have only a modest effect on performance because the mental model related to being inside a car, train, or bus does not build the necessary concepts.

Teaching Tip

An effective strategy at the elementary level, where we find most of our nonnative English speakers, is to use pictures to help students visualize (and thereby internalize) the conceptual relations associated with the prepositions "in" and "on." For vehicles, the conceptual relation involves not only size but also whether the transport is public or private. Thus, we get in small, personal vehicles—cars, trucks, SUVs, and mini-vans—but we get on trains, buses, trolleys, and airplanes. When students see the pictures and appropriate example sentences underneath, they form mental models of the conceptual relations.

Language Is Grounded in Experience

Although language appears to be innate in many respects, we cannot say the same about communicative competence, particularly with regard to how we convey and interpret meaning. Cognitive grammar endorses the Lockean perspective that ideas and meaning are grounded in experience, which varies from person to person. Differences exist because people have different histories. Children, for example, may be born with an innate sense of morality, but it must be developed through input and guidance, which may explain why the first several years of parenting involve intense focus on appropriate versus inappropriate behavior, on the moral education of the child. The fact that parents in all cultures, without any conscious consideration of what they are doing, devote so much attention to helping their children develop language and a sense of right and wrong strongly suggests innateness to some degree. Without slighting the growing body of research indicating that personality—and thus behavior—is largely determined by biology, we can state that differences in behavior can be attributed, in part, to differences in parenting (see Barber, 1996; Baumrind, 1989, 1991; Chao, 1994; Darling & Steinberg, 1993; Heath, 1983; Maccoby & Martin, 1983; Miller, Cowan, P., Cowan, C., & Hetherington, 1993; Pinker, 2002; Schwarz, Barton-Henry, & Pruzinsky, 1985; Steinberg, Darling, & Fletcher, 1995; Steinberg, Dornbusch, & Brown, 1992; Weiss & Schwarz, 1996).

Applying this perspective to language is revealing. Formalist models of language are problematic, in part, because they assume that all sentences begin with the lexicon, that language exists in the mind as words. But words per se do not exist anywhere in the brain; instead, we find cell assemblies representing words through cortical dynamics (Pulvermuller, 2003). If we accept the argument for the lexicon merely as a metaphor, it may seem reasonable, given the nature of language, but there is no evidence to support it. Even if words are indeed stored in the brain, it does not follow that language begins with words. As Fauconnier and Turner (2002) noted, at the heart of language are the "powerful and general abilities of conceptual integration" (p. 180).

More critical, however, is that formalist models of language treat meaning as though it exists exclusively in the mind of the language producer. Meaning is subordinated to a focus on derivations and structure, even though "structure" per se is dismissed as an "artifact" that has no "theoretical status" (Chomsky, 1995, pp. 25–26). Lengthy discussions of structural derivations in the MP present a view of language processing that is exclusively bottom up, and it ignores the fact that a great deal of language processing is top down (Abbott, Black, & Smith, 1985; Fodor, Bever, & Garrett, 1974; Kintsch & van Dijk, 1978; Johnson-Laird, 1983; Sanford & Garrod, 1981; Smith, 1983).

Again, this is not a trivial matter. Formalist grammars cannot provide a satisfactory model of language processing because they do not account for a variety of factors associated with language as a communicative act that conveys meaning. Consider the following sentences:

3. The house had a three-car garage.
4. The House approved the minimum-wage bill.
5. The Louvre and the National house many of the world's great treasures.

The meaning of the word *house* in these sentences derives from our experience with the world. Producing and comprehending 4, for example, requires a knowledge of government that is quite removed from grammar.

Construing Meaning

The following hypothetical scenario illustrates a more difficult problem for formalist grammars: A couple (Fritz and Macarena) has put their home up for sale; they meet with a potential buyer (Rita) and give her a tour. Rita comments on how lovely the home is and asks the purchase price. Fritz and Macarena provide a figure, and Rita looks around slowly and then makes the following statement:

6. The house needs new paint.

What, exactly, does this statement mean? In formalist accounts, the meaning is inherent in the statement as a matter of fact. That is, the statement maps a certain real-world condition onto a linguistic form that is determined by the lexicon and the grammar. However, as Lee (2001), and others (Williams, 1993, 2003a) have pointed out, meaning in human communication rarely consists of this sort of mapping. Instead, it involves a complex array of contextual or situational factors that lead those participating in the language event to construe statements in different ways. On this account, in our scenario, Rita's utterance of sentence 6 does not have the same meaning for her as it does for Fritz and Macarena. For her, the sentence may signify the prospect of money saved in the purchase, whereas for Fritz and Macarena it may signify money lost if they sell to Rita. We find a further illustration of this phenomenon if we conclude our scenario with Rita purchasing the house. Sentences 7 and 8 convey this fact. Both map the same real-world condition into very similar grammatical structures—yet they mean very different things:

7. Fritz and Macarena sold their house to Rita for a good price.
8. Rita bought Fritz and Macarena's house for a good price.

The range of factors that can influence how we construe the meaning of statements is very large. Lee (2001) argued that all language use exists in frames that consist of background knowledge and context and that language is understood in relation to these frames. On this account, "if I approach the boundary between land and sea from the land, I refer to it as 'the coast,' whereas if I approach it from the sea, I call it 'the shore'" (Lee, p.10). Lee suggested that frames can help explain the misunderstandings that often occur in cross-cultural communication, which "have nothing to do with the meaning of linguistic forms in the narrow sense.... In a frame-oriented approach, ... knowledge differences based on an individual's life experiences (including growing up in a particular culture) can be built into the model" (p. 11). Thus, we understand why it is so difficult to get jokes in another language—they are culture specific. As Woody Allen (1982) noted in the movie *Stardust Memories,* he was lucky to have been born in a society that puts a big value on jokes: "If you think of it this way ... if I had been an Apache Indian, those guys didn't need comedians at all, right?" (p. 342).

Frames must also include emotional states. Our emotions influence what we say and how it is understood. When we process language, we do not merely look for the meaning of the words—we commonly try to recognize and understand the intentions underlying the words. With regard to oral discourse, understanding the intentions is often more important than the words themselves. Using this analysis, we see that there are two reasons why formalist grammars cannot explain how we understand that sentences 7 and 8 have different meanings: (a) the computational system does not allow for construal and does not provide a model of language acquisition that includes mental models of spaces, frames, and propositions; and (b) their bottom-up model of processing is incompatible with the top-down mechanisms necessary for extracting the meaning from such sentences. As teachers, we cannot separate form from substance or meaning. If rhetoric tells us anything, it is that a writer/speaker must be aware of how an audience understands the message. Yet formalist grammars ignore the fact that language is a social action, that form and meaning are inseparable, and that the meaning of any sentence does not reside exclusively in the mind of the one who produces it but also exists in the minds of those who read or hear each sentence.

APPLYING KEY IDEAS

Although it seems clear that grammar is largely a manifestation—rather than the sole determiner—of meaning, it is equally clear that poor grammar, in the form of ungrammatical constructions, can interfere with meaning. Ungrammatical sentences force the audience to *guess* at the intended meaning. This problem is particularly acute in writing. Using the information in the foregoing sections, develop three activities that engage students in the connection between meaning and grammar. Share these activities with classmates and develop a portfolio of lessons that can be used in teaching.

The Importance of Context

If we accept the proposal that frames greatly affect understanding, we begin to recognize that students face significant obstacles when writing. One of the bigger—but often unrecognized—problems is that teachers and students usually do not share common frames associated with writing assignments. Teachers have an understanding of each assignment that leads them to have fairly specific expectations for student responses, yet students will have a different understanding, as well as a perception of the teacher's expectations that are far off target. Furthermore, when students are writing about anything other than themselves, they generally lack sufficient background knowledge for meaningful communication. And because writing tasks commonly lack a context, students frequently do not recognize that they must create a context for each essay they produce. The necessary frames are missing and must be created. Adding to students' difficulties: The lack of a context makes formulating a viable intention quite challenging because the language act associated with most classroom writing tasks is artificial. Intention grounds all oral discourse, yet writing typically is produced in response to a teacher's assignment. Students' "intention," then, is merely to meet the demands of the assignment, which renders the intention and the language act arhetorical. On this basis, we understand that even if a student is able to construct an appropriate frame for a given paper, the paper will fail as a social action if there is no viable underlying intention.

These problems are not insurmountable, but they are troubling and challenging. Too often, we find our schools skirting the problems by relying exclusively on self-expressive or personal writing, which simply creates more problems. Viable assignments must engage students in the sort of writing they will encounter in college and the workplace, and it most certainly has nothing to do with self-expression. Such assignments also must be highly contextualized without being overly long. They must provide students with success criteria as a means of sharing expectation frames. Students should not have to guess what a successful response entails.

Teaching Tip

Cognitive grammar suggests that students can improve their writing if they understand the need to contextualize the writing task. Students have a tacit understanding of the importance of context in speech; this is part of their communicative competence. Therefore, asking them to discuss a paper in work groups and then to produce an oral composition prior to writing may serve as a bridge between speech and writing that leads to better contextualization.

COGNITIVE GRAMMAR AND LANGUAGE ACQUISITION

Chapter 2 noted that there are two dominant models of language acquisition, the induction model and the association model. The differences between these models is central to cognitive grammar and mark a clear departure from formalist approaches. Let's examine the process of acquisition and the two dominant models more closely.

The Induction Model

The question that has fascinated researchers for the last 50 years is not whether language is grammatical but rather how children grasp the full complexities of grammar with little effort and without being taught. Parents and other adults do not teach infants grammar—they just talk to them. Nevertheless, without any explicit instruction, children can utilize most possible grammatical constructions by age 4. By age 10 or 11, they can utilize all. Production typically lags behind comprehension, however, and writing generally has a more complex structure than speaking, which explains why most people, but especially children, find it difficult to generate the complex grammatical constructions found in writing.

The nature of parental input complicates the question of acquisition. As Chomsky (1965, 1972) observed, children manage to produce grammatical sentences at an early age on the basis of often distorted linguistic input, that is, the "baby talk" that adults always use when speaking to infants. Because the utterances children produce are grammatical but are not mere repetitions of adult speech, Chomsky proposed that humans have an innate language acquisition device that induces grammar rules from limited and distorted data. In this account, for the first 2 years of life, children's language acquisition device is processing input and developing the grammar rules of the home language. There are fits and starts, but then the induction is completed and the child applies those rules consistently.

The minimalist program focuses on the role of universal grammar in acquisition, but it also is an induction model based on the idea that the language children hear from adults is impoverished. Under what he called "principles and parameters theory," Chomsky (1981, 1995, 2000) linked acquisition to a finite set of innate parameters for grammar. The parameters define not only what is and what is not grammatical but also what can and cannot be grammatical in a given language. Any input that does not fit the parameters is ignored or discarded. Thus, even though baby talk constitutes distorted input, it nevertheless is congruent with the parameters for grammar and is accepted as meaningful (also see Hudson, 1980; Slobin & Welsh, 1973; Comrie, 1981; Cullicover, 1999; Jackendoff, 2002; Newmeyer, 1998; Pinker, 1995; and Prince & Smolensky, 1993).

One might be tempted on this basis to suggest that parents play a major role in helping children develop grammar through their interventions when children generate incorrect utterances. Observations of parent–child interactions, however, have not supported this suggestion (Bohannon & Stanowicz, 1988; Bowerman, 1982; Demetras, Post, & Snow, 1986; Hirsh-Pasek, Treiman, & Schneiderman, 1984; Marcus, 1993). Parental interventions are somewhat random, and they often are unrelated to grammar, typically addressing, instead, matters of pronunciation and factuality.

Anyone who has raised children or spent a great deal of time with children knows that acquisition depends significantly on a matching procedure. Beyond the cooing and baby talk that is part of the bonding that parents and children experience, there is a consistent instructional agenda that involves introducing children to objects in their world and providing them with the names for those objects. In the case of a ball, for example, a parent will hold up a ball and utter the word "ball." Eventually, the day will come when the child makes his or her first attempt at producing the word, and in most instances it comes out as something other than "ball." "Ba" is a very common first effort. Normally, the parent will correct the child's utterance, stretching out the word and emphasizing the /l/ sound, and the child will respond by trying his or her best to mimic the parent. This procedure ultimately results in a close match between the two utterances.[2]

Such observations suggest that sociolinguistic conventions play a significant role in our understanding of language. The nature of parental interventions, however, are such that they cannot account for the rapid expansion of grammatical utterances or the fact that 90% of these utterances are grammatically correct by age 3.5.

Overgeneralization of Past Tense. We saw in chapter 5 that formalist grammars are computational and rule driven. Their treatment of tense illustrates how the process is understood to work. Formalist grammars propose that regular past tense is governed by a rule-based submodule. When producing a sentence like *Fred walked the dog,* the submodule is activated; it then takes the verb form *to walk* from the lexicon and applies something like the following rule: "Add the suffix *-ed* to the untensed verb." Irregular verbs are handled differently. Between the ages of 2 and 3, we observe children regularizing irregular verbs by adding the past-tense suffix. Instead of using *held,* for example, they will produce *holded.* After 6 to 8 months, they begin using the irregular forms correctly. The assumption is that during this period children's regular tense submodule is overgeneralizing the rule and that eventually the submodule determines that the rule does not apply. Pinker (1999) speculated that a second tense submodule, this one for irregular verbs, is then activated. However, this submodule does not apply

---

[2]The inability to achieve an exact match results in language change over generations.

a rule for tense but instead serves as a storage bin for the list of irregular verbs and their associated past-tense forms.

This model seems overly complex, and it also appears to be incongruent with the idea that the grammar submodules are innate and governed by universal grammar. We should be able to predict that such submodules have built-in provisions for handling irregular verbs, which occur in just about every language.

An important characteristic of rule-driven systems is that they consistently produce correct output. They are deterministic, so after a rule is in place there is no reason to expect an error. The rule necessarily must produce the same result each time. The process is similar to a game like basketball: There is a rule that stipulates that when a player makes a basket outside the three-point line his or her team gets three points. As long as a player makes a basket outside this line, the result is always the same. But we just don't find this situation in language. People produce frequent errors in speech and writing, which suggests that, whatever mechanisms are responsible for generating sentences, they in fact do not produce correct output consistently.[3]

The Association Model

Cognitive grammar simplifies the logical problems associated with acquisition by rejecting the rule-governed model of mind and language, replacing it with an association model based on the work in cognitive science by Rumelhart and McClelland (1986) and others working in *connectionism* (also see Searle, 1992). Rejecting the rule-governed model of mind offers significant advantages.

Neural Connections.   Cognitive science research has suggested that the process of induction associated with formalist models of acquisition does not correctly describe what happens as children acquire language. One of the problems is that the competence-performance distinction does not really tell us much about the nature of errors in language. More broadly, these models do not seem congruent with what neuroscience has discovered about how the mind actually works.

The association model of acquisition that emerged out of connectionism is easy to understand. Connectionism describes learning in terms of *neural networks*. These networks are physiological structures in the brain that are com-

---

[3]Many people assume that frequent errors appear in writing rather than speech. Close observation, however, shows that speech is typically more prone to errors than writing. The difference is that speech occurs so rapidly that most of us are not able to detect the errors; writing, on the other hand, lends itself to close examination, which quickly reveals even the smallest error. Also, when listening to language, we focus nearly all of our attention on meaning and message, whereas when reading—especially student papers—we give significant attention to form.

posed of cells called neurons and the pathways—dendrites and axons—that allow neurons to communicate with one another through synapses, junction switches that facilitate information processing. Learning involves changes in the brain's cell structure, changes that literally grow the network to accommodate the new knowledge. The more a person learns, the more extensive the neural network.

Rule-governed models like the minimalist program assume that mental activity or thought is verbal—any given sentence begins as mentalese. Connectionism, on the other hand, suggests that it is a mistake to assume that cognitive activities are verbal just because everyone reports hearing a mental voice when thinking. Instead, as we saw earlier, it proposes that mental activities are primarily (though not exclusively) imagistic.[4] Our language itself contains the essence of this proposal, for "seeing" is synonymous with understanding. We "look" at problems and try to "focus" on issues. When listening to someone speak, we try to "see" their point. We process the world as we "see" it, not as we smell, hear, or taste it. Visualization is at the core of understanding and language and also appears to be at the core of mental activities.

This point is important for a number of reasons, but one of the more relevant is that it allows language processing to be understood as a matter of matching words with mental representations and internalized models of reality. On this account, the structure of language is not governed by rules but by *patterns of regularity* (Rumelhart & McClelland, 1986). As we shall see, the difference here is significant.

Let's note first that these patterns begin establishing themselves at birth.[5] When children encounter the world, their parents and other adults provide them with the names of things. Children see dogs, for instance, and they immediately are provided the word "dog," with the result being that they develop a mental image, or model, related to "dog-ness": four legs, hairy, barks, licks, pet, and so on. As a child develops and has more experience with dogs, his or her mental model for "dog-ness" grows to include the range of features that typify dogs. These features are part of the mental representation and the string of sounds, or phonemes, that make up the word "dog." The representations exist as cell structures in the brain.

---

[4]Some educators have proposed that, if mentation is largely imagistic, then immersing children in highly visual activities will enhance learning. As Katz (1989) noted, however, such activities usually do not include a verbal component. Images appear to be native to mental operations, whereas language is not. Thus, language must arise out of social interactions.

[5]Pinker and Prince (1988) and Pinker (2002) strongly criticized connectionism, arguing that it is essentially identical to the behaviorism model (long obsolete), which proposed that language acquisition was based solely on experience with and memorization of linguistic input. There are, however, some significant differences. Connectionism, for example, recognized that language ability is innate and genetically based, whereas behaviorism did not. Indeed, behaviorism rejected all notions of innateness.

The brain acts as a self-organizing system and does not rely on extensive or explicit guidance from the environment (Elman et al., 1996; Kelso, 1995). Self-organized systems usually are in a state of delicate equilibrium determined in large part by preexisting conditions and to a lesser extent by the dynamics of their environment, which provide data through a feedback mechanism (Smolin, 1997). One result for cognition and language is that even meager input can have a significant influence (Elman et al., 1996). Although to casual observers the linguistic input children receive may appear to be limited and distorted, to a child's developing brain this input is both rich and meaningful. Adult language is absolutely necessary if children are to develop language, but infants bring significant innate resources to the endeavor.

The self-organizing characteristics of the brain allow children to categorize similar representations appropriately and cross-reference them in various ways. Dogs and cats might exist in a category for pets, but they would be cross-referenced not only with a category for four-legged animals but also with words that begin with the letter *d* and words that begin with the letter *c*. Cross-referencing here is not metaphorical: It consists of actual neural connections that link related neurons. The result is a very complex neural network of related items with all their associated features. Exactly how all these items and features are sorted, stored, and cross-referenced remains a mystery, but once a mental representation is established in the brain, the child is able to process it at will. For example, the mental image of a dog eventually becomes linked to all its associated features, both as a sound and as a graphic representation of the word—*d-o-g*.

A similar process seems to be at work with respect to grammar. Children use their innate ability to organize the world around them to identify the patterns of regularity—the grammar—that appear in the language they hear during every waking hour (Williams, 1993). Chomsky (1957, 1965) argued that this process is not possible because language has an infinite possible number of grammatical utterances and that the human brain is incapable of remembering them all. He concluded, therefore, that the brain must have some mechanism for generating the full range of possible utterances on the basis of a relatively small number of generative rules.

There are at least two errors in this conclusion. First, as de Boysson-Bardies (2001) pointed out, "the human brain contains 10^{10} neurons"; ... [each] "neuron forms about 1,000 connections and ... can receive 10,000 messages at the same time"; "the number of junctions may be reckoned at 10^{15}—more than the number of stars in the universe" (p. 14). In other words, the human brain has essentially unlimited storage and processing capacity. The suggestion that the brain is incapable of memorizing innumerable grammatical patterns seems a bit ridiculous in this light. The real cognitive challenge is not storage but retrieval.[6] Second, although any language has an infinite possible number of grammatical utterances, it is a mistake to confuse grammatical utterances with *grammatical patterns*. As it turns out, the number of acceptable patterns in any given language is relatively small, and these patterns seem to be based on brain architecture. The linear flow of information input through the senses into the brain is replicated via the linear flow of electrochemical signals through the neural pathways, which in turn is reflected in the linear flow of speech and writing.

Cognitive processing tends to be hierarchical, moving from most to least important. In addition, we excel at establishing cause–effect relations, so much so that this ability begins developing within hours of birth (Carey, 1995; Cohen, Amsel, Redford, & Casasola, 1998; Springer & Keil, 1991). These features would lead us to predict that languages will tend to be structured around agency, with subjects in the initial position, which is exactly what we find.

From this perspective, there is no need to propose either a mechanism for inducing grammar rules or parameters or a generative grammatical component. We have only two major sentence patterns in English—SVO and SVC—and all the other patterns are essentially variations of these. The constituents that make up these patterns are universal across all known languages. That is, some combination of subject, verb, object, and complement forms the basic pattern of all languages. Thus, even if we ignored the inherent restrictions on grammar imposed by brain architecture, we could not argue that the number of grammatical patterns is theoretically infinite. Returning to an example in chapter 5—*The day was very ... n hot*—we must reject any suggestion that such sentences reveal anything significant about grammar, for the addition of the adverbial *very* does not affect the underlying sentence pattern, SVC. Furthermore, for the two primary sentence patterns, there are only 12 possible grammatical combinations ($3! + 3! = 12$), and many of these, such as OSV, are extremely rare, attested in fewer than a half dozen languages.

Because humans excel at pattern recognition, the limited number of grammatical patterns in all languages is easily within the range of our capacity. The task is so simple that even people with seriously limited intelligence have no difficulty developing language that is grammatically correct.

Explaining Language Errors.   Cognitive grammar proposes that language production begins with an intention that activates the neural network. The network produces logical propositions in the form of images in many instances,

---

[6]We often hear the assertion that people only use 10% of their brain. The reality is that people use all their brain all the time, even when sleeping. This does not mean, however, that they use it to capacity. We find an illustrative analogy in the act of lifting a book: All the arm muscles are working—they just aren't working to capacity. Lifting a dumbbell uses exactly the same muscles but to fuller capacity.

words in some others, or a combination of both that in turn produce a mental model through conceptual blending. The mental model activates that part of the network where sentence patterns are stored. The structure of the propositions inherent in the mental model specifies a range of possible sentence patterns. One is selected as a "best fit" and is then filled with words that match the model and the person's intention. Cognitive grammar accounts for the high degree of creativity in language on the basis of the essentially limitless supply of mental propositions and the flexibility inherent in English word order. Language's creative characteristics are not the result of a generative grammar.

This model of production allows cognitive grammar to offer a viable explanation of errors in language without recourse to rules or competence and performance. It is often the case that, when speaking, we intend to say one thing and end up saying something different. We usually catch these "slips of the tongue" and self-correct, but the question remains: What caused the error? Consider the following example: The family and I are going to drive to the beach, and before we leave I want my son to bring in the dog and put out the cat. But what I actually utter is "Bring in the cat and put out the dog." Why did my intention fail to produce the desired sentence?

Our experiences of the world are defined and processed as patterns. Mammals have four limbs, people laugh when they are happy, birds fly, dogs bark, the sun rises in the morning and sets in the evening. Many patterns necessarily overlap because they have similar characteristics. Numerous people, for example, have to remind themselves that tomatoes are a fruit, not a vegetable, and that dolphins are mammals, not fish. Language acquisition at the word level involves recurrent encounters with, say, dogs and cats, resulting in mental models of "dog-ness" and "cat-ness." Hearing the word or deciding to utter it triggers an association between one set of neural patterns and another set that contains subsets of the various features related to the target. Each triggering increases the strength of the connection between the appropriate patterns, raising the probability of correctly matching strings of phonemes.

In the case of dogs and cats, we can imagine several subsets, clustered, perhaps, under the general set of pets or mammals, depending on how one primarily categorizes these animals. The subsets will contain not only the features of dogs and cats—hairy, lovable, licks, ownership, and so forth—but they also will contain entries for other animals, such as mice, guinea pigs, turtles, and skunks. In my scenario, when I formulated the intention to tell my son to bring in the dog and put out the cat, the entire network associated with pets/mammals was activated. Because the individual representations of dogs, cats, skunks, and guinea pigs have numerous overlapping features and because they are all interconnected, they will compete as targets (see Rumelhart & McClelland, 1986). This competition suggests not only that it is possible for a feature characteristic of both dogs and cats to dominate but that in fact it will occur. As a result, we can predict that in some instances, on a probabilistic or statistical basis, a person will call a dog a cat and vice versa: "The connecting strengths of the association between the string of phonemes characterized as 'dog' and the features characterizing 'dog-ness' are insufficient to provide consistency" (Williams, 1993, p. 559).

We can apply the same principles to grammar and usage errors. For example, we may instruct students on the ungrammaticality of *The reason is because* and *I feel badly*, providing them with the correct forms: *The reason is that* and *I feel bad*. The lesson will be stored in the brain as associated structural patterns that we can symbolically represent in the following diagrams:

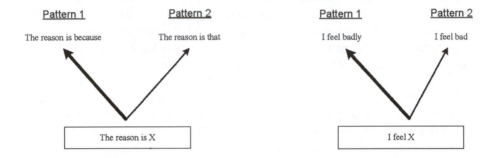

FIG. 6.1.   Graphic Representation of Connection Strengths.

In both cases, there are two potential targets activated by the trigger. After our instruction, it is possible that students will select the correct target. However, because they are immersed in a language environment where the overwhelming majority of people, regardless of education, produce the erroneous strings, the connection strength for the incorrect form will be far greater than the connection strength for the correct form. On this basis, we can predict with confidence that instruction will have a limited effect on performance unless it is reinforced consistently both in and out of school—and unless our students are motivated to change their language.

Cognitive grammar proposes that language acquisition is intimately allied with experiences and internal representations of reality. Sentence production and grammaticality, indeed language as a whole, are "tied to associations between various patterns of regularity generalized through interaction with the environment" (Williams, 1993, p. 561). From this perspective, the act of producing an utterance involves matching a mental model of the intended representation of reality against the range of linguistic patterns available from experience.

The implications for teaching are straightforward but unsurprising. Children benefit from being immersed in a language-rich environment that includes reading, writing, and active modeling of speech. Cognitive grammar, therefore, provides a theoretical foundation for what many teachers already do. What is not quite so obvious is that this model of acquisition suggests that the environment should be highly diverse, exposing children to multiple genres and audiences so as to broaden their linguistic skills. The writing-across-the-curriculum (WAC) movement has demonstrated the advantages inherent in such an approach, but it is not widely implemented in our public schools, and where it is, the results have not been particularly significant owing to faulty implementation. Because WAC requires knowledge of the writing conventions in a range of disciplines—and because most language arts teachers lack such knowledge—all but a handful of programs and textbooks have settled on a journalistic approach. That is, they ask students to read and write *about* science, *about* social science, and *about* humanities. They do not ask students to read and write science, social science, or even humanities, where the typical assignment is a response paper that expresses what students *feel* about a work of literature rather than examining its literary elements and making an argument. Insights from cognitive grammar allow us to predict that students' language skills will show more growth if they actually are asked to engage in reading and writing in these disciplines rather than about them.

Overgeneralization of Tense Revisited. Earlier, we examined the phenomenon of tense overgeneralization and saw how it is used to support the induction model of language acquisition. In this account, children apply the past-participle affix to irregular verbs consistently after they formulate the rules associated with verb forms. However, this account is incongruent with what we actually observe. Sometimes children use the regular and irregular forms correctly, sometimes incorrectly; moreover, adults make the same errors, indicating that, contrary to the induction account, consistency does not come with age. This inconsistent behavior is almost impossible to explain adequately with a rule-governed model, but it is easily understood in terms of competing forms: The connecting associations related to past-tense forms are insufficiently developed in children to allow one form to dominate.

With the association model, errors occur because in the neural network there are many similar patterns of regularity with numerous overlapping features, and these patterns are activated simultaneously by an intention. In the case provided (Fig. 6.1), the model would propose that the patterns for these two structures coexist in the network owing to the fact that they both appear in speech. Whether a person uses one or the other depends not on internal rules or external stimuli that interfere with the application of those rules but on other factors (Goldrick & Rapp, 2001). Age increases the connection strengths within the network, so as people grow older they produce fewer errors. However, this model predicts that, statistically, errors always will occur on a random basis regardless of age. This prediction is born out by the fact that everyone produces errors of one type or another while speaking, even though grammar is inherent in their language subsystems. Errors in writing have the same basis. In this context, language acquisition is not, as formalist grammars propose, a process of developing the grammar tools necessary for producing language; rather, it is a process of developing the neural network, which provides the tools for language.

By the same token, this model allows us to understand why language instruction in our schools is slow and difficult. Children come to school with the home language well established. The connection strengths for nonstandard language have had years of reinforcement, whereas there may be no connections at all for certain features of Standard or formal Standard English. For most children, age will simply increase the disparity because of insufficient exposure over the course of their lives to Standard and formal Standard models.

The Role of Grammar in Acquisition.   Grammar is an important part of the whole language apparatus, but it is only one part. Grammar, from any perspective, is a pattern of word combinations. Cognitive grammar dismisses the idea of an innate universal grammar without dismissing the idea of linguistic universals. It also rejects the proposal that grammar has a generative component for producing language. Language production is the result of complex cognitive and physiological processes associated with intention, motivation, socialization, image formation, and logical propositions.

In addition, production must involve a fundamental communicative competence that includes a wide array of behaviors—such as recognition and interpretation of facial expressions and body language, necessary for turn taking in conversations; recognition and understanding of situation and audience, which govern the level of formality in language use (when talking to the boss, we don't use the same language that we use when having pizza and beer with friends); and prosody, which is not limited to the metrical structure of poetry but also includes the rhythm of spoken language.

Prosody is critically important to language because when rhythm patterns in speech do not match what the hearer expects, communication is seriously hampered. The difficulty in understanding foreign accents, for example, is frequently a matter of prosody, not grammar. Given the importance of prosody in language production, we should find it interesting that formalist accounts of acquisition give relatively little attention to this feature of linguistic performance. Pinker (1995), for example, provided a lengthy discussion of language acquisition (almost 50 pages) but devoted only five paragraphs to prosody. Moreover, these five paragraphs are limited to questioning the link between prosody and grammar: Do children use prosody to determine grammar? As a strong advocate of Chomskian linguistics, Pinker concluded that grammar may influence prosody, but he then took the strange step of recognizing that the mapping between syntax and prosody is "inconsistent" (p. 164).

More relevant is the question of how children master the rhythmic patterns of their home language in the course of language acquisition. When we examine speech as an acoustical signal, it is continuous, yet we do not hear speech as a continuous stream; we hear it as segments that follow a specific pattern. Numerous studies have shown that infants only a few days old are able to distinguish the prosodic patterns of different languages, such as English and Japanese (Bagou, Fougeron, & Frauenfelder, 2002; Bahrick & Pickens, 1988; Christophe & Morton, 1998; Dehaene-Lambertz & Houston, 1998). This ability seems congruent with the universal human talent for pattern recognition, but it raises interesting and as yet unanswered questions. If language acquisition relies on a process of induction, what is there in speech rhythms that children induce? Are there "rules" of prosody? Are prosodic patterns simply internalized on the basis of exposure?

Cognitive grammar does not view language as being the product of children's mastery of grammar but rather views grammar as being a byproduct of language. It follows that grammar is not a theory of language or of mind, which makes the question of underlying linguistic structures irrelevant. Grammar, from this perspective, is nothing more than a system for describing the patterns of regularity inherent in language. The surface structure of sentences is linked directly to the mental proposition and corresponding phonemic and lexical representations. A formal grammatical apparatus to explain the relatedness of actives and passives, for example, and other types of related sentences is not necessary.

Consider again the issue of passive constructions:

- Fred kissed Macarena.
- Macarena was kissed by Fred.

In cognitive grammar, how these sentences might be related grammatically is of little consequence. More important is what they convey. Our intuition may tell us that these sentences are related, but our language sense also tells us that they have different meanings and emphases. At the very least, *Fred* is the focus of the active form, whereas *Macarena* is the focus of the passive. However, many readers/hearers would also note that *Macarena* seems to be a willing participant in the first sentence but an unwilling participant in the second.

The Implications for Grammatical Analysis.

This kind of analysis allows us to understand why cognitive grammar maintains that the role of grammar is merely to describe surface structures. As Langacker (1987) noted, cognitive grammar "is defined as those aspects of cognitive organization in which resides a speaker's grasp of established linguistic conventions. It can be characterized as a structured inventory of conventional linguistic units" (p. 57). On this account, grammatical analyses focus on conventional linguistic knowledge, that is, on the knowledge gained from experience with real language rather than language manufactured to meet the needs of syntactic analysis. Because phrase-structure grammar is ideally suited for describing "conventional linguistic units," cognitive grammar relies on phrase structure for the symbolic representation of syntax.

Using phrase-structure grammar for syntactic analysis raises the question of phrase-structure rules, but those working in cognitive grammar do not recognize the formulaic descriptions familiar from chapter 2 as being rules in any meaningful sense. Langacker (1990), for example, referred to phrase-structure rules as "general statements" (p. 102). Thus, there is no reason to assume that the NP VP notation specifies a rule, but there is every reason to recognize that it describes a grammatical relation.

Issues of meaning become self-evident because there is no effort to develop an intervening stage between cognition and utterance. This position has the immediate benefit of linking syntax and semantics, which Langacker (1987, 1990) supported when he cautioned against efforts to separate syntax and semantics, arguing that in cognitive grammar "symbolic structure is not distinct from semantic or phonological structure" (p. 105).

Chomsky's (1957) charge that phrase-structure grammar fails to provide a theory of language is viable only if one assumes that grammar should be theoretical. There is no compelling reason to make this assumption. Cognitive grammar proceeds from a different assumption—that the first goal is to develop a viable theory of cognition that will include language and grammar.

I would argue that cognitive grammar enables a deeper understanding of what many teachers already know—the key to helping students become better writers lies in getting them to become effective, self-motivated readers and in giving them frequent opportunities to write. The feedback from peers and teachers that are part of theory-based language arts classes strengthens the connecting pathways that build the neural network associated with language in general and writing in particular.

Cognitive grammar also helps us better understand why grammar instruction does not lead to improved writing. The ability to identify a noun or a verb is linked to a specific set of mental models and has, at best, only a tenuous relation through the neural network with the models associated with written discourse. There are indications that knowledge of grammar may be stored in an area quite far removed from knowledge of writing, stored in different parts of the network in a way that makes association difficult. Grammar instruction is likely to strengthen connecting associations in that part of the network responsible for grammar, but there is no evidence that it strengthens connections between these different parts of the network.

The implications for teaching are significant: "There is a sense in which writers, even experienced ones, must approach every writing task as though it were their first. They are faced with individual acts of creation each time they attempt to match a mental model of the discourse with the premises, paragraphs, examples, proofs, sentences, and words that comprise it" (Williams, 1993, p. 564). If cognitive grammar offers an accurate model of language, then the focus of our language arts classes must be on immersing students in language in all its richness and engaging them in examinations and discussions of content and form. Mastery of grammar and usage will follow.

APPLYING KEY IDEAS

1. In what ways does the rejection of grammar "rules" affect notions of correctness in language?
2. Parents and people who work with children know that the very young never seem to tire of repetitive interactions. How might this observation be linked to cognitive grammar?
3. Some people see important connections between critical thinking skills and the idea that thought is largely imagistic rather than verbal. Reflect on this notion, and then list some of the connections you see.
4. What are some of the pedagogical implications of cognitive grammar with respect to teaching grammar to students?
5. Although linguists focus almost exclusively on spoken language, teachers generally focus on writing, and historically grammar has been seen, incorrectly, as a means of improving writing skill. Does cognitive grammar have any implications for teaching reading and writing?

7

Dialects

WHAT IS A DIALECT?

Language varies over time, across national and geographical boundaries, by gender, across age groups, and by socioeconomic status. When the variation occurs within a given language, we call the different versions of the same language *dialects*. Thus, we describe English, for example, in terms of British English, Canadian English, American English, Australian English, Caribbean English, and Indian English. Within the United States, we speak of Southern English, Boston English, New York English, West Coast English, and so on.

Dialects are largely the result of geographical and socioeconomic factors, although many people mistakenly associate dialects with ethnicity (Haugen, 1966; Hudson, 1980; Trudgill, 2001; Wolfram, Adger, & Christian, 1998). They differ with respect to accent, prosody, grammar, and lexicon. Measurable differences exist between the language that men and women use—women tend to be more concerned about correctness than men—but dialects are not related to gender, overall. The influence of geography is evident in the observation that a person from Arizona, for example, is highly unlikely to utter "I have plenty enough," whereas this utterance is common in many parts of North Carolina. The influence of SES (socioeconomic status) is evident in the observation that someone from the upper third of the socioeconomic scale would be likely to utter "I'm not going to the party," whereas someone from the lower third would be more likely to utter "I ain't goin' to no party." Some dialectic features differ both by region and SES, as in the case of:

- Fred jumped *off* the table.

- Fred jumped *off of* the table.

Figure 7.1, put together by William Labov, Sharon Ash, and Charles Boberg, illustrates the major regional dialects in North America:

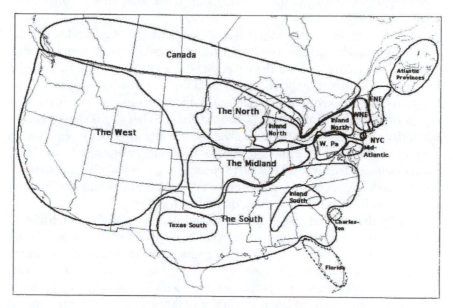

FIG. 7.1.   Major North American dialects. Reprinted from *The Atlas of North American English* with permission.

HOW DO DIALECTS DEVELOP?

When we look at the history of language, we find that all languages fit into specific language families. The largest of these is Indo-European, which includes English, Spanish, German, French, Greek, Iranian, and Russian. About half of the world's population speaks an Indo-European language as their first language.

Research has shown that Indo-European emerged in the Transcaucus area of eastern Anatolia about 6,000 years ago. Language itself predates Indo-European by many thousands of years, but we have not been able to look sufficiently far into the past to trace its history beyond this point. Scholars generally agree that Cro-Magnon man used language 40,000 years ago, but there is significant disagreement over whether Neanderthals did. The question of when mankind began using language is important because it can help us understand human evolution. As mentioned in the previous chapter, some scholars argue that language evolved from preexisting cognitive abilities, whereas others argue that no evidence exists for this view and that language seems to have emerged rapidly with the appearance of the Cro-Magnons. If the latter view is correct, language has a very short history.

There are approximately 5,000 different languages, so the fact that half the world's population speaks some variation of Indo-European is remarkable. How could it achieve such a dominant place? Recent research on mitochondrial DNA (MDNA) may provide an answer. MDNA is present in every cell in the body, and it remains virtually unchanged (aside from random mutations) as it passes from mother to daughter. Geneticist Brian Sykes (2002) analyzed and quantified the mutations of this relatively stable type of DNA in an effort to learn more about human evolution, and his discoveries were significant. First, modern humans are not at all related to Neanderthals, as some anthropologists had claimed, and second, modern Europeans are descendants of one of seven women who lived at different times during the Ice Age.

Initially, the idea that today's Europeans are all descended from such a small number of women may be hard to accept, but biologists know that most lines do not survive more than a few generations. Family trees tend to be narrow at the top and bottom, with a bulge in the middle. Only the most vigorous lines last. We therefore can describe the probable scenario for Indo-European. No doubt there were many unrelated languages in use 10,000 years ago, at the time of the great agricultural revolution, but these languages disappeared as the people speaking them died out. Those who spoke Indo-European, on the other hand, survived and spread throughout the Old World. Some of the migrants invaded Anatolia from the East around 2000 B.C. and established the Hittite kingdom, where the official language was among the first of the Indo-European languages to find its way into writing (Bryce, 2002).

All living languages change, and the migration of the original speakers of Indo-European from the Transcaucus would have accelerated the rate of change as bands separated and lost contact. Jacob Grimm—famous for authoring, with his brother Wilhelm, *Grimms' Fairy Tales*— proposed the "law of sound shift" in 1822. He argued that sets of consonants displace one another over time in predictable and regular ways. Soft voiced consonants in Indo-European—such as *b, d,* and *g*—shifted to the hard consonants *p, t,* and *k* in German. On the basis of Grimm's law, it is possible to trace the evolution of certain words from Sanskrit, the oldest Indo-European language still in use, to their modern equivalents. For example, the Sanskrit word *char* (to pull) evolved into the English *draw* and the German *tragen* without changing meaning.

In most instances, language change is always subtle. Exceptions are related to advances in science and technology and to conquest. The word *modem,* for example, did not exist in the 1960s; it emerged owing to developments in computers. Prior to the Norman invasion of England in 1066, English contained few French terms, but it quickly absorbed hundreds of them afterward. Barring such events, language change is the result of children's efforts to match the adult speech they hear around them. The match never is exact, and over time the minute variations between the language of children and the language of adults produces changes in lexicon, accent, and even grammar. Within a given group, the changes tend to be uniform; thus, everyone in that group is essentially using the same language at any point in time. Geographical barriers, however, inhibit uniform change whenever they prevent easy and frequent travel between any two groups. In cases where travel is infrequent, the language of groups with a common base dialect always is moving in different directions at any given time. As a result, significant dialectical differences may appear within three generations.

The United States and Britain provide an interesting illustration of the factors underlying dialect shift. The ocean separating the two countries ensured that a variety of differences would emerge, even though at one point American colonists spoke the same dialects as their English brethren. Some of the differences are related to vocabulary: Americans use the word *truck* for a vehicle designed for transporting goods, whereas Britons use the word *lorry*. Other such differences abound.

With regard to pronunciation, postvocalic *r* (as in *car*) has disappeared in much of England, but it is present throughout most of the United States (an exception, however, is the South, where postvocalic *r* no longer exists in many areas). Interestingly, the shift has not been in the direction one might expect. Language change in America has been slow and conservative, whereas it has occurred much faster in Britain. The reason is that during most of the 230 years since independence, America's population was smaller and more isolated than the population of Britain. Large, cosmopolitan populations experience more rapid linguistic change than small, isolated populations. On this basis, one could assume that the rapid growth in the U.S. population since 1960 has resulted in significant linguistic changes and that these changes will accelerate in the years ahead, in light of projections that show the population doubling by 2030. The first assumption appears to be accurate.

Socioeconomic factors also affect dialects, but they play a more complex role. Every language has a prestige dialect associated with education and financial success. The prestige dialect in the United States is known as Standard English, and it is spoken by a large number of people. Those who do not grow up speaking Standard English are motivated to learn it because it is the language of school and business. In this text, we have referred to formal Standard English as yet another dialect, associated most commonly with writing, especially academic writing, and members of the educated elite. The number of people who use formal Standard English when speaking is relatively small, but it nevertheless is the most widely accepted dialect. Given the importance of Standard and formal Standard dialects and their numerous differences from nonstandard dialects, we can understand why a significant portion of the U.S. population must be considered bidialectical.

Because SES is closely tied to level of education (Herrnstein & Murray, 1994), nonstandard speakers who are not fully bidialectical tend to be undereducated, and they also tend to be linked to the working-class poor. Education, however, is not an absolute indicator of dialect: Anecdotal evidence suggests that colleges and universities are more tolerant of nonstandard English than they used to be, and a number of factors have made public schools more sensitive to, and indeed more tolerant of, nonstandard English. As a result, it is fairly easy to observe college graduates—and, increasingly, college and public school faculty—uttering nonstandard expressions such as "I ain't got no money" and "Where's he at."

STUDENTS AND DIALECTS

Students who want to succeed academically have good reasons to shift from their home dialect, and many do so. This motivation continues in the workplace, where employers deem nonstandard home dialects unacceptable for many positions. Language is perhaps the most important factor in defining who we are, and we judge and are judged continually on the basis of the language we use. Consequently, the desire to be identified with an elite group leads many people to drop their home dialect for Standard English, if not formal Standard English.

Changing one's home dialect is not easy. First, there is the challenge of mastering a new set of linguistic features, such as vocabulary, accent, rhythm, and in some cases, grammar. Motivation appears to be the key. We note, for example, that when aspiring actors and actresses come to Los Angeles, the first thing many do is hire a diction coach to help them replace their New York or Southern or even Australian dialects. The efforts are nearly always successful: Few people remember that superstar Mel Gibson grew up in Australia and that he spoke Australian English in his first films. We also note how quickly dislocated teenagers shift dialects. When on the faculty at the University of North Carolina years ago, I worked with many students from the

Northeast who blended New York and Southern dialects within a few months of their arrival in Chapel Hill. Within a year, only traces of their home dialect remained. The desire of teenagers to conform to a peer group is well known and accounts for the rapid dialect shift.

But adopting a new dialect can be problematic when there is little motivation. We define ourselves and develop our identity through the interactions we have with those closest to us—our families and friends. Adopting the prestige dialect may make some students feel that they are losing their connection with home and community. At the university level, we often hear students talking about the difficulties they face when they go home for a break and find that the language they now use is different from what their parents and friends speak. Some feel that they are outsiders in their own homes. First-generation college students are especially prone to this experience. Although nearly all parents want their children to get a college education, ours is a very class-conscious society, and education that threatens to move children too far outside the boundaries of their communities is often seen as a threat by friends and family, in spite of their good intentions and best wishes.

This conflict is especially acute in our public schools owing to the huge influx of immigrants that began in the mid-1980s and continues today. Census Bureau data indicate that a large percentage of these immigrants are in the country illegally, which necessarily erects a barrier to any notion of assimilation. One result is that emotional (as well as fiscal) ties to the home country remain quite strong. Ghettoization is rampant as immigrants seek to find comfort in communities that perpetuate their home values, customs, ideals, and language.

The result is a serious dilemma for immigrants, our schools, and the nation. Some states, such as California, Arizona, and Colorado, have dismantled bilingual education programs, and in many other states the pressure to reclassify children as English proficient is so strong that it frequently occurs too soon. Consequently, becoming bilingual is a real challenge for the children of immigrants. On achieving bilingual proficiency, they then face an equally difficult challenge—Standard English. Those who do not master the prestige dialect are likely to remain insiders in their communities but outsiders with respect to the workplace and the broader society. Most people try to solve this problem by becoming bidialectical, over time learning how to use both dialects with varying degrees of success. Others may find jobs that do not require much proficiency in the prestige dialect.

Many of our students who speak Black English Vernacular (BEV) or Chicano English—the two most pervasive nonstandard dialects in the country—resist using Standard English in school because they do not want to be identified with the white mainstream. Meanwhile, the white population is diminishing. Again turning to California, which often is an early indicator of trends, the population in 1970 was 80% white; by 1998, it had dropped to just over 50% (Reyes, 2001). What I have observed in many schools with a predominantly Hispanic student body is that some white students use Chicano English in order to fit in. Frequently, anyone—white, black, or Hispanic—who uses Standard English is ostracized by peers. The mysterious popularity of "gangster chic" has exacerbated this unfortunate situation.

The role language plays in personal and cultural identity has motivated numerous well-meaning educators to argue that our schools should not teach Standard English or expect students to master its conventions. In 1974, the National Council of Teachers of English (NCTE), for example, passed a resolution proclaiming that students have a right to their own language and arguing that conventions of Standard English should be abolished because they are elitist and/or discriminatory.[1] Although this resolution originally sought to address the difficulties of our black students whose home dialect is BEV, some teachers feel that it is even more relevant today, in the face of uncontrolled immigration from Mexico, Central America, and China that has altered the very foundation of public education by creating student populations at many schools that are 100% nonnative English speaking. The link between education and income, however, cannot be denied. Reed (2004) reported that Hispanics as a group have the lowest levels of educational achievement and also the highest poverty rate; about 25% of all Hispanics live at the poverty level, and for illegal immigrants the number is probably higher. Meanwhile, as Weir (2002) indicated, the rapid growth of the U.S. population has led to an equally rapid increase in competition and sorting, with education being the most significant factor in the growing disparity in income that is turning America into a two-tiered society. Given the important role language plays in academic success and thus in economic success, we have no choice but to recognize that students need to expand their repertoire of language skills and conventions, not reduce them, which necessarily would be the outcome of any serious effort to enforce the idea that students have a right to their own language. In the hard realities of the marketplace, students may have this right, just as they have the right to wear a T-shirt and jeans to an interview for a banking job. But in exercising this right, they also must be prepared to accept the consequences, which in both cases would be the same—unemployment.

---

[1]The NCTE resolution is in stark contrast to the TESOL (Teachers of English to Speakers of Other Languages) resolution of 1981: "Whereas speakers of nonstandard English should have the opportunity to learn standard English and teachers should be aware of the influence on nonstandard English on the acquisition of standard English, and whereas TESOL is a major organization which exerts influence on English language education throughout the educational community, be it therefore resolved that TESOL will make every effort to support the appropriate training of teachers of speakers of nonstandard dialects by disseminating information through its established vehicles."

We have an obligation to be sensitive to the situation that our students find themselves in. At the same time, it is important to recognize that positions like the NCTE resolution oversimplify a complex problem. As teachers, we have an even greater obligation to provide students with the tools they need to realize their full potential, which they must do within the framework of sociolinguistic realities. It may be entirely wrong and unfair, but people nevertheless view certain dialects negatively. Wolfram, Adger, and Christian, (1998) reported that these negative views are held even by those who speak nonstandard dialects.

Some people may argue that it's a mistake to put so much emphasis on the socioeconomic value of helping students master Standard and formal Standard English. Doing so serves to commodify education, making it a means to a dubious end. There is truth in this argument. However, we must be careful not to press this argument too forcefully—the value of economic security and social mobility cannot realistically be denied, especially for students from poor families. The ease with which even the best and the brightest fall into ideologically induced incoherence on this point is stunning. We need only look at professional publications over the last two decades to see it everywhere. Some years ago, for example, Anthony Petrosky (1990) criticized schools in the Mississippi Delta because they were too successful at graduating students who went on to college and made successful careers for themselves in other states. Petrosky complained that learning Standard English, or what he called "instructional language," maintained the "existing class and socioeconomic order by allowing the students who do well the opportunity to leave the Delta ...; this opportunity can be said to reinforce the values necessary to maintain the authority, the priorities, and the language that allow those values to exist in the first place" (p. 66). In other words, if the schools had not provided instruction in Standard English, the students who left the Delta would not have had the opportunity to do so, and they would not have had the opportunity to pursue careers in medicine, teaching, engineering, law, and so on. Instead, like their less capable, less diligent cohorts who did not master the Standard dialect, they would have been forced by circumstance to remain in the Delta, where unemployment hovered around 20% and the number of people living below the national poverty level was as high as 68% in 1994 (U.S. Department of Commerce, Bureau of the Census, County & City Data Book, pp. 2–3). Such arguments seem to confuse dignity and value. Without question, there can be dignity in poverty, but *value?* It is relatively easy for those who do not have to deal with closed socioeconomic doors to engage in this sort of political posturing. In the name of ideology, they are always too ready to sacrifice the dreams others have for a better life.

Fortunately, most teachers understand that education is the key to opportunity, that opportunity is a clear good, and that mastery of Standard English is a key to education. Large numbers of educators believe that schools must adopt an *additive stance* with respect to dialects, and they view mastery and use of Standard English as complementing the home dialect, whatever it may be. This additive stance calls for legitimizing and valuing all dialects while simultaneously recognizing the appropriateness conditions that govern language use in specific situations. From this perspective, there are situations in which Black English, for example, is appropriate and Standard English is not; and there are situations in which Standard English is appropriate and Black English is not. The goals of schools, therefore, should include helping students recognize the different conditions and mastering the nuances of Standard English. Sadly, this commonsense approach tends to get lost in all the noise surrounding language policy and language curricula. Those involved simply cannot reach agreement on fundamental principles. Education is intensely political.

APPLYING KEY IDEAS

Reflect on the foregoing discussion and your own views on the question of teaching the prestige dialect in our schools. What is your position? Write a page or two explaining your position and its implications for your teaching. Share your writing with your class and determine whether there is any consensus. Based on the outcome of the class discussion, what conclusions can you draw about the status of Standard English instruction in our schools of tomorrow?

Evaluate your own dialect. If your goal as a teacher is to provide a model of Standard English for students, what adjustments may you have to make in your language?

SLANG

Although slang is a variation of a language, it is not the same as a dialect. Slang differs from a dialect in several ways. For example, it is limited to a relatively small group of people, whereas a dialect is used by large numbers. Slang typically is associated with young people between the ages of 12 and 25, who use it as a means of group bonding that distinguishes insiders from outsiders, especially with respect to age and gender—boys tend to use more slang than girls. The lexicons of dialects remain stable over time, as we see in the case of the word *elevator* in American English and *lift* in British English. Slang, on the other hand, is in perpetual motion even within a given group, which results in the rapid emergence and disappearance of terms. Only a few slang terms from each generation survive beyond their initial time frame. For example, the word *cool* as a superlative dates back to the 1930s but nevertheless is used extensively in both the United States and Great Britain today. On the other hand, we just don't hear anyone using the word *groovy*, a superlative that was pervasive during the 1960s.

The dynamic character of slang is rooted in the sociological factors that stimulate it—the changes that are part of adolescence. They inevitably become less important as people mature into adulthood. Teenagers feel that they are different from other people, so they use slang as a way of validating their perception, attempting to solidify their group identity by erecting linguistic barriers to all who are different, particularly adults. As they themselves become adults, the imperative disappears for most, which is why we encounter few adults who use slang. When we do, we commonly feel uncomfortable; it just doesn't seem appropriate to see a 60-year-old talking like a 15-year-old.

Some people argue that adults have their own version of slang, called *jargon*. Jargon signifies technical terms used in trades and professional work. It performs nearly all of the same functions as slang, for it also separates insiders from outsiders. Some professions, such as law, make their domain even more opaque to outsiders by seasoning jargon with Latin. Likewise, physicians write prescriptions in Latin, which has the effect of preventing most people from knowing what they are purchasing at the pharmacy. Like slang, jargon commonly serves as a kind of insider code that allows people to reduce into a single term complex ideas that may require dozens of words to explain. Teachers, for example, often use the expression *zone of proximal development*, coined by Vygotsky (1978), to describe a sophisticated concept in education. A significant difference between slang and jargon, however, is that jargon tends not to disappear over time; indeed, in many instances it becomes more dense.

Teaching Tip

Students everywhere seem to be interested in slang. An activity involving slang, therefore, can serve as an effective way of getting them more interested in language. One such activity begins by having students work in small groups to make a list of slang terms and expressions they know. Then have them record additional examples of slang outside of class, preferably off campus, perhaps at a mall. Allow them to discuss their observations and compare them to the initial lists they created. For the second part of the activity, have students observe TV news broadcasts and documentaries. A second discussion should follow, in which students explore differences and similarities in the language they observed. What are the factors associated with slang use?

DEVELOPMENT OF A PRESTIGE DIALECT

All countries have prestige dialects, and, in most cases, sheer historical accident led to the dominance of one variety of a language rather than another.
Haugen (1966) suggested that all standard dialects undergo similar processes
that solidify their position in a society. First, a society will select, usually on the
basis of users' socioeconomic success, a particular variety of the language to be
the standard. At some point, the chosen variety will be codified by teachers and
scholars who write grammar books and dictionaries for it. The effect is to stabi-
lize the dialect by reaching some sort of agreement regarding what is correct
and what is not. The dialect then must be functionally elaborated so that it can
be used in government, law, education, technology, and in all forms of writing.
Finally, the dialect has to be accepted by all segments of the society as the standard, particularly by those who speak some other variety (Hall, 1972;
Macaulay, 1973; Trudgill, 2001).

NONSTANDARD DIALECTS

Although many people think of nonstandard dialects exclusively in terms of
Black English and Chicano English, dialects cannot be viewed simply in terms
of ethnicity. Many African Americans speak BEV, but not all do. Not surprisingly, the determining factor nearly always is SES, not ethnicity. Thus, we find
nonstandard dialects in all communities—white, Asian, Hispanic, and
black—that have low incomes.

For most of America's history, the difficulties of travel in such a large country made geography the most important factor in language variation. Regional
dialects still abound, but Wolfram et al. (1998) reported a leveling of regional
differences. Labov (1996), however, noted that:

> Sociolinguistic research on linguistic change in progress has found rapid
> development of sound changes in most urbanized areas of North Amer-
> ica, leading to increased dialect diversity. It appears that the dialects of
> New York, Philadelphia, Detroit, Chicago, Saint Louis, Dallas, and Los
> Angeles are now more different from each other than they were 50 or 100
> years ago. (p. 1)

The data may not be in conflict. It is possible that leveling is occurring across
regions, moving Western and Southern dialects, for example, closer, while the
opposite is true in the nation's major urban centers. At this point, the findings
are unclear and require further research.

Nevertheless, we can speculate about the factors that might be influencing
dialect change. Leveling may well be the result of increased American mobil-

ity. People relocate more frequently today than ever before, and the result is an unprecedented blending of various dialects, especially in the South, which has seen tremendous population growth owing to an influx of Northerners looking for jobs, lower taxes, and warm weather.

Another factor may be the overall shift of Black English toward Standard English, through the ongoing process of decreolization.[2] This shift is surprising because in many respects segregation—or, more accurately, self-segregation—today is stronger than at any time since the early 1960s. Blacks and whites alike generally call bussing a failure; educators as well as parents are reassessing the educational benefits to minority children of integrated classrooms; and self-segregated schools, usually with an Afrocentric curriculum, are being hailed by many African Americans as the best answer to the persistent achievement problems black children experience in integrated schools (see Orfield, 2004). These factors should result in more separation between Standard English and Black English. However, they are mitigated by the fact that, at the same time, affirmative action has been successful in increasing the educational and economic opportunities among African Americans to such a degree that Black English speakers have more contact with standard speakers than in the past.

In addition, Herrnstein and Murray (1994) reported that the black middle class has been growing steadily for about 25 years, providing a compelling incentive to shift toward Standard English as families move into middle- and upper-middle-class communities. Likewise, Robert Harris (1999) noted that in 1998:

> the Joint Center for Political and Economic Studies, a Washington, D.C.-based think tank devoted to black economic and political participation in American society, reported that for the first time in its surveys of black opinion, more African Americans than whites responded favorably when asked whether they were better off financially than in the previous year. This unprecedented optimism among African Americans reflects the growth of a strong black middle class, the lowest poverty rate since measurements were started in 1959, and unemployment below 10 percent. These are heady but fragile times for the newly emergent black middle class. (p. 1)

The motivation to use Standard English would be strong among children of the growing black middle class, who must match their dialect to that of their socioeconomic peers if they hope to become insiders. Although the white middle class has been shrinking during this same period, there are no incentives to adopt a nonstandard dialect—to shift downward—among adults, although there is for their children. Peer pressure will motivate them to embrace a nonstandard dialect.

---

[2]Some evidence of recreolization dos exist. For example, young Black English speakers who want to emphasize an action will add a second participle to a verb to produce *walked-ed, talked-ed,* and *stopped-ed.*

Two factors may be responsible for the rapid changes Labov (1996) reported. One is that our urban centers have been magnets for immigrants. Many cities, such as Los Angeles, have seen their populations more than double since 1970. The influx of new residents, the majority for whom English is a second language, would create a dynamic linguistic environment that is conducive to linguistic change. In addition, the American economy has grown significantly since 1970. Real GDP in 1970 was $3,771.9 billion; by 2003, this figure had jumped to an astounding $10,398 billion (U.S. Department of Commerce, Bureau of Economic Analysis, 2004a).

We can make such numbers more personal, perhaps, by considering the nation's median price for homes as a reflection of the increase in wealth. In 1970, the median price of a home nationally was $24,400. In 2001, the most recent year for which data are available, the price was $174,100. In the West, which saw dramatic population growth during this period, the numbers are even more striking: $24,000 and $214,400, respectively (U.S. Department of Housing and Urban Development, 2004).[3] One result of such affluence is what James Twitchell (2003) referred to as the "opulux culture"—America's infatuation with designer labels, custom kitchens, and German luxury cars. Another, however, is a concomitant increase in sophistication and cosmopolitanism, two of the more salient factors associated with rapid dialect change.[4]

Although change is a natural part of all living languages, there is cause for concern. The Usage Notes in earlier chapters detailed many features of nonstandard English, yet for a growing number of young people, the problems they face owing to their use of nonstandard English are more severe than any we have discussed. Their language exemplifies what linguists call *restricted code,* language that is impoverished with respect to syntax, vocabulary, meaning, and the ability to communicate beyond the most rudimentary level. Restricted codes today seem unrelated to race or SES. The following example came from a white, middle-class 10th-grade student in a history course who was asked to summarize how a congressional bill becomes a law:

---

[3]By April 2004, the median home price in California had more than doubled to $453,590 (*San Jose Business Journal,* May 24, 2004).

[4]The increase in wealth represented in these numbers does not mean that everyone is better off today than in 1970. They actually tell much of the story of the shrinking middle class. In 1970, the average annual income was $15,000 (Puget Sound Regional Council, 2001, p. 2); in April 2004, the average annual income was $27,455 (U.S. Department of Commerce, Bureau of Economic Analysis, 2004b, p. 1). Thus, whereas home prices (based on 2001 data) have increased 7.1 times, income has not even doubled. The situation is worse for people living in California, where home prices have increased an astounding 18.6 times. All things being equal, the average worker in California today would have to earn $279,000 to have the same buying power that he or she had in 1970.

Well, uhm, it's like, you know, the Congress, like, you know, uhm, they meet, right? And, uhm, they talk about stuff, you know, and uhm, like, the stuff gets written down, you know, and, well, like, that's how it happens.

This student clearly has a problem with logical thinking, but logical thinking is linked to language in important ways. The imprecision, particularly the absence of a vocabulary that allows him to convey what he knows, is characteristic of restricted code. Healy (1990) argued that nonstandard usage among our students "may account for many of the problems in logical thinking ... that are becoming so evident in our high schools" (p. 110). She went on to note that "the most difficult aspect of writing clearly ... is that it demands the ability to organize thought" (p. 111). In a similar vein, Orr (1987) suggested that many school problems are rooted in the fact that nonstandard speakers do not know what words mean. Reporting her experience as a teacher, Orr stated:

In a chemistry class a student stated that ... the volume of a gas would be half more than it was. When I asked her if she meant that the volume would get ... larger, she said, "No, smaller." When I then explained that half more than would mean larger, indicating the increase with my hands, she said she meant twice and with her hands indicated a decrease. When I then said, "But twice means larger," ... she said, "I guess I mean half less than." (p. 27)

A few studies and much anecdotal evidence suggest that the number of students who speak restricted-code nonstandard English is increasing, that their language is becoming ever more impoverished (Bohannon & Stanowicz, 1988; Healy, 1990; Vail, 1989). As a result, teachers must look even more closely at their goals and methods than they did in the past. Not all nonstandard speakers use a restricted code, but growing numbers of standard speakers do, which is alarming. For those who do not, instruction in the standard conventions can lead to measurable improvement in language skills, especially with respect to writing, but the real key lies in strategies that improve vocabulary and logical, precise use of language. For those who use a restricted code, like the two students just mentioned, their language limits their ability to communicate beyond the most superficial level and raises serious obstacles to academic success.

DIALECTS AND EDUCATION

Because socioeconomic status is closely tied to level of education (Herrnstein & Murray, 1994), nonstandard speakers tend to be undereducated, and they also

tend to be linked to the working-class poor.[5] Education, however, is not an absolute indicator of dialect. The language skills of college graduates appear to have
declined significantly over the last 25 years (Healy, 1990). Moreover, the shrinking of the middle class has led increasingly to comments about class warfare,
with predictable aversion and animosity toward the educated elite who have high
incomes. Being identified as a member of the elite has tangible liabilities, especially for politicians. Thus, we frequently see candidates doffing their suits and
ties for polo shirts and jeans. They not only declare that they feel the pain of voters but make every effort to utter that declaration in a homespun dialect intended
to project the image of Everyman. Some would argue on this ground that President George W. Bush represents the perfect politician, because voters so easily
see themselves in his Texas dialect and his linguistic misadventures. Given these
realities, our complaints about the decline in student language skills over the last
two decades necessarily must be viewed in the context of a major shift toward
nonstandard English among the well-educated nationwide.

Not surprisingly, several reports have shown that literacy levels in the public
schools and in higher education have plummeted since the mid-1960s. Chall
(1996) and Coulson (1996) reported serious declines in language and literacy
levels for students in all age groups. Chall, for example, described her experience
at a community college where the "freshmen tested, on the average, on an
eighth-grade reading level. Thus, the average student in this community college
was able to read only on a level expected of junior high school students" (p. 309).
Findings like these are not limited to community colleges. Entering freshmen at a
major research university in North Carolina, ranked among the top 25 schools in
the nation, are tested each year for reading skill, and their average annual scores
between 1987 and 1994 placed them at about the 10th-grade reading level.[6]

---

[5]We must be careful about our understanding of what it means to be poor in America. Rector and
Johnson (2004) reported that:

> only a small number of the 35 million persons classified as 'poor' by the Census Bureau fit that
> description. While real material hardship certainly does occur, it is limited in scope and severity.
> Most of America's "poor" live in material conditions that would be judged as comfortable or
> well-off just a few generations ago.... Forty-six percent of all poor households actually own their
> own homes. The average home owned by persons classified as poor by the Census Bureau is a
> three-bedroom house with one-and-a-half baths, a garage, and a porch or patio. Seventy-six per-
> cent of poor households have air conditioning. By contrast, 30 years ago, only 36 percent of the
> entire U.S. population enjoyed air conditioning. Only 6 percent of poor households are over-
> crowded. More than two-thirds have more than two rooms per person. The average poor Ameri-
> can has more living space than the average individual living in Paris, London, Vienna, Athens,
> and other cities throughout Europe. Nearly three-quarters of poor households own a car; 30 per-
> cent own two or more cars. Ninety-seven percent of poor households have a color television; over
> half own two or more color televisions. Seventy-eight percent have a VCR or DVD player; 62
> percent have cable or satellite TV reception. Seventy-three percent own microwave ovens, more
> than half have a stereo, and a third have an automatic dishwasher. (pp. 1–2)

[6]During this period, students took the Nelson-Denny reading test, which was administered by the
university's learning skills center. I reviewed the data in my capacity as an administrator at the school.

Efforts to explain the drop in language skills have focused on two factors: the high number of hours per week that children watch television (approximately 30) and the widespread shift from phonics as the basis for reading instruction to whole-language approaches. There is no question that television exerts an insidious influence on children's language development, if for no other reason than that it isolates young people from the social interactions with adults and peers that are crucial to good language skills. Instead of playing and having conversations with other children, too many young people are rooted in front of a TV set afternoons, evenings, and weekends.

Most of the programs children watch are cartoons, hardly a language-rich genre. Many parents justify the hours their children spend watching cartoons by believing that an hour or so of *Sesame Street* each day provides a restorative educational balance. The reasoning is similar to that displayed by the overweight person who orders a diet soda to wash down the chili cheese fries. Furthermore, the few studies that have examined the pedagogical foundations and benefits of *Sesame Street* suggested not only that the show did not employ sound pedagogical principles but also that it does more harm than good (Burns & Anderson, 1991; Meringoff, 1980; Singer, 1980).

The issue of reading instruction may be important. Certainly, many people feel that the shift in numerous schools from phonics to whole-language approaches during the 1980s had a deleterious effect on language in general and reading in particular. Reading leads to larger vocabularies and richer sentence structures, which have beneficial effects on language skills, and if whole-language approaches lead to greater difficulty in reading, students will be less likely to reap these benefits. The problem with this argument is that most schools that experimented with whole language have shifted back to phonics. Indeed, the 2002 No Child Left Behind Act essentially mandated this change. Thus, the issue of reading instruction seems moot. The only thing we know for sure is that the amount of reading young people do today is significantly lower than it was just 30 years ago (Healy, 1990). In fact, many young people today never do any pleasure reading.

Meanwhile, it is reasonable to conclude that the plunge in language skills among students is linked to a decline in skills among teachers. Approximately 60% of all university professors today are first-generation college graduates, and it is safe to assume that a large portion came from working-class backgrounds where nonstandard English was the norm and the Standard English of the schools the exception. Having established their careers and no longer facing the compulsion to be insiders, these teachers are in a position to abandon the Standard English that they mastered in order to succeed and to slip comfortably into the home dialects of their childhood. On many college campuses today, the speech of students and faculty is almost indistinguishable.

As far as I can determine, no study has examined the role, if any, that non-standard English among teachers plays in children's language and literacy development. As indicated earlier, some teachers and social commentators have lauded the shift to nonstandard English as part of an effort to bridge the widening gap between the educated elite and the undereducated underclass. This is misguided populism at its worst. When students with low skills become teachers with low skills, we can predict that they probably will produce students with low skills. The cycle becomes self-perpetuating.

BLACK ENGLISH

The serious study of Black English Vernacular was impeded for decades by myths and misconceptions, and it was not until the early 1970s that scholars began to move beyond the myths and examine BEV in a principled way. Dillard (1973) reported, for example, that until the 1960s it was often argued that Black English was a vestige of a British dialect with origins in East Anglia (also see McCrum, Cran, & MacNeil, 1986). According to this view, American blacks had somehow managed to avoid significant linguistic change for centuries, even though it was well known that all living languages are in a constant state of change. This romantic notion of a dialect somehow suspended in time is totally without substance. Dillard also described the "physiological theory," which held that Black English was the result of "thick lips" that rendered blacks incapable of producing Standard English. More imaginative and outrageous was Mencken's (1936) notion that Black English was the invention of playwrights: "The Negro dialect, as we know it today, seems to have been formulated by the songwriters for the minstrel shows; it did not appear in literature until the time of the Civil War; before that, as George P. Krappe shows ..., it was a vague and artificial lingo which had little relation to the actual speech of Southern blacks (p. 71)."

Mencken didn't mention how blacks were supposed to have gone to the minstrel shows so that they might pick up the new "lingo," nor why in the world they would be motivated to do so.

Pidgins

Linguists today support the view that Black English developed from the pidgin versions of English, Dutch, Spanish, and Portuguese used during the slave era. A pidgin is a contact vernacular, a form of language that arises spontaneously whenever two people lack a common language. It is a mixture of two (or possibly more) languages that has been modified to eliminate the more difficult features, such as irregular verb forms (Kay & Sankoff, 1974; Slobin, 1977). Function words like determiners (*the, a, an*) and prepositions (*in, on, across*) are commonly dropped. Function markers, such as case, are eliminated, as are tense and plurals.[7]

European slavers came from England, France, Spain, Portugal, and Holland. Their human cargo came from a huge area of Western Africa, including what is now Gambia, the Ivory Coast, Ghana, Nigeria, and Zaire. These languages mixed together to serve as the basis for the early pidgins. McCrum et al. (1986) suggested that the pidgins began developing shortly after the slaves were captured, because the traders separated those who spoke the same language to prevent collaboration that might lead to rebellion. Chained in the holds of the slave ships, the captives had every incentive to continue using pidgin to establish a linguistic community. It is more likely, however, that the pidgins already were well established among the villages responsible for capturing and selling tribesmen and tribeswomen to the European slavers. Trade in humans as well as commodities had a long history in the region, and those who were captured may have grown up using one or more pidgins for trade in addition to their native languages. At the very least, they would have started using a pidgin almost immediately after capture. They would not have waited until they were placed on ships headed for the New World.

Creolization

Once in America, the slaves had to continue using pidgin English to communicate with their owners and with one another. Matters changed, however, when the slaves began having children. A fascinating phenomenon occurs when children are born into a community that uses a pidgin: They spontaneously regularize the language. They add function words, regularize verbs, and provide a grammar where none really existed before. When the children of the pidgin-speaking slaves began speaking, they spoke a Creole, not a pidgin. A Creole is a full language in the technical sense, with its own grammar, vocabulary, and pragmatic conventions.

Why, then, is Black English classified as a dialect of English rather than a Creole? The answer is that the Creole spoken in North America underwent a process of *decreolization*. True Creoles, like those spoken in the Caribbean, experienced reduced contact with the major contributory languages. Papiamento, the Creole spoken in the Dutch Antilles, offers a good example. This language is a mixture of Dutch, French, and English. Although Dutch has long been the official language of the Antilles, the linguistic influences of French and English disappeared about 200 years ago, and the influence of Dutch has waned

---

[7]The broken English that Johnny Weissmuller used in the Tarzan movies from the 1930s and 1940s, which still air on TV, reflects accurately the features of a pidgin.

significantly in this century. As a result, Papiamento continued to develop in its own way; it did not move closer to Standard Dutch. A different process occurred in the United States. The influence of Standard English on the slave Creole increased over the years, especially after the abolition of slavery. Thus, the Creole that was spoken by large numbers of slaves shifted closer and closer to Standard English, until at some point it stopped being a Creole and became a dialect. It is closer to English than to any other language, which is why speakers of Standard English can understand BEV but not a Creole.

Although the process of decreolization was powerful, Black English preserved many features of its Creole and pidgin roots, which extend to the West African tribal languages as well as to Dutch, French, Portuguese, and Spanish. The most visible of these features are grammatical, and for generations these grammatical differences have led large numbers of Americans to assume that BEV was merely a degenerate version of Standard English. Speakers were believed to violate grammatical rules every time they used the language. Works like Dillard's (1973) and Labov's (1970, 1971, 1972), however, demonstrated that Black English has its own grammar, which is a blend of Standard English and a variety of West African languages seasoned with European languages.

Many people observe that there is a strong similarity between Black English and the English used by white Southerners, but the dialects are not the same, even though they are quite similar. Blacks and whites have lived in close-knit communities in the South for generations. Throughout the slave era, white children played with black children, who exerted a powerful influence on the white-minority dialect. (As Slobin [1977] indicated, language change occurs primarily in the speech of children.) Because whites were the minority, the various Southern dialects shifted toward Black English as Black English simultaneously shifted toward the various Southern dialects until they were closer to each other than to any other American dialect.

Socioeconomic status is often a more salient factor in dialect variation in the South than region, although region continues to play a major role owing to the tendency among Southerners to resist the increase in mobility that has characterized other parts of the nation. Anyone traveling from Virginia to South Carolina will recognize three distinct dialect variations linked to region; these variations, in turn, are part of the larger Southern dialect, as shown in Fig. 7.1. The Research Triangle area in North Carolina—composed of Raleigh, Durham, and Chapel Hill—has four distinct dialect variations, even though there are no geographical factors hindering travel or communication. These variations are linked to SES and education.

The Place of BEV in our Schools

During the 1960s, as a result of the Civil Rights Movement, we saw a significant effort to reexamine the place of BEV in our schools. School policies at the time did not allow the use of Black English for recitation and writing and insisted, instead, on fairly strict adherence to standard conventions. Many educators, parents, and social activists charged that these policies were discriminatory and placed an unfair burden on African-American children. Robinson (1990), for example, suggested that Standard English is an obstacle to learning and that BEV should be legitimized in the schools. Several years later, in what may be seen as a logical conclusion to the reexamination that began in the 1960s, the Oakland, California, school district made national headlines by proclaiming that BEV—or "ebonics," as the district labeled it—was not a dialect but rather an independent language and decided that it would be the language of instruction in the district's predominantly black schools.

This approach was not really new. In the 1970s, several schools in California's Bay Area issued specially prepared textbooks written in BEV rather than Standard English and used BEV as the language of instruction. The situation in Oakland, however, garnered much more attention and hostility. The question is why.

The school board's declaration that BEV is "genetic" may have been one reason; its decision to ignore decades of linguistic research into BEV as a dialect may have been another. I would suggest, however, that a number of other factors were also at work.

In the 1970s, the Civil Rights Movement was still strong, and there generally was wide support for policies intended to improve the academic performance of minority students. Affirmative action programs, for example, were endorsed by a significant majority of the population. Over time, however, this support began to wane. Blacks made impressive and highly visible advances politically (at one point, nearly every major city in the country had a black mayor), educationally, and economically, and many whites began to feel that society had done enough to level the playing field. When Dinesh D'Souza published *Illiberal Education* in 1991 and reported that a black applicant to UC Berkeley was 8,000 times more likely to be admitted than an Asian applicant with better qualifications, the resulting outrage laid the foundation for the slow but steady dismantling of affirmative action programs nationwide. Also, other issues began to press: women's rights, gay rights, abortion rights, illegal immigration, and the steady erosion of middle-class buying power. The well of compassion for just causes was being sucked dry.

For many, what exacerbated matters beyond measure was the sudden influence of postmodernism. Any significant discussion is far beyond the scope of this book, but suffice it to say that postmodernism's Marxist roots gave its advocates an aggressive edge that most commonly found expression in remarkably successful efforts to impose politically correct behavior on everyone. As I've noted elsewhere (Williams, 2003a):

> Western society, insofar as it is defined as the prevailing traditions and institutions that are deemed to be of historical significance, is fundamentally evil, according to Marcuse [who in many respects can be considered a founding father of postmodernism], and must be overturned by any means necessary. For example, in 1965, he argued that only those with left-wing views should be afforded the right of free speech. This right should be denied to those with incorrect thoughts by invoking the "natural right" of "oppressed and overpowered minorities to use extralegal means" to silence opposing points of view. (p. 89)

In the ensuing "culture wars" of the 1990s, those advocating political correctness effectively silenced not only opposing points of view but discussion in general. When this was combined with the rapid rise of identity politics, which seemed eager to sacrifice the commonweal for personal gain, the result was a seething resentment among many that seriously undermined support for minority issues (see Williams, 2002). Thus, when the issue of ebonics came up in Oakland, it acted as a spark that ignited a tinderbox of frustration and latent resentment nationwide.

Also, a court ruling on BEV almost 20 years earlier, in 1979, made it appear that the Oakland school board was engaged in political grandstanding. The case involved a group of attorneys who sued the Ann Arbor School District board on behalf of 11 children who spoke Black English and who were failing in school. The suit alleged that the district had not prepared teachers to instruct children whose home dialect was BEV. Although this case raises the question of how judges who know nothing about linguistics or education can make rulings on complex topics after only a few hours of testimony, it nevertheless set an inescapable precedent. Ruling for the plaintiffs, the court (Memorandum Opinion and Order, 1979) found that:

> Black English is not a language used by the mainstream of society—black or white. It is not an acceptable method of communication in the educational world, in the commercial community, in the community of the arts and science, or among professionals (p. 1378).

The district was ordered to provide teachers with 20 hours of linguistic training that gave them insight into the structure of Black English. This training, however, did not include any instruction on how to utilize the new knowledge to teach better, nor did it provide any reduction in the underlying tension between home and school dialects. If anything, the suit and the subsequent order exacerbated the overall problem by declaring, as a legal finding of fact, that Standard English is the language of schools and by simultaneously holding schools and teachers accountable for the failure of students whose home dialect causes difficulties when it comes to literacy. The ruling, in other words, was profoundly illogical.

When we consider the place of BEV—or any other nonstandard dialect, for that matter—in our schools, we ought to look beyond politics and consider what is best for students. As teachers, we have an obligation to provide children with the tools they need to realize their full potential as individuals and as members of society. The politics of education too easily can blind us to the needs of our students, which certainly was the case in the Bay Area when various schools shifted instruction and textbooks to BEV. I worked with about a dozen of these students in the early 1970s after they enrolled in college. They discovered that they were underprepared for college work. Even worse, they could not read their college texts. All but a few dropped out. It is worth asking how many of these students would have been able to complete college if they had not been caught up in an experiment.

To date, no evidence exists to suggest that substituting Black English for Standard English improves academic performance. Too often, the gap in educational performance between blacks and Hispanics on the one hand and whites and Asians on the other receives little notice. This gap, however, is huge and warrants our full attention. Data from the 1999 NAEP report indicated a 4-year gap between black and Hispanic students and their white and Asian counterparts. In a follow-up study, Thernstrom and Thernstrom (2003) reported that black high school seniors have lower test scores in reading, writing, math, history, and geography than 8th-grade white students. On this basis, it seems that efforts to validate the use of nonstandard English in education will do little to modify the status of students from disadvantaged backgrounds.[8] They do not expand students' language skills in any way that will help them overcome the very real obstacle to educational success and socioeconomic mobility that nonstandard English presents. These efforts merely keep these students ghettoized. Equally troubling is that the argument for shifting to BEV as the dialect of instruction seems, inher-

---

[8]Thernstrom and Thernstrom (2003) argued that the primary source of these performance gaps lies in home environments. Their research indicated that white and Asian-American parents commonly have high expectations for their children and demand that they work hard. Hispanic children are handicapped by the limited education of their parents, which makes it difficult for them to preach the benefits of education and the necessity of making short-term sacrifices to achieve long-term goals. The poor academic performance of African-American students, Thernstrom and Thernstrom argued, rests in "the special role of television in the life of black children and the low expectations of their parents" (p. 211).

ently, to be founded on a disturbingly racist point of view: There is the undeni-
able—and unacceptable—hint that students who speak Black English are
incapable of mastering Standard English.

Adopting an additive stance with respect to dialects eliminates many of the
difficulties associated with BEV and instruction. The mastery and use of Standard English complements the home dialect, whatever it may be. An additive
stance also calls for legitimizing and valuing all dialects while simultaneously
recognizing the appropriateness conditions that govern language use in
specific situations.

Black English Grammar

Black English grammar differs from Standard English grammar in several
ways. For example, it normally omits the *s* suffix on present-tense verbs (*He
talk pretty fast*), except in those instances where the speaker overcorrects in an
effort to approximate standard patterns (*I goes to work*). It drops the *g* from participles (*He goin' now*), and it also uses four separate negators: *dit'n, not, don'*
and *ain'*. Consider the following sentences:

1. Fred dit'n come yesterday.
2. Macarena not comin'.
3. Fritz don' eat them pies.
4. Fritz don' be goin' the store.
5. Macarena ain' eat.
6. She don' be eatin'.

Agreement.   In Standard English, verbs agree in number with their subjects in the present tense. In BEV, they usually do not. We therefore observe the
following differences:

7. I love you, Macarena. (standard)
8. I loves you, Macarena (black)

Aspect.   One of the more significant differences between Standard English and Black English is that the two dialects treat tense and aspect differently.
On page 71, we examined aspect as a feature of the English verb form, looking
specifically at progressive and perfect forms. At that point, we considered the
fact that Standard English marks verb tenses as past or present and that it provides the option of indicating the static or ongoing nature of an action (aspect)
through the use of these two verb forms. Black English, in contrast, allows for

optional tense marking but requires that the action be marked as momentary or continuous.

Aspect also allows speakers to stretch out the time of a verb, an important characteristic of Black English, which uses the verb form *be* to accomplish the task. Sentences 9 and 10, for example, have quite different meanings:

9. Macarena workin'.
10. Macarena be workin'.

In sentence 9, Macarena may be working today, at this moment, but she normally doesn't. In sentence 10, on the other hand, Macarena has been conscientiously working for a long time. We see similar examples in the following:

11. Fritz studyin' right now.
12. Fritz be studyin' every afternoon.

Studyin' agrees in aspect with *right now,* and *be studyin'* agrees in aspect with *every afternoon*. It therefore would be ungrammatical in Black English to say or write *Fritz studyin' every afternoon* or *Fritz be studyin' right now* (Baugh, 1983; Fasold, 1972; Wolfram, 1969).

Black English uses *been,* the participial form of *be,* as a past-perfect marker: *Been* signals that an action occurred in the distant past or that it was completed totally (Rickford, 1975). In this sense it is similar to the past-perfect form *have* + *verb* and *have* + *been* in Standard English, as the following sentences illustrate:

13. They had told us to leave. (standard)
14. They been told us to leave. (black)
15. Kerri had eaten all the cake. (standard)
16. Kerri been eat all the cake. (black)
17. She had been hurt. (standard)
18. She been been hurt. (black)

Been is also used to assert that an action initiated in the past is still in effect, as in the following:

19. Macarena has known Fritz more than 3 months now. (standard)
20. Macarena been been knowin' Fritz more than 3 month now. (black)

Questions in Black English generally take two forms, depending on the aspect involved. Someone inquiring about a short-term state, for example, might ask:

21. Is you hungry?

The same question concerning a long-term state, however, would be structured as:

22. Do you be hungry?

We also see from sentence 21 that *is* can function in two ways in BEV, as an emphasis marker and as a question marker. Thus, sentence 23 is perfectly grammatical:

23. I is hungry.

A variant would be:

24. I'm is hungry.

As a question, sentence 23 also would have two variants:

25. Is I hungry?
26. Is I'm hungry?

Other important features of BEV grammar are shown here:

- The present tense is used in narratives to indicate past action, as in *They goes to the market.*
- When cardinal adjectives precede nouns, the noun is not pluralized, as in *The candy cost 1 dollar and 50 cent.*
- Relative pronouns in the subject position of a relative clause can be dropped, as in *Fritz like the woman has red hair.*
- The possessive marker is dropped, as in *He found Macarena coat.*
- Whereas Standard English alternates a negative and a positive in a sentence (*I never want to see you again*), Black English uses double negatives, as in *He don' never goin' call.*

APPLYING KEY IDEAS

1. In addition to your own dialect, how many others are there in your community that you are aware of?
2. How many dialects do you understand?

3. What may be some factors, not mentioned in this chapter, that inhibit the acquisition and use of Standard English among children?
4. Listen carefully to a dialect in your community and list the features that differ from your home dialect.
5. Television news anchors generally speak what is known as "broadcast standard," a hybrid dialect that is often identified as coming closest to spoken Standard English. What are some features of your home dialect that differ from broadcast standard?
6. What value is there in knowing that BEV is well structured according to its own grammar?
7. What are some possible connections between BEV and academic performance?
8. Team up with two other students in your class. Using what you have learned to this point, develop a set of three activities that engage nonstandard dialect-speaking students in using Standard English. Share these activities with other members of the class to develop a lesson portfolio.

CHICANO ENGLISH

The term *Chicano* emerged during the 1960s as a label rooted in efforts to raise the cultural awareness and identity among Mexican Americans, and it emphasizes their unique position between two heritages. *Chicano English* (CE) is the term used to describe the nonstandard dialect spoken by many second and third-generation Mexican Americans, most of whom do not speak Spanish, although they may understand it slightly (see Garcia, 1983). CE is also used to describe the dialect spoken by first-generation immigrants who have lived in the United States long enough to have acquired sufficient mastery of English to be able to carry on a conversation exclusively in it and thus are considered to be bilingual (see Baugh, 1983).

Chicano English is influenced linguistically by monolingual Spanish speakers, monolingual English speakers, and bilingual Spanish-English speakers. CE is not the same as *Spanglish*—a blend of English and Spanish frequently used by native Spanish speakers who have picked up a few words of English. Although Spanglish was once ridiculed and derided as *pocho* English because of its long association with *pachucos*, young gang members notorious in places like East Los Angeles, Spanglish is now widely used throughout Mexican-American communities. We look at Spanglish later in the chapter.

Interest in CE is fairly recent, largely because until the 1980s the focus of language policy in the United States as it relates to dialects was on Black English. The central issue with regard to the Hispanic population was bilingual education. The explosion of immigration from Mexico and Central America that began in 1985 altered this situation, but the level of research in CE remains very low. Carmen Fought's (2002) *Chicano English in Context* is the first book-length investigation of CE in 20 years.

There are several reasons for this general lack of interest. The most pressing appears to be the overwhelming number of students entering our schools who are monolingual in a language other than English. Schools reasonably identify these students as their first priority. As soon as these English language learners (ELL) are reclassified as English proficient, they are treated essentially like native speakers and receive no accommodation. Another factor is the politics of education, which set priorities in terms of funding and policy. Research requires money. Even though our Hispanic population now outnumbers our black population, Hispanics have, historically, been uninvolved politically. Quite simply, they don't vote in high numbers, so they receive little attention from government. Thus, there is no money available to research CE.

CHICANO ENGLISH GRAMMAR

Even though most speakers of Chicano English have little or no Spanish, Spanish exerts a significant influence on their dialect. We can see this influence in various structural and phonetic features of CE. For example, Spanish is an inflected language, so it relies less on word order than English does. As a result, the sentence *Macarena ate the apple* can be expressed in two ways in Spanish:

- Macarena comió la manzana. (Macarena ate the apple.)

or

- Comió la manzana Macarena. (literal translation: Ate the apple Macarena.)

Although CE does not allow the structure shown in the second sentence, it does allow for a variation that involves pleonasm, or redundancy, that is related to the freer word order we see in Spanish. A pronoun marks the subject, which is repeated as a noun at the end of the sentence, as in:

- He hit the ball, Fred.
- She gave me a ride, my mother.

Spanish also uses the double negative, which is reflected in the grammar of CE. Students regularly produce statements such as *I didn't do nothing* and *She don't want no advice.*

Spanish signifies third-person possession through prepositional phrases rather than possessive nouns, as in the following sentence:

- Vivo en la casa de mi madre. (literal translation: I live in the house of my mother.)

We therefore frequently find students producing sentences of the following type in CE:

- The car of my brother is red.
- The ring of my financée was expensive.

Because Spanish has a single preposition (*en*) that corresponds to both *in* and *on* in English, speakers of CE commonly use *in* where Standard English requires *on,* as in the following:

- Macarena got in the bus before she realized that she didn't have no change.
- We got in our bikes and rode down the hill.

Other syntactic influences on Chicano English include topicalization, dropped inflections, inappropriate use of do-support, dropping *have* in perfect verb forms, and transformation of mass nouns into count nouns. Examples of these influences are shown in the following sentences:

- My brother, he lives in St. Louis. (topicalization)
- My parents were raise old-fashion. (dropped inflections)
- My father asked me where did I go. (inappropriate do-support)
- I been working every weekend for a month. (dropping *have*)
- When we went to the mountains, we saw deers and everything. (mass noun to count noun)

As indicated earlier, CE is subject to various influences. In the case of dropped *have,* we cannot say that this is the result of Spanish interference; Spanish forms the perfect verb form with *haber* plus the past participle of the main verb. Thus, *I have been working every weekend for a month* would have a form essentially identical to the Spanish:

- Yo hube estado trabajando cada finde semana por una mes.

On this account, it seems reasonable to conclude that the dropped *have* that we find in CE is the influence of nonstandard English dialects.

CHICANO ENGLISH IN THE CLASSROOM

Very little research examines the influence of CE on academic performance. Castaneda and Ulanoff (2004) observed elementary children in grades 3, 4, and 5 and students in one high school in Southern California and reported that the elementary students were reluctant to use CE in the classroom. The high school students, however, were different. Castaneda and Ulanoff noted that they:

> often chose to use Chicano English as a "political" and/or "solidarity" statement within the context of school activities.... [For both groups, it] was more common to hear Chicano English spoken on the playground or at lunch than in the context of classroom interaction.... The high school students demonstrated more proficiency with standard English and so their use of Chicano English appeared to be something done purposely, at times for group identity, at times to demonstrate resistance to norms. (p. 7)

Regrettably, Castaneda and Ulanoff (2004) were unable to assess possible correlations between academic performance and CE, but we can predict that manifestations of "solidarity" and "resistance" would not win the hearts of many teachers. Resistance seldom characterizes students who are succeeding. When we consider that the dropout rate for Mexican-American students has hovered around 30% for decades, the Castaneda and Ulanoff report is not encouraging.

Chicano English and Writing

What little research exists on CE and writing performance is so old as to be almost irrelevant but nevertheless warrants a review. The available studies are not particularly useful because they looked at sentence-level issues rather than the whole essay. Amastae (1981) evaluated writing samples collected from students at Pan American University in Texas over a 4-year period to determine the range of surface errors and the degree of sentence elaboration as measured by students' use of subordination. Spanish interference did not seem to be a major source of error in the compositions, but the students used very little subordination (also see Edelsky, 1986), which would tend to make their writing seem less than fluid, perhaps even choppy. Because subordination is generally viewed as a measure of writing maturity (K. Hunt, 1965), its absence in the essays of Chicano English speakers could adversely affect how teachers judge their writing ability.

As far as I could determine, not a single study of CE has examined rhetorical features such as topic, purpose, and audience. Without this research, it is impossible to determine best practices for students who use Chicano English because we don't really know what the issues are. Carol Edelsky's (1986) study of bilingual, elementary-age Spanish-speaking students examined rhetorical features of writing, but we have no basis for applying her findings to CE speakers, although it is tempting to assume that what works for speakers of Standard English and BEV would work for speakers of CE. Along these lines, Edelsky's study concluded that bilingual students benefited from process pedagogy.

Drawing on what we know about the influence of BEV on the academic performance of black students may be the most productive approach for understanding CE in the classroom, particularly when students are asked to write. We know that use of BEV at school seriously hinders academic success (Delpit, 1988; Michaels, 1982) and that there are significant BEV interference issues in these students' writing. We must carefully consider that nonstandard dialects in the classroom have negative effects along two dimensions. The first and most obvious for CE is that the dialect does not conform to the conventions of Standard English that are an important part of our writing pedagogy. If a student writes *She don't want no advice*, he or she has failed to demonstrate mastery of that part of the lesson to be learned. But I would suggest that the second dimension is more problematic: All nonstandard dialects manifest the features of conversations. An important part of formal schooling is to help students develop a repertoire of language skills that allows them to function appropriately in a variety of situations, and another important part is to help them recognize what those situations are and what is appropriate in each. The implication, therefore, is that students whose dialect is CE will benefit from well-structured writing assignments that give them opportunities not only to practice the conventions of Standard English but also to identify the situations that require those conventions.

Teaching Tip

Unless students read, it is very difficult for them to begin internalizing the differences between writing and conversation. A useful strategy, therefore, consists of engaging students in reading materials that reflect a variety of genres. Discussion of these materials must not focus exclusively on content but also must include questions of form. An effective lesson would involve a topic that students are interested in. Have them talk about the topic in small groups, using a recorder to tape their discussion. Have students transcribe their group's discussion. Then ask them to read an essay or article on the same topic and compare it with the transcripts of their discussions. Examine closely differences in ideas and structure, pointing out those features that are characteristic of conversation and those that are characteristic of writing.

SPANGLISH

Over the last couple of decades, as the native Spanish speaking population has grown exponentially, Spanglish has become increasingly widespread. As the name suggests, Spanglish is a combination of Spanish and English. It is not quite the same thing as "code-switching," which is discussed in the next section. Spanglish is a hybrid dialect of *Spanish, not English,* that typically is used by immigrants from Mexico who have resided in the United States for some time but who have acquired only a smattering of English. Equivalent Spanish words are dropped from the lexicon and replaced by the hybrid terms, such as "wachar" for "watch," "parquear" for "park," and "pushar" for "push." A native English speaker who does not know Spanish would have a hard time even recognizing Spanglish, and it is the case that many native Spanish speakers who are not immigrants disparage those who use Spanglish.

We can get a sense of the differences between Spanish and Spanglish by comparing the sentences below, which translate into "I'm going to park my car":

- Voy a estacionar mi auto. (Standard Spanish)
- Voy a parquear mi caro. (Spanglish)

Neither "parquear" ("park") nor "caro" ("car") exist in Standard Spanish; the equivalent words are *estacionar* and *auto*.

It is entirely possible that Spanglish represents a kind of contact vernacular or pidgin that native Spanish speakers are developing to cope with their new English-language environment. At this point, however, we just don't have enough data to make any concrete conclusions. Because Spanglish is spoken by those who essentially have no English, the problems it presents in our schools are addressed as ELL issues, not dialectical ones.

CODE SWITCHING

Different dialects often have differences in grammar, as in the case of Black English Vernacular and Standard English. They also have different usage conventions. Because our society is highly mobile, large numbers of people are bidialectical, which has the benefit of allowing them to shift between different language situations. We frequently find that speakers of Standard English use nonstandard grammar and/or usage and that speakers of nonstandard English use Standard grammar and/or usage.

When people shift from one form of language to another, they are engaged in what is called *code switching*. In its broadest sense, code switching refers to the act of using different language varieties.

We can account for code switching on the basis of linguistic variation, which exists not only across dialects but also within them. Sources of variation include age, occupation, location, economic status, and gender. Women, for example, tend to be more conscientious about language than men. As a result, in a family whose dialect is nonstandard, the woman's language will be closer to Standard English than the man's (Trudgill, 2001), especially in situations that call for Standard English. We therefore may observe a woman using Standard English in the workplace but nonstandard at home.

The phenomenon of linguistic variation led William Labov (1996) to suggest that every dialect is subject to "inherent variability." In his analysis, speakers of a particular dialect fail to use all the features of that dialect all the time, and the constant state of flux that we see in language causes some degree of variation. This principle accounts for the fact that Standard English speakers periodically reduce sentences like "I've been working hard" to "I been working hard." More common, however, is variation of nonstandard features to standard features, nearly always as a result of sociolinguistic pressures to conform to the mainstream. On this account, people who speak nonstandard English typically will attempt to adopt Standard features in any situation in which they are interacting with someone they perceive as socially superior. This effort to conform can be readily observed in classrooms when we ask students who use nonstandard English to write a paper and then read it aloud. The writing will contain numerous nonstandard dialect features, but as the student is reading, he or she will correct many of them. In these cases, the students are engaged in code switching.

We can learn the degree of bidialectalism of our students from these observations, which in turn can help us construct assignments and activities that make students more aware of code switching and their level of Standard English mastery. Also, they teach us that the inherent variability of language makes dialects unstable and therefore malleable. The language people use at any given time can be located on a continuum that ranges in some cases from formal Standard written English to informal nonstandard spoken English. People move back and forth on the continuum as context demands and as their linguistic skills allow. This movement can be with different dialects or with different languages.

When teachers witness code switching on a daily basis, it is easy for them to assume that students like those reported by Castaneda and Ulanoff (2004) are simply being perverse when they fail to modify their speech and writing to Standard English on a permanent basis. Most of the available research on code switching suggests, however, that it is acquired behavior rather than learned (Baugh, 1983; Genishi, 1981; Labov, 1971, 1972a, 1972b; McClure, 1981;

Peck, 1982). If this is the case, then code switching would be largely unconscious. I would argue that such a conclusion is faulty.

Existing research shows that those who speak English as a second language tend to code switch under two conditions: (a) when speaking with an audience they know is bilingual, and (b) when they need a word in L2 that they don't have or can't remember. The situation is slightly different for nonstandard-English speakers. They generally do not code switch when speaking with others who are bidialectal. Instead, they will use one dialect or the other, depending on the social relationship that exists among the group and on the setting. The dominant factor, however, is the social relationship: As it becomes more intimate, there is a greater tendency to use the home dialect, even in those situations in which other speakers do not share and have a hard time understanding that dialect. As the bidialectal speaker shifts further along the continuum toward nonstandard speech, the monodialectal participant may have to ask "What?" several times as a reminder that he or she is not understanding some of the nonstandard language. At such moments, the bidialectal speaker must make a conscious decision to shift in the other direction along the continuum. Whenever these social factors do not obtain, it is considered rude to use the nonstandard dialect.

The model of cognitive grammar described in the previous chapter allows us to understand this behavior by positing that, among bidialectal speakers, both the standard and the nonstandard forms coexist in their neural networks. This seems commonsensical: If they didn't, Standard English and nonstandard English speakers would not be able to understand one another, yet they generally do. The case of negatives provides a useful example. For Standard English speakers, the negative/positive pattern dominates, whereas for nonstandard English speakers the negative/negative pattern dominates. On this basis, we must conclude that use of the nondominating form is a conscious decision.

This analysis allows us to understand Castaneda and Ulanoff's (2004) observations. Recall that the elementary-school children in their study were reluctant to use Chicano English, whereas the high schoolers used it to express "solidarity" and "resistance." Recall also the discussion of moral behavior in chapter 6. The children in elementary school recognized that it would be rude for them to use CE in the classroom, so they refrained. Teenagers, on the other hand, often are unconcerned about being rude. In both cases, to use or not to use CE was a conscious decision. Does this mean that teachers are witnessing a kind of perversity when students choose to use CE or BEV in the classroom? Well, in some cases, yes. We must keep in mind that the key to dialect shift is motivation.

The situation is not quite the same with respect to writing, however. Here, students are struggling not just with differences between Standard and nonstandard English but also with the differences inherent in formal Standard English, as well as the natural inclination to focus on content rather than form. What this means, of course, is that our students whose home dialect is nonstandard will have a harder time and will need more support than those whose home dialect is Standard English.

APPLYING KEY IDEAS

1. Reflect on how you respond when you hear someone using either BEV or CE. Does your response include an assessment of that person's status, job, or education? If so, what can we learn about teaching students whose home dialect is BEV or CE?
2. Form a group with three classmates to discuss how you might motivate BEV and CE speakers to use Standard English. Develop a sequence of lessons and activities that include at least one simulation exercise that could be used in teaching.

References

Abbott, V., Black, J., & Smith, E. (1985). The representation of scripts in memory. *Journal of Memory and Language, 24*, 179–199.

Alcock, J. (2001). *The triumph of sociobiology*. New York: Oxford University Press.

Aldrich, R. (1999). When the pupil:teacher ratio was 1,000 to one. *Times Educational Supplement*. Retrieved December 20, 2003, from http://www.tes.com.uk/seach/ search_display.asp?section=archive&sub_secton=friday.

Allen, Woody. (1982). *Four films of Woody Allen: Annie Hall, Interiors, Manhattan, Stardust Memories*. New York: Random House.

Amastae, J. (1981). The writing needs of Hispanic students. In B. Cronnell (Ed.), *The writing needs of linguistically different students*. Washington, DC: SWRL Educational Research and Development.

Andrews, L. (1995). Language awareness: The whole elephant. *English Journal, 84*(1), 29–34.

Andrews, L. (1998). *Language exploration and awareness: A resource book for teachers* (2nd ed.). Mahwah, NJ: Lawrence Erlbaum Associates.

Bagou, O., Fougeron, C., & Frauenfelder, U. (2002). Contribution of prosody to the segmentation and storage of "words" in the acquisition of a new mini-language. Retrieved May 5, 2004, from http://www.lpl.univ-aix.fr/projects/aix02/sp2002/ pdf/bagou-fougeron-frauenfelder.pdf.

Bahrick, L., & Pickens, J. (1988). Classification of bimodal English and Spanish language passages by infants. *Infant Behavior and Development, 11*, 277–296.

Bain, A. (1866). *English composition and rhetoric*. New York: Appleton-Century-Crofts.

Baldassare, M., & Katz, C. (2003). *The faces of diversity: Melting pot or great divide?* San Francisco: Public Policy Institute of California. Retrieved January 15, 2004, from http://www.ppic.org/main/commentary.asp?i=403.

Barber, B. K. (1996). Parental psychological control: Revisiting a neglected construct. *Child Development, 67*(6), 3296–3319.

Barkow, J., Cosmides, L., & Tooby, J. (Eds.). (1992). *The adapted mind*. Oxford, England: Oxford University Press.

Bateman, D., & Zidonis, F. (1966). *The effect of a study of transformational grammar on the writing of ninth and tenth graders*. Champaign, IL: National Council of Teachers of English.

Baugh, J. (1983). *Black street speech: Its history, structure, and survival*. Austin, TX: University of Texas Press.

Baumrind, D. (1989). Rearing competent children. In W. Damon (Ed.), *Child development today and tomorrow* (pp. 349–378). San Francisco: Jossey-Bass.

Baumrind, D. (1991). The influence of parenting style on adolescent competence and substance use. *Journal of Early Adolescence, 11*(1), 56–95.

Bhatnagar, S., Mandybur, G., Buckingham, H., & Andy, O. (2000). Language representation in the human brain: Evidence from cortical mapping. *Brain and Language, 74,* 238–259.

Bloom, P. (1994). Generativity within language and other cognitive domains. *Cognition, 60,* 177–189.

Bloomfield, L. (1933). *Language.* New York: Holt, Rinehart & Winston.

Boas, F. (1911). *Handbook of American Indian languages.* Washington, DC: Smithsonian Institution.

Bohannon, J., & Stanowicz, L. (1988). The issue of negative evidence: Adult responses to children's language errors. *Developmental Psychology, 24,* 684–689.

Bowerman, M. (1982). Evaluating competing linguistic models with language acquisition data: Implications of developmental errors with causative verbs. *Quaderni di Semantica, 3,* 5–66.

Braddock, R., Lloyd-Jones, R., & Schoer, L. (1963). *Research in written composition.* Champaign, IL: National Council of Teachers of English.

Bradshaw, J., Ford, K., Adams-Webber, J., & Boose, J. (1993). Beyond the repertory grid: New approaches to constructivist knowledge acquisition tool development. *International Journal of Intelligent Systems, 8*(2), 287–333.

Bryce, T. (2002). *Life and society in the Hittite world.* Oxford, England: Oxford University Press.

Burns, J., & Anderson, D. (1991). Cognition and watching television. In D. Tupper & K. Cicerone (Eds.), *Neuropsychology of everyday life* (pp. 93–108). Boston: Kluwer.

Calabretta, R., Nolfi, S., Parisi, D., & Wagner, G. (2000). Duplication of modules facilitates the evolution of functional specialization. *Artificial Life, 6,* 69–84.

California's median home price increases 24.6 percent in April. (2004, May 24). *San Jose Business Journal.* Retrieved June 4, 2004, from http://sanjose.bizjournals.com/sanjose/stories/2004/05/24/daily19.html.

Calkins, L. (1983). *Lessons from a child.* Exeter, NH: Heinemann.

Callaghan, T. (1978). The effects of sentence-combining exercises on the syntactic maturity, quality of writing, reading ability, and attitudes of ninth grade students. *Dissertation Abstracts International, 39,* 637-A.

Calvin, W. (2004). *A brief history of the mind: From apes to intellect and beyond.* New York: Oxford University Press.

Carey, S. (1995). On the origin of causal understanding. In D. Sperber, D. Premack, & A. Premack (Eds.), *Causal cognition: A multidisciplinary debate* (pp. 269–308). Sixth Symposium of the Fyssen Foundation. Oxford, England: Clarendon Press.

Carruthers, P., & Chamberlain, A. (2000). *Evolution and the human mind: Modularity, language and meta-cognition.* Cambridge, England: Cambridge University Press.

Castaneda, L., & Ulanoff, S. (2004, April). *Chicano talk: Examining social, cultural, linguistic features and schooling.* Paper presented at the annual meeting of the American Educational Research Association, San Diego, CA.

Chall, J. (1996). American reading achievement: Should we worry? *Research in the Teaching of English, 30,* 303–310.

Chao, R. K. (1994). Beyond parental control and authoritarian parenting style: Understanding Chinese parenting through the cultural notion of training. *Child Development, 65*(4), 1111–1119.

Chomsky, N. (1955). The logical structure of linguistic theory. Mimeograph. MIT, Cambridge, MA.

Chomsky, N. (1957). *Syntactic structures.* The Hague, Netherlands: Mouton.

Chomsky, N. (1965). *Aspects of the theory of syntax.* Cambridge, MA: MIT Press.

Chomsky, N. (1972). *Language and mind.* New York: Harcourt Brace Jovanovich.

Chomsky, N. (1981). *Lectures on government and binding.* Dordrecht, Netherlands: Foris.

Chomsky, N. (1995). *The minimalist program.* Cambridge, MA: MIT Press.

Chomsky, N. (2000). *New horizons in the study of language and mind.* Cambridge: Cambridge University Press.

Christensen, F. (1967). *Notes toward a new rhetoric: Six essays for teachers.* New York: Harper & Row.

Christophe, A., & Morton, J. (1998). Is Dutch native English? Linguistic analysis by 2-month-olds. *Developmental Science, 1,* 215–219.

Clark, A. (1993). *Associative engines: Connectionism, concepts, and representational change.* Cambridge, MA: MIT Press.

Cmiel, K. (1991). *Democratic eloquence: The fight over popular speech in nineteenth-century America.* Berkeley, CA: University of California Press.

Cobb, L. (1835). *Cobb's juvenal reader no. 1.* Philadelphia: James Kay Jr. & Brothers.

Cohen, L. B., Amsel, G., Redford, M. A., & Casasola, M. (1998). The development of infant causal perception. In A. Slater (Ed.), *Perceptual development visual, auditory, and speech perception in infancy* (pp. 167–209). Hove, England: Psychology Press.

Coles, W., & Vopat, J. (1985). *What makes writing good: A multiperspective.* Lexington, MA: Heath.

Combs, W. (1977). Sentence-combining practice: Do gains in judgments of writing "quality" persist? *Journal of Educational Research, 70,* 318–321.

Comrie, B. (1981). *Language universals and linguistic typology: Syntax and morphology.* Chicago: University of Chicago Press.

Connors, R. (2000). The erasure of the sentence. *College Composition and Communication, 52,* 96–128.

Connors, R., & Lunsford, A. (1988). Frequency of formal errors in current college writing, or Ma and Pa Kettle do research. *College Composition and Communication, 39,* 395–409.

Coulson, A. (1996). Schooling and literacy over time: The rising cost of stagnation and decline. *Research in the Teaching of English, 30,* 311–327.

Crosby, A. (1997). *The measure of reality: Quantification and Western society, 1250–1600.* Cambridge, England: Cambridge University Press.

Crowley, S. (1990). *The methodical memory: Invention in current-traditional rhetoric.* Carbondale, IL: Southern Illinois University Press.

Crowhurst, J., & Piche, G. (1979). Audience and mode of discourse effects on syntactic complexity in writing at two grade levels. *Research in the Teaching of English, 13,* 101–109.

Cullicover, P. (1999). *Syntactic nuts: Hard cases in syntax.* Oxford, England: Oxford University Press.

D'Souza, D. (1991). *Illiberal education: The politics of race and sex on campus.* New York: The Free Press.

Daiker, D., Kerek, A., & Morenberg, M. (1978). Sentence-combining and syntactic maturity in freshman English. *College Composition and Communication, 29,* 36–41.

Darling, N., & Steinberg, L. (1993). Parenting style as context: An integrative model. *Psychological Bulletin, 113*(3), 487–496.

Davis, J. (2004). *The journey from the center to the page: Yoga principles & practices as muse for authentic writing.* New York: Penguin Putnam.

Day, P., & Ulatowska, H. (1979). Perceptual, cognitive, and linguistic development after early hemispherectomy: Two case studies. *Brain and Language, 7,* 17–33.

de Boysson-Bardies, B. (2001). *How language comes to children: From birth to two years* (M. DeBevoise, Trans.). Cambridge, MA: MIT Press.

Dehaene, S. (1999). Fitting two languages into one brain. *Brain, 122,* 2207–2208.

Dehaene-Lambertz, G., & Houston, D. (1998). Faster orientation latencies toward native language in two-month-old infants. *Language and Speech, 41,* 21–31.

DeLoache, J., Miller, K., & Pierroutsakos, S. (1998). Reasoning and problem-solving. In D. Kuhn & R. Siegler (Eds.), *Handbook of child psychology* (Vol. 2, pp. 801–842). New York: Wiley.

Delpit, L. (1988). The silenced dialogue: Power and pedagogy in educating other people's children. *Harvard Educational Review, 58,* 280–298.

Demetras, M., Post, K., & Snow, C. (1986). Feedback to first language learners: The role of repetitions and clarification questions. *Journal of Child Language, 13,* 275–292.

Dennis, M., & Kohn, B. (1975). Comprehension of syntax in infantile hemiplegics after cerebral hemidecortication: Left hemisphere superiority. *Brain and Language, 2,* 475–486.

Dennis, M., & Whitaker, H. (1976). Language acquisition following hemidecortication: Linguistic superiority of the left over the right hemisphere of right-handed people. *Brain and language, 3,* 404–433.

Dillard, J. (1973). *Black English: Its history and usage in the United States.* New York: Vintage Books.

Dionysius Thrax. (1874). The grammar of Dionysius Thrax (T. Davidson, Trans.). *Journal of Speculative Philosophy, 8,* 326–339.

Dykema, K. W. (1961). Where our grammar came from. *College English, 22,* 455–465.

Edelsky, C. (1986). *Writing in a bilingual program: Había una vez.* Norwood, NJ: Ablex.

Edmondson, W. (2000). *General cognitive principles and the structure of behavior.* Retrieved April 10, 2002, from http://www.cs.bham.ac.uk/~whe/seqimp.pdf.

Eisenstein, E. (1980). *The printing press as an agent of change.* Cambridge, England: Cambridge University Press.

Elbow, P. (1973). *Writing without teachers.* New York: Oxford University Press.

Elbow, P. (1981). *Writing with power.* New York: Oxford University Press.

Elley, W., Barham, I., Lamb, H., & Wyllie, M. (1976). The role of grammar in a secondary school English curriculum. *New Zealand Journal of Educational Studies, 10,* 26–42. (Reprinted in *Research in the Teaching of English, 10,* 5–21)

Elman, J., Bates, E., Johnson, M., Karmiloff-Smith, A., Parisi, D., & Plunkett, K. (1996). *Rethinking innateness: A connectionist perspective on development.* Cambridge, MA: MIT Press.

English Review Group. (2004). *The effect of grammar teaching (syntax) in English on 5 to 16 year olds' accuracy and quality in written composition.* London: EPPI Centre.

Fabbro, F. (2001). The bilingual brain: Cerebral representation of languages. *Brain and Language, 79,* 211–222.

Fasold, R. (1972). *Tense marking in Black English: A linguistic and social analysis.* Washington, DC: Center for Applied Linguistics.

Fauconnier, G., & Turner, M. (2002). *The way we think: Conceptual blending and the mind's hidden complexities.* New York: Basic Books.

Fernald, A. (1994). Human maternal vocalizations to infants as biologically relevant signals: An evolutionary perspective. In P. Bloom (Ed.), *Language acquisition: Core readings* (pp. 51–94). Cambridge, MA: MIT Press.

Fernald, A., Swingley, D., & Pinto, J. (2001). When half a word is enough: Infants can recognize spoken words using partial phonetic information. *Child Development, 72,* 1003–1015.

Ferrie, J. (1999). *How ya gonna keep 'em down on the farm [when they've seen Schenectady]?: Rural-to-urban migration in 19th century America, 1850–1870.* NSF report (Grant No. SBR-9730243). Retrieved December 25, 2003, from http://www.faculty.econ.northwestern.edu/faculty/ferrie/papers/urban.pdf.

Fleming, D. (2002). The end of composition-rhetoric. In J. Williams (Ed.), *Visions and revisions: Continuity and change in rhetoric and composition* (pp. 109–130). Carbondale, IL: Southern Illinois University Press.

Fodor, J. (1983). *The modularity of mind.* Cambridge, MA: MIT Press.

Fodor, J., Bever, T., & Garrett, M. (1974). *The psychology of language.* New York: McGraw-Hill.

Fought, C. (2002). *Chicano English in context.* New York: Palgrave MacMillan.

Gale, I. (1968). An experimental study of two fifth-grade language-arts programs: An analysis of the writing of children taught linguistic grammar compared to those taught traditional grammar. *Dissertation Abstracts, 28,* 4156A.

Garcia, E. (1983). *Early childhood bilingualism.* Albuquerque, NM: University of New Mexico Press.

Gardner, H. (1983). *Frames of mind: The theory of multiple intelligences.* New York: Basic Books.

Gardner, H. (1993). *Multiple intelligences: The theory in practice.* New York: Basic Books.

Gardner, H. (2000). *Intelligence reframed: Multiple intelligences for the 21st century*. New York: Basic Books.

Geiger, R. (1999). The ten generations of American higher education. In P. Altback, R. Berdahl, & P. Gumport (Eds.), *American higher education in the twenty-first century: Social, political, and economic challenges* (pp. 38–69). Baltimore: Johns Hopkins University Press.

Genishi, C. (1981). Code switching in Chicano six-year-olds. In R. Duran (Ed.), *Latino language and communicative behavior* (pp. 133–152). Norwood, NJ: Ablex.

Glencoe/McGraw-Hill. (2001). *Glencoe writer's choice: Grammar and composition*. Columbus, OH: Glencoe/McGraw-Hill.

Glenn, C. (1995). When grammar was a language art. In S. Hunter & R. Wallace (Eds.), *The place of grammar in writing instruction, past, present, and future*. Portsmouth, NH: Boynton Cook Heinemann.

Goldrick, M., & Rapp, B. (2001, November). *Mrs. Malaprop's neighborhood: Using word errors to reveal neighborhood structure*. Poster presented at the 42nd annual meeting of the Psychonomic Society, Orlando, FL.

Gould, S. J. (1991). Exaptation: A crucial tool for evolutionary psychology. *Journal of Social Issues, 47,* 43–65.

Green, E. (1973). An experimental study of sentence combining to improve written syntactic fluency in fifth-grade children. *Dissertation Abstracts International, 33,* 4057A.

Greenwood, J., Seshadri, A., & Vandenbroucke, G. (2002). The baby boom and baby bust: Some macroeconomics for population economics. *Economie d'avant garde*. Research report no. 1. Retrieved June 6, 2004, from http://www.econ.rochester.edu/Faculty/Greenwood Papers/bb.pdf.

Grodzinsky, Y. (2000). The neurology of syntax: Language use without Broca's area. *Behavioral and Brain Sciences, 23,* 5–51.

Grossberg, S. (1999). The link between brain, learning, attention, and consciousness. *Consciousness and Cognition, 8,* 1–44.

Hall, M. (1972). *The language experience approach for the culturally disadvantaged*. Newark, DE: International Reading Association.

Halliday, M. (1979). One child's protolanguage. In M. Bullowa (Ed.), *Before speech*. Cambridge, England: Cambridge University Press.

Harris, R. A. (1993). *The linguistics wars*. New York: Oxford University Press.

Harris, R. L. (1999). The rise of the black middle class. *World and I Magazine, 14,* 40–45.

Hartwell, P. (1985). Grammar, grammars, and the teaching of grammar. *College English, 47,* 107–127.

Haugen, E. (1966). *Language conflict and language planning: The case of modern Norwegian*. Cambridge, MA: Harvard University Press.

Haussamen, B., Benjamin, A., Kolln, M., & Wheeler, R. (2003). *Grammar alive: A guide for teachers*. Urbana, IL: National Council of Teachers of English.

Healy, J. (1990). *Endangered minds: Why children don't think and what we can do about it*. New York: Simon & Schuster.

Heath, S. (1983). *Ways with words*. Cambridge, England: Cambridge University Press.

Hendriks, P. (2004). *The problem with logic in the logical problem of language acquisition*. Retrieved April 1, 2004, from http://www.ai.mit.edu/people/jimmylin/papers/Hendricks00.pdf.

Henry, J. (2003, November 16). Literacy drive fails to teach 11-year-olds basic grammar. *London Daily Telegraph*. Retrieved December 25, 2003, from http://www.telegraph.co.uk/education/main.jhtml.

Hernandez, A., Martinez, A., & Kohnert, K. (2000). In search of the language switch: An fMRI study of picture naming in Spanish–English bilinguals. *Brain and Language, 73,* 421–431.

Herrnstein, R., & Murray, C. (1994). *The bell curve: Intelligence and class structure in American life*. New York: Free Press.

Hillocks, G. (1986). *Research on written composition: New directions for teaching*. Urbana, IL: National Conference on Research in English.

Hirsch, E. D. (1988). *Cultural literacy: What every American needs to know.* New York: Vintage.

Hirsh-Pasek, K., Treiman, R., & Schneiderman, M. (1984). Brown and Hanlon revisited: Mothers' sensitivity to ungrammatical forms. *Journal of Child Language, 11,* 81–88.

Homer. (1998). *The Iliad.* (R. Fagles, Trans.). New York: Penguin.

Howie, S. (1979). A study: The effects of sentence combining practice on the writing ability and reading level of ninth grade students. *Dissertation Abstracts International, 40,* 1980A.

Hudson, R. (1980). *Sociolinguistics.* Cambridge, England: Cambridge University Press.

Hunt, K. (1965). Grammatical structures written at three grade levels. *NCTE Research Report Number 3.* Champaign, IL: National Council of Teachers of English.

Hunt, R. W. (1980). *The history of grammar in the Middle Ages: Collected papers.* Amsterdam: John Benjamins.

Hymes, D. (1971). Competence and performance in linguistic theory. In R. Huxley & E. Ingram (Eds.), *Language acquisition: Models and methods* (pp. 3–28). New York: Academic Press.

Illes, J., Francis, W., Desmond, J., Gabrieli, J., Glover, G., Poldrack, R., Lee, C., & Wagner, A. (1999). Convergent cortical representation of semantic processing in bilinguals. *Brain and Language, 70,* 347–363.

Jackendoff, R. (2002). *Foundations of language: Brain, meaning, grammar, evolution.* New York: Oxford University Press.

Johnson, D., & Lappin, S. (1997). A critique of the minimalist program. *Linguistics and Philosophy, 20,* 272–333.

Johnson-Laird, P. (1983). *Mental models.* Cambridge, MA: Harvard University Press.

Johnson-Laird, P. (2001). Mental models and deduction. *Trends in Cognitive Science, 5,* 434–442.

Kapel, S. (1996). *Mistakes, fallacies, and irresponsibilities of prescriptive grammar.* Retrieved December 21, 2003, from http://www.newdream.net/~scully/toelw/Lowth.htm.

Katz, L. (1989). *Engaging children's minds.* Norwood, NJ: Ablex.

Kay, P., & Sankoff, G. (1974). A language-universals approach to pidgins and Creoles. In D. De-Camp & I. Hancock (Eds.), *Pidgins and Creoles: Current trends and prospects* (pp. 61–72). Washington, DC: Georgetown University Press.

Kelso, J. (1995). *Dynamic patterns: The self-organization of brain and behavior.* Cambridge, MA: MIT Press.

Kerek, A., Daiker, D., & Morenberg, M. (1980). Sentence combining and college composition. *Perceptual and Motor Skills, 51,* 1059–1157.

Kim, K., Relkin, N., Lee, K., & Hirsch, J. (1997). Distinct cortical areas associated with native and second languages. *Nature, 388,* 171–174.

Kinneavy, J. (1979). Sentence combining in a comprehensive language framework. In D. Daiker, A. Kerek, & M. Morenberg (Eds.), *Sentence combining and the teaching of writing* (pp. 60–76). Conway, AR: University of Akron and University of Arkansas.

Kintsch, W., & van Dijk, T. (1978). Toward a model of text comprehension and production. *Psychological Review, 85,* 363–394.

Kitahara, H. (1997). *Elementary operations and optimal derivations.* Cambridge, MA: MIT Press.

Klein, P. (1998). A response to Howard Gardner: Falsifiability, empirical evidence, and pedagogical usefulness in educational psychologies. *Canadian Journal of Education, 23,* 103–112.

Klima, E. (1964). Negation in English. In J. Fodor & J. Katz (Eds.), *The structure of language* (pp. 246–323). Englewood Cliffs, NJ: Prentice-Hall.

Kohn, B. (1980). Right-hemisphere speech representation and comprehension of syntax after left cerebral injury. *Brain and Language, 9,* 350–361.

Kolln, M. (1996). Rhetorical grammar: A modification lesson. *English Journal, 86,* 25–31.

Kratzer, A. (1996). Severing the external argument from its verb. In J. Rooryck & L. Zaring (Eds.), *Phrase structure and the lexicon* (pp. 109–137). Dordrecht, Netherlands: Kluwer.

Labov, W. (1970). *The study of nonstandard English.* Urbana, IL: National Council of Teachers of English.

Labov, W. (1971). The notion of system in Creole studies. In D. Hymes (Ed.), *Pidginization and creolization of language* (pp. 447–472). Cambridge, England: Cambridge University Press.

Labov, W. (1972a). *Language in the inner city: Studies in the Black English vernacular*. Philadelphia: University of Pennsylvania Press.

Labov, W. (1972b). *Sociolinguistic patterns*. Philadelphia: University of Pennsylvania Press.

Labov, W. (1996). The organization of dialect diversity in North America. Retrieved June 3, 2004, from http://www.ling.upenn.edu/phono_atlas.ICSLP4.html.

Lamb, S. (1998). *Pathways of the brain: The neurocognitive basis of language*. Amsterdam: John Benjamins.

Langacker, R. (1987). *Foundations of cognitive grammar: Vol. 1. Theoretical prerequisites*. Stanford, CA: Stanford University Press.

Langacker, R. (1990). *Concept, image, and symbol: The cognitive basis of grammar*. New York: Mouton de Gruyter.

Langacker, R. (1999). *Grammar and conceptualization*. Berlin, Germany: Mouton de Gruyter.

Lee, D. (2001). *Cognitive linguistics: An introduction*. Melbourne, Australia: Oxford University Press.

Lees, R. (1962). The grammatical basis of some semantic notions. In B. Choseed & A. Guss, *Report on the eleventh annual roundtable meeting on linguistics and language studies* (pp. 5–20). Washington, DC: Georgetown University Press.

Lester, M. (1990). *Grammar in the classroom*. New York: Macmillan.

Lester, M. (2001). Grammar and usage. In *Glencoe writer's choice: Grammar and composition* (pp. T25–T30). Columbus, OH: Glencoe/McGraw-Hill.

Lindemann, E. (1985). At the beach. In W. Coles & J. Vopat (Eds.), *What makes writing good* (pp. 98–113). Lexington, MA: Heath.

Locke, J. (2000). *Some thoughts concerning education*. Oxford, England: Oxford University Press.

Lowth, R. (1979). *A short introduction to English grammar*. Delmar, NY: Scholars Facsimilies & Reprints. (Original work published 1762)

Macaulay, R. (1973). Double standards. *American Anthropologist, 75,* 1324–1337.

Maccoby, E. E., & Martin, J. A. (1983). Socialization in the context of the family: Parent–child interaction. In P. H. Mussen (Series Ed.) & E. M. Hetherington (Vol. Ed.), *Handbook of child psychology: Vol. 4. Socialization, personality, and social development* (4th ed., pp. 1–101). New York: Wiley.

Macrorie, K. (1970). *Telling writing*. New Rochelle, NY: Hayden.

Marcus, G. (1993). Negative evidence in language acquisition. *Cognition, 46,* 53–85.

McClure, E. (1981). Formal and functional aspects of the code-switched discourse of bilingual children. In R. Duran (Ed.), *Latino language and communicative behavior: Advances in discourse processes* (Vol. 6, pp. 69–94). Norwood. NJ: Ablex.

McCrum, R., Cran, W., & MacNeil, R. (1986). *The story of English*. New York: Viking.

McGinnis, M. (2002). Object asymmetries in a phrase theory of syntax. In J. Jensen & G. van Herck (Eds.), *Proceedings of the 2001 CLA Annual Conference* (pp. 133–144). Ottawa: Cahiers Linguistiques d'Ottawa. Retrieved June 8, 2004, from http://www.ucalgary.ca/~mcginnis/papers/CLA01.pdf.

Memorandum Opinion and Order. (1979). Martin Luther King Junior Elementary School Children, et al. v. Ann Arbor School District, 73 F. Supp. 1371, 1378 (E.D. Mich. 1979).

Mencken, H. (1936). *The American language: An inquiry into the development of English in the United States*. New York: Knopf.

Meringoff, L. (1980). Influence of the medium on children's story apprehension. *Journal of Educational Psychology, 72,* 240–249.

Michaels, B. (1982). *Black rainbow*. New York: Congdon & Weed.

Miller, N., Cowan, P., Cowan, C., & Hetherington, E. (1993). Externalizing in preschoolers and early adolescents: A cross-study replication of a family model. *Developmental Psychology, 29*(1), 3–18.

Morgan, H. (1996). An analysis of Gardner's theory of multiple intelligence. *Roeper Review, 18,* 263–269.

Müller, R., & Basho, S. (2004). Are nonlinguistic functions in "Broca's area" prerequisites for language acquisition? FMRI findings from an ontogenetic viewpoint. *Brain and Language, 89,* 329–336.

Müller, R., Kleinhans, N., & Courchesne, E. (2001). Rapid communication: Broca's area and the discrimination of frequency transitions: A functional MRI study. *Brain and Language, 76,* 70–76.

National Center for Education Statistics. (1993). *Literacy from 1870 to 1979: Educational characteristics of the population.* Retrieved December 24, 2003, from http://nces.ed.gov/naal/historicaldata/edchar.asp.

National Commission of Excellence in Education. (1983). *A nation at risk: The imperative for educational reform.* Washington, DC: U.S. Government Printing Office.

Nelson, K. (1973). Structure and strategy in learning to talk. *Monographs of the Society for Research in Child Development, 38* (1–2, Serial No. 149).

Newmeyer, F. (1998). On the supposed "counterfunctionality" of universal grammar: Some evolutionary implications. In J. Hurford, M. Studdert-Kennedy, & C. Knight (Eds.), *Approaches to the evolution of language* (pp. 305–319). Cambridge, England: Cambridge University Press.

Newport, E., Gleitman, H., & Gleitman, E. (1977). Mother, I'd rather do it myself: Some effects and non-effects of maternal speech style. In C. Snow & C. Ferguson (Eds.), *Talking to children: Language input and acquisition* (pp. 109–150). Cambridge, England: Cambridge University Press.

Noden, H. (1999). *Image grammar: Using grammatical structures to teach writing.* Portsmouth, NH: Heinemann.

Odell, L., Vacca, R., Hobbs, R., & Irvin, J. (2001). *Elements of language: Introductory course.* Austin, TX: Holt, Rinehart & Winston.

Ojemann, G. A. (1983). Brain organization for language from the perspective of electrical stimulation mapping. *Behavioral and Brain Sciences, 2,* 189–207.

Orfield, G. (2004). *Still separate after all these years: An interview with Professor Gary Orfield.* Retrieved June 11, 2004, from http://www.gse.harvard.edu/news/ features/orfield05012004. html.

Orr, E. (1987). *Twice as less.* New York: Norton.

Paradis, M. (1999, August). *Neuroimaging studies of the bilingual brain: Some words of caution.* Paper presented at the 25th Lacus Forum, University of Alberta, Edmonton, Canada.

Patterson, N. (2001). Just the facts: Research and theory about grammar instruction. In J. Hagemann (Ed.), *Teaching grammar: A reader and workbook* (pp. 31–37). Boston: Allyn & Bacon.

Peck, M. (1982). *An investigation of tenth-grade students' writing.* Washington, DC: United Press of America.

Pedersen, E. (1978). Improving syntactic and semantic fluency in writing of language arts students through extended practice in sentence-combining. *Dissertation Abstracts International, 38,* 5892-A.

Perani, D., Paulesu, E., Galles, N., Dupoux, E., Dehaene, S., Bettinardi, V., Cappa, S., Fazio, F., & Mehler, J. (1998). The bilingual brain: Proficiency and age of acquisition of the second language. *Brain, 121,* 1841–1852.

Perron, J. (1977). *The impact of mode on written syntactic complexity.* Athens, GA: University of Geogia Studies in Language Education Series.

Petrosky, A. (1990). Rural poverty and literacy in the Mississippi Delta: Dilemmas, paradoxes, and conundrums. In A. Lunsford, H. Moglen, & J. Slevin (Eds.), *The right to literacy* (pp. 61–73). New York: Modern Language Association.

Pinker, S. (1994). *The language instinct: How the mind creates language.* New York: Morrow.

Pinker, S. (1995). Language acquisition. In L. Gleitman & M. Liberman (Eds.), *Language: An invitation to cognitive science* (pp. 135–182). Cambridge, MA: MIT Press.

Pinker, S. (1999). *Words and rules.* New York: Basic Books.

Pinker, S. (2002). *The blank slate: The modern denial of human nature.* New York: Viking.

Pinker, S., & Prince, A. (1988). On language and connectionism: Analysis of a parallel distributed processing model of language acquisition. *Cognition, 28,* 73–193.

Plato. (1937). Protagoras. In B. Jowett (Ed. & Trans.), *The dialogues of Plato* (Vol. 1, pp. 81–132). New York: Random House.

Plato. (1937). Phaedrus. In B. Jowett (Ed. & Trans.), *The dialogues of Plato* (Vol. 1, pp. 233–284). New York: Random House.

Prince, A., & Smolensky, P. (1993). *Optimality theory: Constraint interaction in generative grammar.* Piscataway, NJ: Rutgers University Center for Cognitive Science.

Puget Sound Regional Council. (2001). *Puget Sound trends.* Retrieved June 3, 2004, from http://www.psrc.org/datapubs/pubs/trends/e3trend.pdf.

Pullum, G. (1996). Learnability, hyperlearning, and the poverty of the stimulus. *Proceedings of the 22nd Annual Meeting: General Session and Parasession on the Role of Learnability in Grammatical Theory* (pp. 498–513). Berkeley Linguistics Society.

Pulvermuller, F. (2003). *The neuroscience of language: On brain circuits of words and serial order.* Cambridge, England: Cambridge University Press.

Pylkkänen, L. (2002). *Introducing arguments.* Unpublished doctoral dissertation, MIT, Cambridge, MA.

Quintilian. (1974). Elementary and secondary education. In F. Wheelock (Ed.), *Quintilian as educator: Selections from the institutio oratoria of Marcu Favius Quintilianus* (H. Butler, Trans.) (pp. 29–78). New York: Twayne.

Rector, R., & Johnson, K. (2004). *Understanding poverty in America.* Retrieved June 3, 2004, from www.heritage.org/research/welfare/bg1713.cfm.

Reed, D. (2004). Recent trends in income and poverty. *California Counts: Population Trends and Profiles, 5,* 1–16.

Reyes, B. (Ed.). (2001). *A portrait of race and ethnicity in California: An assessment of social and economic well-being.* San Francisco: Public Policy Institute of California.

Rickford, J. (1975). Carrying the new wave into syntax: The case of Black English been. In R. Fasgold & R. Shuy (Eds.), *Analyzing variation in language* (pp. 162–183). Washington, DC: Georgetown University Press.

Robinson, J. (1990). *Conversations on the written word: Essays on language and literacy.* Portsmouth, NH: Boynton Cook.

Rose, M. (1984). *Writer's block: The cognitive dimension.* Carbondale, IL: Southern Illinois University Press.

Rueda, R., Saldivar, T., Shapiro, L., Templeton, S., Terry, C., & Valentino, C. (2001). *English.* Boston: Houghton Mifflin.

Rumelhart, D., & McClelland, J. (1986). *Parallel distributed processing: Explorations in the microstructure of cognition* (Vols. 1 & 2). Cambridge, MA: MIT Press.

Schilperoord, J. (1996). *It's about time. Temporal aspects of cognitive processes in text production.* Amsterdam: Rodopi Bv Editions.

Sampson, G. (1997). *Educating Eve: The "Language Instinct" debate.* London: Cassell.

Sanford, A., & Garrod, S. (1981). *Understanding written language.* New York: Wiley.

Schmid, H. (2000). *English abstract nouns as conceptual shells: From corpus to cognition.* Berlin, Germany: Mouton de Gruyter.

Schroeder, M., & Aeppel, T. (2003, October 10). Skilled workers mount opposition to free trade, swaying politicians. *The Wall Street Journal,* pp. 1–3. Retrieved January 19, 2004, from http://www.interesting-people.org/archives/interesting-people/ 200310/msg00095.html.

Schwarz, J., Barton-Henry, M., & Pruzinsky, T. (1985). Assessing child-rearing behaviors: A comparison of ratings made by mother, father, child, and sibling on the CRPBI. *Child Development, 56*(2), 462–479.

Searle, J. (1992). *The rediscovery of the mind.* Cambridge, MA: MIT Press.

Singer, J. (1980). The power and limitations of television: A cognitive–affective analysis. In P. Tannenbaum (Ed.), *The entertainment functions of television* (pp. 31–66). Hillsdale, NJ: Lawrence Erlbaum Associates.

Slobin, D. (1977). Language change in childhood and history. In J. Macnamara (Ed.), *Language, learning and thought* (pp. 185–214). New York: Academic Press.

Slobin, D., & Welsh, C. (1973). Elicited imitation as a research tool in developmental psycholinguistics. In C. Ferguson & D. Slobin (Eds.), *Studies of child language development* (pp. 485–496). New York: Holt, Rinehart & Winston.

Smith, F. (1983). *Essays into literacy.* London: Heinemann.

Smolin, L. (1997). *Life of the cosmos.* New York: Oxford University Press.

Society for Neuroscience. (2002). *Brain facts.* Washington, DC: Society for Neuroscience.

Springer, K., & Keil, F. (1991). Early differentiation of causal mechanisms appropriate to biological and nonbiological kinds. *Child Development, 62,* 767–781.

St. Augustine. (1994). *On dialectic* (de dialectica) (J. Marchand, Trans.). Retrieved December 30, 2003, from http://www.ccat.sas.upenn.edu/jod/texts/dialecticatrans.html.

Steinberg, D. (1993). *Introduction to psycholinguistics.* New York: Addison-Wesley.

Steinberg, L., Darling, N., & Fletcher, A. (1995). Authoritative parenting and adolescent adjustment: An ecological journey. In P. Moen, G. Elder, & K. Luscher (Eds.), *Examining lives in context: Perspectives on the ecology of human development* (pp. 423–466). Washington, DC: American Psychological Association.

Steinberg, L., Dornbusch, S., & Brown, B. (1992). Ethnic differences in adolescent achievement: An ecological perspective. *American Psychologist, 47*(6), 723–729.

Sullivan, M. (1978). The effects of sentence-combining exercises on syntactic maturity, quality of writing, reading ability, and attitudes of students in grade eleven. *Dissertation Abstracts International, 39,* 1197-A.

Sykes, B. (2002). *The seven daughters of Eve.* New York: Norton.

Taylor, J. (2002). *Cognitive grammar.* Oxford, England: Oxford University Press.

Thernstrom, A., & Thernstrom, S. (2003). *No excuses: Closing the racial gap in learning.* New York: Simon & Schuster.

Trudgill, P. (2001). *Sociolinguistics: An introduction to language and society* (4th ed.). New York: Penguin.

Twitchell, J. (2003). *Living it up: America's love affair with luxury.* New York: Simon & Schuster.

U.S. Census Bureau. (2000). *Educational attainment in the United States.* Retrieved February 10, 2004, from http://www.census.gov/population/www/ socdemo/education/p20-536.html.

U.S. Department of Commerce, Bureau of Economic Analysis. (2004a). *Real disposable income per capita.* Retrieved June 3, 2004, from http://www.bea.gov/briefrm/ percapin.htm.

U.S. Department of Commerce, Bureau of Economic Analysis. (2004b). *2003 comprehensive revision of the national income and product accounts.* Retrieved June 3, 2004, from http://www.bea.gov/bea/dn/home/gdp.htm.

U.S. Department of Commerce, Bureau of the Census. *County & city data book, 1994.* Retrieved June 4, 2004, from http://www.usccr.gov/pubs/msdelta/ch1. htm.

U.S. Department of Education. (1983). *A nation at risk. National Commission on Excellence in Education.* Retrieved June 8, 2004, from http://www.ed.gov/pubs/ NatAtRisk/risk.html.

U.S. Department of Education. (1999). *1998 writing: Report card for the nation and the states.* Washington, DC: U.S. Government Printing Office.

U.S. Department of Housing and Urban Development. (2004). *U.S. housing market conditions: Historical data.* Retrieved June 3, 2004, from http://www.huduser.org/periodicals/ushmc/winter2001/histdat08.htm.

U.S. Office of Management and Budget. (2004). Federal support for education: Fiscal years 1980 to 2000. *Education Statistics Quarterly.* Retrieved January 25, 2004, from http://nces.ed.gov/pubs2001/quarterly/winter/crosscutting/c_section1.html.

Vail, P. (1989). *Smart kids with school problems.* New York: Plume.

Vygotsky, L. (1978). *Mind in society* (M. Cole, U. John-Steiner, S. Scribner, & E. Souberman, Eds.). Cambridge, MA: Harvard University Press.

Weaver, C. (1996). *Teaching grammar in context.* Portsmouth, NH: Boynton Cook.

Weir, M. (2002). The American middle class and the politics of education. In O. Zunz, L. Schoppa, & N. Hiwatari (Eds.), *Social contracts under stress: The middle classes of America, Europe, and Japan at the turn of the century* (pp. 178–203). New York: Russell Sage Foundation.

Weiss, L., & Schwarz, J. (1996). The relationship between parenting types and older adolescents' personality, academic achievement, adjustment, and substance use. *Child Development, 67*(5), 2101–2114.

Wheelock, F. (Ed.) (1974). *Quintilian as educator: Selections from the institutio oratoria of Marcu Favius Quintilianus* (H. Butler, Trans.). New York: Twayne.

White, R. (1965). The effect of structural linguistics on improving English composition compared to that of prescriptive grammar or the absence of grammar instruction. *Dissertation Abstracts, 25*, 5032.

Whitehead, C. (1966). The effect of grammar diagramming on student writing skills. *Dissertation Abstracts, 26*, 3710.

Williams, J. (1993). Rule-governed approaches to language and composition. *Written Communication, 10*, 542–568.

Williams, J. (1998). *Preparing to teach writing: Research, theory, and practice* (2nd ed.). Mahwah, NJ: Lawrence Erlbaum Associates.

Williams, J. (2002). Rhetoric and the triumph of liberal democracy. In J. Williams (Ed.), *Visions and revisions: Continuity and change in rhetoric and composition* (pp. 131–162). Carbondale, IL: Southern Illinois University Press.

Williams, J. (2003a). *Preparing to teach writing: Research, theory, and practice* (3rd ed.). Mahwah, NJ: Lawrence Erlbaum Associates.

Williams, J. (2003b). Grammar and usage. In I. Clark (Ed.), *Concepts in composition: Theory and practice in the teaching of writing* (pp. 313–337). Mahwah, NJ: Lawrence Erlbaum Associates.

Witte, S. (1980). Toward a model for research in written composition. *Research in the Teaching of English, 14*, 73–81.

Wolfram, W. (1969). *A sociolinguistic description of Detroit Negro speech*. Washington, DC: Center for Applied Linguistics.

Wolfram, W. (1998). Linguistic and sociolinguistic requisites for teaching language. In J. Simmons & L. Baines (Eds.), *Language study in middle school, high school, and beyond* (pp. 79–109). Newark, DE: International Reading Association.

Wolfram, W., Adger, L., & Christian, A. (1999). *Dialects in schools and communities*. Mahwah, NJ: Lawrence Erlbaum Associates.

Index